GREEN LANTERN
AND
PHILOSOPHY

The Blackwell Philosophy and Pop Culture Series
Series Editor: William Irwin

South Park and Philosophy
Edited by Robert Arp

Metallica and Philosophy
Edited by William Irwin

Family Guy and Philosophy
Edited by J. Jeremy Wisnewski

The Daily Show and Philosophy
Edited by Jason Holt

Lost and Philosophy
Edited by Sharon Kaye

24 and Philosophy
*Edited by Jennifer Hart Weed,
Richard Davis, and Ronald Weed*

Battlestar Galactica and
Philosophy
Edited by Jason T. Eberl

The Office and Philosophy
Edited by J. Jeremy Wisnewski

Batman and Philosophy
*Edited by Mark D. White and
Robert Arp*

House and Philosophy
Edited by Henry Jacoby

Watchmen and Philosophy
Edited by Mark D. White

X-Men and Philosophy
*Edited by Rebecca Housel and
J. Jeremy Wisnewski*

Terminator and Philosophy
*Edited by Richard Brown and
Kevin Decker*

Heroes and Philosophy
Edited by David Kyle Johnson

Twilight and Philosophy
*Edited by Rebecca Housel and
J. Jeremy Wisnewski*

Final Fantasy and Philosophy
*Edited by Jason P. Blahuta and
Michel S. Beaulieu*

Alice in Wonderland and
Philosophy
Edited by Richard Brian Davis

Iron Man and Philosophy
Edited by Mark D. White

True Blood and Philosophy
*Edited by George Dunn and
Rebecca Housel*

Mad Men and Philosophy
*Edited by James South and Rod
Carveth*

30 Rock and Philosophy
Edited by J. Jeremy Wisnewski

The Ultimate Harry Potter and
Philosophy
Edited by Gregory Bassham

The Ultimate Lost and
Philosophy
Edited by Sharon Kaye

Spider-Man and Philosophy
*Edited by Jonathan
J. Sanford*

GREEN LANTERN
AND
PHILOSOPHY
NO EVIL SHALL ESCAPE THIS BOOK

Edited by Jane Dryden
and Mark D. White

WILEY

John Wiley & Sons, Inc.

For general information about our other products and services, please contact our Customer Care Department within the United States at (800) 762-2974, outside the United States at (317) 572-3993 or fax (317) 572-4002.

Wiley also publishes its books in a variety of electronic formats. Some content that appears in print may not be available in electronic books. For more information about Wiley products, visit our web site at www.wiley.com.

ISBN 978-0-470-57557-4 (cloth); ISBN 978-1-118-00327-5 (ebk.);
ISBN 978-1-118-00328-2 (ebk.); ISBN 978-1-118-00329-9

Printed in the United States of America

10 9 8 7 6 5 4 3 2 1

CONTENTS

PART FIVE
DON'T TELL KRONA: METAPHYSICS, MIND, AND TIME

PART SIX
CAN GREEN LANTERN MAKE A BOXING GLOVE HE CAN'T LIFT?: POWERS AND LIMITATIONS

ACKNOWLEDGMENTS

No Gratitude Shall Escape Our Sight

We would like to thank some of our personal Guardians for helping to make this dream a reality. Eric Nelson and Connie Santisteban of Wiley gave us our rings and our batteries and taught us the most important oath of all: Don't miss deadlines! Though they granted us this power, Bill Irwin taught us how to use it and gave invaluable advice on the constructs we developed. Finally, we thank our fellow members in the Philosophy Corps for their dedication to the mission; we hope none of them become Red Lanterns because of us!

Jane would like to thank Caitlyn Pascal and Dawn Wintour, who got her started reading comics back in the day. Mark would like to thank Jeff Peters, whose love of Green Lantern helped to reignite Mark's green flame after many years away from the Corps.

Finally, we would like to thank all the amazingly imaginative and intelligent creators who have powered the Green Lantern mythos for all these decades: Mort Finger, Art Nodell, Julius Schwartz, John Broome, Gil Kane, Denny O'Neil, Neal Adams, Marv Wolfman, Joe Staton, Alan Moore, Len Wein,

Dave Gibbons, Steve Englehart, Gerard Jones, Ron Marz, Judd Winick, Peter Tomasi, and, of course, Geoff Johns. Without them, Green Lantern would just be a run-of-the-mill hero with sparkly jewelry; because of them, Green Lantern is a legend. This book is dedicated to them.

INTRODUCTION

Welcome to the Corps!

We admit it: If we could be any superheroes, we'd like to be Green Lanterns. Why Green Lanterns, you ask? First, there's the vast array of vivid and compelling characters who fill the pages of the Green Lantern comics: Hal, Kyle, John, and Guy, of course, but also Alan Scott, Arisia, Ganthet, Soranik Natu, Kilowog, Katma Tui, Salaak, Mogo–even Sinestro.[1] They're so different from one another, and yet they seem like folks we'd like to know—and would very much like to join. (And not to brag, but we look quite good in green.)

And then there's the concept of the Green Lantern Corps itself, an intergalactic police force composed of members from different species on different worlds who all have to get along with one another and work together to ensure peace and order in the universe. The United Nations only needs to worry about different countries and humans getting along—the Green Lantern Corps needs to worry about different planets and species! Each member of the Corps has a unique set of values and way of life, but they all swear to fight evil, putting aside their differences to further a common goal.

But more than anything, it's the rings. The power of a Green Lantern ring inspires a sense of possibility and wonder the first time you read a comic or see one on the big screen. Anyone who dreams of how to make the world a better place can imagine ways to make that dream come true with a Green Lantern ring. Given enough willpower, a Green Lantern can make the ring do whatever he or she can imagine. And each Lantern's constructs reflect his or her personality, from Hal Jordan's simple boxing gloves to John Stewart's architecturally sound structures to Kyle Rayner's artistic flights of fancy.

With these fantastic concepts and characters, the philosophical questions just flow. How do all the Green Lanterns work together? What limits does justice place on the use of a Green Lantern ring? Can a Green Lantern do literally anything at all? What roles do willpower and imagination play when a Green Lantern uses the ring? What do the differently colored corps reveal about the nature of our emotions, and how should emotion affect a Green Lantern's judgment and decisions?

Until recently, Green Lantern has been somewhat of a second-tier superhero. None of the characters who have donned the green ring are as well-known as DC Comics' "big three" (Superman, Batman, and Wonder Woman), and despite Kyle Rayner's Nine Inch Nails shirt in his first appearance, none of the Green Lanterns have the outcast, antihero, angsty appeal of Marvel's X-Men. But with movies, an animated series, and a prominent place in major DC crossover events, Green Lantern is beginning to shine. Sadly, none of us can wear real Green Lantern rings—but whether you're a new fan or an elder from Oa, you're welcome into the Philosophy Corps as we plunge fearlessly and honestly forward.[2]

NOTES

1. You will no doubt notice the absence of Itty in this book. The truth is, all of us here love him, so much so that every chapter seemed to focus on him, so we had to institute a "no Itty" rule out of fairness to the other characters in the Green Lantern stories, like Hal and Sinestro. (Look for *Itty and Philosophy: Size Doesn't Matter* soon after the volumes on Doiby Dickles and G'nort.)

2. What color, you ask? Philosophers still can't agree on the true nature of color, much less a color for the rings!

PART ONE

WILL AND EMOTION: THE PHILOSOPHICAL SPECTRUM

THE BLACKEST NIGHT
FOR ARISTOTLE'S
ACCOUNT OF EMOTIONS

Jason Southworth

Since 2005's *Green Lantern: Rebirth,* writer Geoff Johns has told a series of stories leading up to *Blackest Night,* introducing to the DC Universe a series of six previously unknown color corps in addition to the classic green: red (rage), orange (avarice), yellow (fear), blue (hope), indigo (compassion), and violet (love).[1] The members of each corps see the emotion they represent as the most important one and believe that acting out of that emotion is the only appropriate way to behave. The Green Lanterns, on the other hand, represent the triumph of willpower or reason over emotion and seek to overcome and stifle these emotional states.[2]

The conflict between the various lantern corps, while providing an interesting series of stories, also sets the stage for thinking about one of the most long-standing questions in ethics: What role should emotion play in moral reasoning?

Color-Coded Morality

With the exception of the Indigo Lanterns (who don't speak a language that can be translated by a Green Lantern power ring, much less your average comics reader), the representatives of the new color corps all make the case that acting out their sections of the emotional spectrum is the only way to achieve justice. Let's consider the ways these Lanterns make their cases for a morality driven by a single emotion.

The first of the new color corps to make itself known to the DC Universe was the Sinestro Corps. Led by the renegade Green Lantern after whom it takes its name, this corps embodies the yellow light of fear. Since the days when he was a Green Lantern, Sinestro has argued that people do the right thing only when they fear the consequences if they don't. It was this principle that led Sinestro to force the residents of his home world, Korugar, to live in fear of his wrath.[3] While this might seem extreme, Sinestro has shown us time and time again that fear is a strong motivator. For instance, when he decided that the Green Lanterns needed to change the Laws of Oa to allow Lanterns to kill, he was able to make the Guardians so afraid that they did as he wished.[4] When discussing Sinestro's motivations, some may say that while he wants others to act out of fear, he holds himself exempt from this standard. But a closer look shows that Sinestro's turn to fear came from his own fears of a prophecy relayed to him by Atrocitus, which said that Korugar would fall into a state of chaos from riots and a violent coup if nothing was done to prevent it.[5]

Like the Sinestro Corps, the Violet Lantern Corps was started by a long-time Green Lantern villain, Star Sapphire. Actually, Star Sapphire is not a person, but an alien gem that possesses the person desired most by Hal Jordan; more often than not, that person is Carol Ferris (his sometimes employer and love interest).[6] Let's set aside the fact that violet light is powering a person whose name refers to a blue gem—and whose costume is pink—and move on to a discussion of the Violet Lanterns' emotional focus. Violet Lanterns, just like John Lennon, will tell you that love is all you need. The leaders of this corps, the Zamarons (a group of female former Guardians), appear to believe that the only appropriate way to reason is to act on one's feelings of love. For instance, the Guardian Scar says that "to believe that love will save the universe is naïve and irresponsible," to which Queen Aga'po of the Zamarons responds, "That is your misguided, and dare I say it, irrational opinion."[7] Scar's claim is deemed irrational because she used something other than love to arrive at it. The goal of the corps is clear: to "wield the violet light energy of love" and "convert all to their way of light."[8] They are so committed to this conversion that they go as far as to kidnap members of the Sinestro Corps and imprison them until they come to see (or are brainwashed to see, according to Green Lantern Arisia) the way of the Star Sapphire Corps.[9] When reasoning means acting out of love, rather than intellect or some other emotion, there doesn't seem to be much room for compromise.

The rage of the Red Lanterns is grounded in a belief that great injustices often go unpunished. The founder of the Red Lantern Corps, Atrocitus, experienced a life filled with such injustices. The Manhunters, the Guardians' initial attempt at an intergalactic police force, concluded that the only way to prevent chaos from consuming the universe was to destroy all life—this led to the murder of all but a handful of people in Atrocitus's space sector.[10] Atrocitus and the other survivors of the massacre attempted to enact justice (or vengeance) on the Guardians for what they had done, and the Guardians responded by imprisoning them. From these experiences, Atrocitus now sees emotionless reasoning—the decision process of the Guardians—as responsible for the destruction of his home world.

Rage is all that Atrocitus feels after centuries of imprisonment, and it alone compels him to act. By his reasoning, emotions other than rage are bad, as they are likely to lead to passivity in the face of injustice by causing us to be concerned with the consequences of our actions. When Atrocitus is reborn as a Red Lantern on Ysmault he blames the Guardians for their sins, which "stretch back eons."[11] All he has left is rage, "the red light [which] is violent action with no consideration for consequence. It is uncontrollable."[12] Atrocitus's rejection of other emotions can be seen in his interactions with members of the other corps; for instance, he rejects the power of hope, saying to Blue Lantern Saint Walker, "You wield coalesced hope. Empty prayers. Disembodied faith."[13]

Perhaps the most surprising emotion that one might advocate as the proper impetus for action is avarice. Larfleeze, the only Orange Lantern (except for Lex Luthor's brief stint in *Blackest Night* #6–8, 2010), explains his commitment to greed, talking to himself in *Green Lantern*, vol. 4, #39 (March 2009). Speaking about the Controllers, the creators of the Darkstars (an earlier alternative to the Green Lantern Corps), he says, "They want to protect the universe their own way. You can't protect anything that big! You can only protect what you can hold." Larfleeze's point seems to be that ownership motivates people to protect things, a common point made in discussions of private property.

Another strange case is that of hope. The Blue Lantern Corps was founded by Ganthet and Sayd in the hopes of preventing the Blackest Night.[14] Given the involvement of these well-spoken former Guardians, you might wrongly expect that they make the reasoned case for hope's importance. Unfortunately, all we are told is that hope is the most powerful emotion, and that those who wear the blue ring are the saints of the universe.[15] These aren't really arguments, but assertions. These Lanterns don't have an argument for hope being the most significant emotion—instead, what they have is *hope* that it is. Similarly, these Lanterns never give reasons why they think they will succeed in their goals; instead, they speak of hope that they will.

Despite not being able to give reasons for the supremacy of hope, the Blue Lanterns still try to dominate the other corps. When Hal Jordan asks Ganthet if he created the Blue Corps to replace "us," meaning the Green Lanterns, Ganthet responds, "No. To aid you."[16] This suggests that the Blue Corps see a place for the two corps to coexist, but then they immediately try to talk Hal into leaving the Green Lanterns for their corps. Additionally, within the first few pages of our meeting the first Blue Lantern, Saint Walker, he uses his ring to soothe the anger he senses in another Green Lantern from Earth, John Stewart.[17] In the end, it seems that while the Blue Lanterns aren't openly hostile toward the Green Lanterns, hope still tries to dominate the green light.

Finding the Perfect Mean: A Job for Golden Lanterns?

While the representatives of the various color corps are able to make convincing cases for the moral significance of their emotions (or at least hope for that significance), philosophers stop short of defending the relevance of a single emotion over all others. Beginning with Plato (circa 428–348 BCE) and Aristotle (384–322 BCE), philosophers have argued that our emotions interact with reason when we engage in moral deliberation.

While Aristotle saw emotions as significant, he understood them very differently than do the members of the color corps, and this understanding is integral to his moral philosophy. For Aristotle, morality is all about becoming a particular kind of person—someone with a well-rounded character and the practical wisdom to recognize the right thing to do in any situation. Aristotle recognized that emotions have a strong influence on our actions, and, realizing their power, he thought carefully about the best way to harness them into service of the good. Emotions are not individual character traits, but rather exist on a series of spectrums. For any emotion, there are two extremes—an excess of the emotion at one end and a deficit of it at the other. In between is just the right amount of that emotion, which Aristotle called a virtue, and the goal of those striving to be good people is to harness this just-right amount of emotion.[18]

Aristotle thought that the key to achieving the proper amount of each emotion is reason, which gives moral agents the guidance needed to temper their emotions and to use them in service of the good. Without reason, agents will act in service of their own appetites, controlled by their passions rather than by a desire to do good.[19] Reason is the cool, unemotional component of our psyches that can carefully assess each situation and determine how much of each emotion is called for. Consider this analogy from Plato: Just as a general is the person in charge, directing his soldiers who do the legwork, so reason should direct the emotions, which provide the motivating force for the action. Just as with the general and the soldiers, both reason and emotion are essential, but the person, like the army, will function well only if reason is in charge.[20]

Let's think about this in terms of an example: the virtue of courage, which is the perfect midpoint between the extreme emotions (or vices) of foolhardiness and cowardice. It is good to act decisively in the face of fear, while running away from battles you are capable of fighting is cowardly and charging headlong into situations you can't handle is foolhardy. Reason tells us when we can handle a frightening situation and when the wise action is to back away. In other words, acting from either extreme is intemperate. Once you are able to use reason to consistently hit the sweet spot—the "Golden Mean"—you possess the virtue of that mean, in this case, courage.[21]

For Aristotelians, the first mistake made by all of the color corps is that they are all acting in excess, something even the characters recognize about one another. Take the following exchange between Atrocitus and Sinestro in *Green Lantern*, vol. 4, #36 (January 2009):

> Atrocitus: You believe fear to be the most powerful force in the universe? Fear is inaction. Fear is hiding away. Fear is cowering and begging. Rage is action. Rage is spilling blood.
> Sinestro: Rage is uncontrollable.

Both observations bear out when we look at the Green Lantern comics. The beings Sinestro and his corps instill with fear are unable to act; even Green Lanterns can't use their power rings when they are afraid. Meanwhile, Atrocitus's rage makes him unfocused. He is so busy fuming and fighting that he misses several opportunities to do what he has set out to do—kill Sinestro and the Guardians. Similarly, the Violet Lantern Fatality removes her former enemy, Green Lantern John Stewart, from battle in an attempt to show him love and forgiveness; however, this renders Stewart unable to save his fellow Green Lanterns, whom he cares for deeply.[22] Fatality's single-minded devotion to love prevents her from recognizing that other elements and emotions are at play. Fatality's focus on love to the exclusion of all other considerations enrages Stewart and causes him to reject her, because it resulted in his failure to help people he cared about.

The Rainbow of Emotions and the Prism of the Will

The second mistake made by the members of the color corps, if we follow Aristotle's account, is that by acting out of a single emotion, they fail to see the interrelation of emotions and the *unity of the virtues*. According to Aristotle, if you have one of the virtues, then you have them all, and his explanation for this involves reason and judgment. In order to always hit the

Golden Mean between emotional extremes, you must possess prudence, or right judgment. Without prudence, while you might still occasionally hit the Mean, you do not fully possess the virtue. With right judgment, you will always reason your way to hitting the mark, and if you have reason enough to do this for one of the virtues, then you have reason enough to do it all of the time (although this will take some practice).[23]

Aristotle is obviously correct that emotions are interrelated, something the color corps fail to acknowledge. On an intuitive level, we can see the interrelation between emotions in the lives of several of the corps' leaders. In the case of Atrocitus, love for his family and his species, along with hope that the Guardians would be brought to justice, led to the development of his rage. In the case of Sinestro, love for his home world and avarice about being the best Green Lantern led to his use of fear to keep his home world free of crime.

Looking at the color corps stories as allegories, we can also see plenty of evidence to suggest that reason alone is not sufficient for moral decision-making. The most significant evidence for this is that the primary hero of the stories, Hal Jordan, invariably puts on one of the rings of the new corps in order to defeat the enemy he is facing. When fighting the Sinestro Corps, Hal puts on several yellow rings. When fighting Larfleeze, it is the combined use of the blue and green rings that enables him to defeat the Orange Lantern.[24] While these moments are exciting for fanboys, we can also see that it is only when the emotions are channeled through the will or reason of the green ring that Hal can win the day. Similarly, throughout the *Blackest Night* miniseries, we see that the new Black Lanterns (the reanimated corpses of fallen heroes, villains, and loved ones) can be injured only when they are attacked by a Green Lantern's light combined with any other color of the emotional spectrum. Again, it seems that reason and emotion are both needed, although ultimately emotion is subservient to reason, as Aristotle recommended.

Aristotle's account of the role of emotions in ethics is not just an indictment of the single-minded emotional approaches of the new corps, but also of the Green Lantern Corps' exclusive focus on will over emotion. Going back to the example of courage, you will recall that acting with no fear is considered vicious. As a person accustomed to thinking of Green Lanterns as heroes, this should shock you. After all, Hal Jordan, the quintessential Lantern, is prone to saying that he's not afraid of anything. But Aristotle is clear: If an individual literally has no fear, he can't be a good person. Consider also that the new third law in the Book of Oa forbids physical relations and love between Green Lanterns, implying that Green Lanterns are often required to ignore these feelings when making decisions.[25] For Aristotle, will alone isn't enough, since it is simply a prism through which emotion needs to be filtered in order to get to right action.

John Stuart Mill's Green Approach to Emotion and Reason

Aristotle gives us good reason to reject the single-minded emotional approaches of the color corps. Does agreeing with Aristotle on that point mean that we must adopt his specific approach to morality, especially his claim about the unity of the virtues? Since this would require us to see the Green Lantern Corps in a negative light as well, it is a good thing that the answer is no.

Another option, more sympathetic to the Green Lantern Corps, can be found in the moral theory known as *utilitarianism*. Rather than focusing on a range of emotions from the outset, utilitarianism begins with the belief that the right action is the one that maximizes happiness and minimizes suffering for everyone impacted by it. Morality, in this view, is focused on producing good consequences and avoiding bad ones. John Stuart Mill (1806–1873), one of the founders of utilitarianism, advises us to achieve this goal by approaching moral decisions from the perspective of a "benevolent, disinterested spectator," concerned equally for everyone's well-being, with no special consideration given to one's own preferences or to the interest of loved ones.[26] It was in an attempt to develop such disinterested spectators to police the universe that the Guardians created the robotic police force, the Manhunters.

Many criticize utilitarianism as being too far removed from human emotion, requiring the evaluator to be a detached observer. If this criticism sounds familiar, it is because it is often leveled against the Guardians as well (in fact, Atrocitus did so earlier in this chapter). So common is this criticism that Mill takes the time to specifically address and respond to it. He argues that the important thing is not the motivation for action, but merely the result, which makes sense if all you are concerned about is consequences. Many people will do the right action for emotional reasons, and that is not a problem in this theory, since the important thing is that good consequences be maximized. Mill thinks the most reliable way to get that result is through dispassionate reason, but he recognizes that there is more than one way to achieve the goal and advocates using whatever method necessary to get there.[27] It was the failure of the Guardians to account for emotion in the programming of the Manhunters that led the robot police force to attempt to wipe all life from the Vega system; it's also what led them to create the Green Lantern Corps. They realized that the best candidates to police a universe full of emotional individuals are beings who understand emotion but strive to overcome it, as Green Lanterns do.

Where the Guardians fail is not in being detached observers, as Green Lanterns like Guy Gardner often argue; rather, they fail in their assumption that they are, in fact, wholly detached. The Guardians, like all other species in the universe, are emotional beings, even if they wish they were not. Often, they make big decisions out of fear. As Sinestro points out, the decision to approve lethal force against Sinestro Corps members was made out of fear.[28] Likewise, when they agreed to let Larfleeze keep his orange ring so long as he stayed in the Vega system, it was because they were afraid of having the power at large in the universe.[29] On the lighter side of the emotional spectrum, Ganthet and Sayd made it clear that Guardians are capable of emotion when, out of hope, they left to form the Blue Lantern Corps.[30]

Mill acknowledges that even the best utilitarian will have other motivations besides utility: "Ninety-nine hundredths of all our actions are done from other motives, and rightly so."[31] However, he cautions that good agents will be aware of the impact of these other motivations and guard against them when engaging in moral decision-making, where they can be detrimental. The Guardians are great at manipulating the emotions of others for positive consequences (for example, by exploiting Larfleeze's desire to kill a Guardian by promising him one of their own if he will help them defeat Nekron).[32] Still, they would have done well to also apply this principle to themselves. Given that they are clearly emotional beings, they should recognize their own emotions and take them into account when computing their moral calculus. If the Guardians were more self-aware, they could have recognized that Scar was in the midst of a breakdown after her battle with the Anti-Monitor, and could have acted to prevent her actions that caused the Blackest Night.[33]

Triumph of the Will

So, where does this leave us? While at first it seemed that the new color corps posed interesting alternatives to the Green Lantern Corps, ultimately they all fall flat. The criticism of these single-emotional approaches from Aristotle, and the characters themselves, show that ultimately something other than just one emotion is needed in our moral decision-making process.

While Aristotle's theory offers one way to approach morality with an understanding of emotion and reason, it criticizes the Green Lantern Corps just as much as the other corps. The alternative approach to moral reasoning offered by utilitarianism offers a way to understand the role of emotion in moral reasoning that is more in line with our intuition that the Green Lantern Corps and the Guardians are getting it right. Not only does this theory allow us to see the Green Lanterns as heroes, but the debate regarding the appropriate amount of emotion in moral reasoning lets us account for the moral growth of the Guardians from their creation of the Manhunters to their realization, only recently, of the emotion within themselves. Now that the Guardians have recognized themselves as emotional beings, they will be able to move forward in a clearer way in their mission to protect the universe.[34]

NOTES

1. White and black corps have also been introduced, but since they represent life and death, rather than emotions, they will not be discussed in this chapter.

2. The way the green light is discussed in the comics can be a little confusing. When the emotional spectrum is discussed, the green light is included, suggesting that it should be understood as an emotion. At other times it is discussed as the ability to overcome fear (when a green ring approaches a new candidate for the corps, for instance). There is a long tradition in philosophy of referring to man's ability to reason as his will, and it is in this tradition that we can best understand what the Green Lantern Corps represents. My discussion of the Corps and the Guardians in the last section of this chapter offers some textual (read: comic book) support for this position.

3. This first came to light in *Green Lantern*, vol. 2, #7 (July–August 1961), reprinted in black and white in *Showcase Presents Green Lantern Volume One* (2005) and in color in *The Green Lantern Chronicles Volume Two* (2009). For a full account of Sinestro's actions on Korugar and the fallout from them, see *Green Lantern: Emerald Dawn II* (1991).

4. Sinestro explains this to Hal Jordan in *Green Lantern*, vol. 4, #26 (February 2008), reprinted in *Green Lantern: Rage of the Red Lanterns* (2009).

5. *Green Lantern*, vol. 4, #35 (November 2008), reprinted in *Green Lantern: Secret Origin* (2008). For more discussion of Sinestro's motivations and how they might be justified, see Dryden's chapter "The Greatest Green Lantern" in this volume.

6. The character of Star Sapphire actually goes all the way back to the Golden Age, making her/its first appearance in *All-Flash Comics* #32 (October–November 1947);

her first Silver Age appearance (as Carol Ferris) was in *Green Lantern*, vol. 2, #16 (October 1962), reprinted in *Showcase Presents Green Lantern Volume One*.

7. *Green Lantern Corps*, vol. 2, #30 (January 2009), reprinted in *Green Lantern Corps: Sins of the Star Sapphire* (2009).

8. *Blackest Night* #0 (May 2009).

9. Ibid.

10. *Green Lantern*, vol. 4, #33 (July 2008), reprinted in *Green Lantern: Secret Origin*.

11. *Final Crisis: Rage of the Red Lanterns* (October 2008), reprinted in *Green Lantern: Rage of the Red Lanterns*.

12. Ibid.

13. *Green Lantern*, vol. 4, #38 (February 2009), reprinted in *Green Lantern: Rage of the Red Lanterns*.

14. *Green Lantern*, vol. 4, #25 (January 2008), reprinted in *Green Lantern: The Sinestro Corps War, Volume 2* (2008).

15. *Green Lantern*, vol. 4, #26 (February 2008), reprinted in *Green Lantern: Rage of the Red Lanterns*.

16. *Green Lantern*, vol. 4, #36 (January 2009), reprinted in *Green Lantern: Rage of the Red Lanterns*.

17. Ibid.

18. A minor point, but one worth mentioning, is that Aristotle had a much more expansive list of emotions than discussed in the current Green Lantern storylines. While the Green Lantern list has just six (plus will), Aristotle not only takes there to be three emotions for every domain (cowardice, foolhardiness, and courage in the domain of fear, for example), he also has a more robust understanding of the domains of emotion, including things like a desire to please others and reaction to the success of others.

19. Aristotle, *Nicomachean Ethics*, Book 2:3–4.

20. Plato lays out this theory in detail in Book IV of the *Republic*.

21. Aristotle, *Nicomachean Ethics*, Book 2:10–12.

22. *Green Lantern*, vol. 4, #42 (June 2009), reprinted in *Green Lantern: Agent Orange* (2009).

23. Aristotle, *Nicomachean Ethics*, Book 6: 12–13.

24. *Green Lantern*, vol. 4, #42.

25. *Green Lantern Corps*, vol. 2, #31 (December 2008), reprinted in *Green Lantern Corps: Sins of the Star Sapphire*. For more on that law and the relationships between emotion and reason, the chapter by Donovan and Richardson in this volume.

26. John Stuart Mill, *Utilitarianism* (Chicago: University of Chicago Press, 1863/1906), 25.

27. Ibid., 26–28.

28. *Green Lantern*, vol. 4, #26.

29. *Green Lantern*, vol. 4, #41 (May 2009), reprinted in *Green Lantern: Agent Orange*.

30. *Green Lantern*, vol. 4, #25.

31. Mill, *Utilitarianism*, 26.

32. *Green Lantern*, vol. 4, #48 (November 2009), reprinted in *Blackest Night: Green Lantern* (2010).

33. *Green Lantern Corps*, vol. 2, #28 (April 2010), reprinted in *Green Lantern Corps: Sins of the Star Sapphire*.

34. I would like to thank Ruth Tallman for her helpful comments on this chapter.

FLEXING THE MENTAL MUSCLE: GREEN LANTERNS AND THE NATURE OF WILLPOWER

Mark D. White

There is a never-ending controversy in the comics world concerning how our heroes are drawn. Usually the discussion focuses on female heroes, who are drawn more like bikini models than world-class athletes, but artists are also criticized for drawing male heroes like body builders. It's understandable that Superman would be drawn with an unrealistically amazing physique (although his powers come from the sun, not from pumping iron). But consider Batman and the Flash, both of whom would be too weighed down by all the muscle they're typically drawn with to use their skills and powers effectively. And then we have Reed Richards, the supergenius Mr. Fantastic, who at times looks almost as big as his buddy the Thing (but with a better complexion).

This last example is even more pointed because the source of Reed's "strength" is his mind, not his body. Green Lanterns also use their minds—more precisely, their willpower, rather than their raw intellect—to harness and command their incredible power rings. Green Lanterns do not have to be muscular—just think of Xax, Ch'p, and especially Eddore—or even brilliant—think of Guy Gardner and G'nort. But all do need to be "strong" in terms of will, capable of focusing their concentration through the ring, and maintaining their resolve until their task is completed. And as we have seen many times in the Green Lantern stories, this takes enormous effort (and sweat).

As Sinestro said to a newly resuscitated Hal Jordan in *Green Lantern: Rebirth*, "Your mind is like a muscle unused for years. You forgot how to use the power ring."[1] But is the connection between willpower and a muscle just a useful metaphor, or something more? With all due respect to our esteemed Korugarian "friend," I think we'll investigate this a little more, asking what the best philosophers and psychologists on Earth have had to say on this matter—and mind.

The Ghost in the Lantern

Before we talk about willpower or strength, let's back up a bit and think about the will in general. Most generally, the will can be understood as a part of the mind that makes decisions distinct from the more mechanical operations of the brain. The concept of the will is not very popular among modern scholars in the area of *philosophy of mind*, however, since it reminds them too much of the theological notion of the soul or the simplistic *dualism* of René Descartes (1596–1650), who maintained that the mind is a separate, ethereal "thing" that exists on a separate plane of existence from the body.[2] Philosopher Gilbert Ryle (1900–1976) famously ridiculed the will (and Descartes' dualism in particular) as "the dogma of the Ghost in the Machine."[3] And most contemporary philosophers agree that the mind is more closely connected to the brain, some even suggesting that the mind is the "software" that runs on the brain's "hardware."[4]

At this level, the discussion of the will is nothing more than the timeless debate about mind and matter, which belongs in the area of philosophy known as *metaphysics*, covering the nature of reality and existence at the most abstract level. The will is also discussed in metaphysics in the context of the existence of *free will*: whether our actions are freely chosen by us or whether they are determined perfectly and precisely by the state of the world and the laws of physics (a view known as *determinism*). But we don't need to wade into these very deep waters to discuss will or willpower as it is used in the world of Green Lantern.[5] For our purposes, we're more interested in what happens *inside* the mind or brain rather than the nature of mind or reality.

Action Theory Comics

The understanding of will and willpower used in the Green Lantern comics belongs in the realm of *action theory*, an area of philosophy that looks at how people make decisions and then act on them. In action theory the will is understood to be a distinct part of our decision-making processes—the part that actually makes a choice after our reason and our judgment deliberate about what to do. But on the whole, philosophers are not much fonder of this concept of the will than they were of the metaphysical one. Most action theorists stick to the *desire-belief model* of action, which is usually traced back to David Hume (1711–1776) and in modern times is often associated with Donald Davidson (1917–2003). This model says that desires and beliefs completely determine a person's action, so there is no need for another part of our minds to rubber-stamp that choice. For example, if Carol Ferris wants to buy a new jet for Ferris Aircraft, and she believes it is possible to buy the jet (that is, it's available and the company has the funds), then she will buy the jet. Generally, if someone wants to do something and also believes she can do that thing, then that is sufficient reason to do that thing.

To be sure, the desire-belief model works very well in most normal instances of decision-making, like Carol's decision to buy the jet. But many choices seem more complicated—particularly after they're made. For instance, if Tom Kalamaku needs a particular wrench to fix a plane, and he believes that wrench is in his toolbox, then we assume he would reach into the toolbox for it. But suppose that even though Tom knows he has to fix this plane, and believes that he can, he nonetheless spends hours on Facebook instead. He may even feel guilty about it, because he knows he should have fixed the plane instead. Why didn't he, then?

Most philosophers, following the belief-desire model, would say that Tom actually must have wanted to spend time on Facebook—after all, that's what he did! But there's a very clear sense in which he wanted to fix the plane—it's his job, he's a responsible guy, and he knew that he had a duty to fix that plane. In other words, his best judgment was that he should fix the plane, but he didn't. This may be strange, but it is by no means uncommon. How many of us know that we should exercise, should eat better, should stop smoking or drinking, yet we don't? Philosophers call this phenomenon *weakness of will*, which poses an enormous problem for the desire-belief model of choice because it makes no room for choices made against one's better judgment.[6]

Will: Rebirth

While most philosophers struggle with trying to explain weakness of will within the desire-belief model, some have suggested that a concept of an independent will can solve this problem and can also make descriptions of human choice more realistic.

Several contemporary philosophers have written that the desire-belief model is too simplistic, and that it leaves no room for actual people. One such scholar, R. Jay Wallace, writes, "Action is traced to the operation of forces within us, with respect to which we as agents are ultimately passive, and in a picture of this kind real agency seems to drop out of view."[7] Another, J. David Velleman, writes that in the standard model, "reasons cause an intention, and an intention causes bodily movements, but nobody—that is, no person—does anything."[8] In other words, the desire-belief model is a version of *psychological determinism*, the idea that our actions are the direct results of psychological factors within our minds (desires and beliefs), which leaves no room for true choice—including, as we saw earlier, choice against our better judgment. But, as Wallace argues, "rational agents are equipped with a capacity for active self-determination that goes beyond the mere susceptibility to desires and beliefs."[9] So the desire-belief model does not seem rich enough to describe our actual choices, which are not always ideal.

In his 2001 book *Rationality in Action*, contemporary philosopher John Searle argues that the standard picture of choice as painted by philosophers is fine for animals, who may have no choice but to satisfy their primal drives, but not for human beings. Searle suggests that true rationality is not deterministic, as the desire-belief model implies, but rather has "gaps," such as that between judgment and decision, in which true choice is made, possibly against a person's best judgment. Furthermore, there is no explaining what happens in the gap: "What fills the gap? Nothing. Nothing fills the gap: you make up your mind to do something, or you just haul off and do what you are going to do."[10] No matter how we may deliberate or mull over a decision, we still have to choose to follow it, and that choice happens in the gap, representing free choice (if not free will in the metaphysical sense).

One advantage of Searle's gap is that it makes weakness of will very easy to understand: it happens when someone chooses, for whatever reason, not to do what he or she judges it best to do! Tom knows he should go home, but doesn't. He made the "wrong" choice according to his judgment, but that was his choice to make. I know I shouldn't have eaten that cherry danish this morning, yet I still did. According to Searle, this type of choice is no big mystery; such choices will only be mysterious for those who are devoted to the desire-belief model. But can we explain why people make such choices? Searle says no, because there is no explaining what happens in the gap—there is no rational process at work to analyze or pick apart. And that is precisely his point: people do have true, free choice, above and beyond their deliberative, calculating decision-making processes, and oddly enough, that is part of what makes us rational in a broader, richer sense.

With Great Will Comes Great Willpower

So let's say we accept the existence of the will in some form—we still need to explore the concept of *willpower* to understand what makes a Green Lantern tick (or grasshopper, as the case may be). What does it mean for the will to have power or strength, and how would we measure that?

As we saw earlier, the will is what enables us to make true choices, whether good or bad. But even though you can make bad choices, ones against your best judgment, you'd rather not! After all, that's what your judgment is for—to help you make the best decisions you can—and your will is just there to carry them out (or not). So we can say that a person's will is strong to the extent that it enables him or her to follow through with his or her best judgment—and the stronger the will, the more willpower the person has.

One early writer on willpower (though he called it "virtue" or "strength") was the philosopher Immanuel Kant (1724–1804). Kant is perhaps best known for the *categorical imperative*, his version of the "moral law," which helps determine duties that should be followed out of respect for that law.[11] But he also recognized that there are many factors that can tempt us away from our duties, such as desires and inclinations. Ideally, people will be *autonomous*, having the "inner freedom" to choose to do the right thing regardless of temptations (or external influence), but no one is perfect (other than God). As Kant wrote, "While the capacity to overcome all opposing sensible impulses can and must be simply *presupposed* in man on account of his freedom, yet this capacity as *strength* is something he must acquire."[12] The stronger (or more virtuous) a person is, the less often he or she will fail in her duties—this was his version of willpower, "the moral strength of a human being's will in fulfilling his duty."[13] And we recognize that strength "only by the magnitude of the obstacles that the human being himself furnishes through his inclination," or the temptations that he (or she) can resist.[14]

This is all well and good, you may say, but how does Kant recommend that we develop this strength? He wrote that "the way to acquire it is to enhance the moral *incentive* (the thought of the law), both by contemplating the dignity of the pure rational law in us and by *practicing* virtue."[15] In other words, we build our strength by using it, whether to follow the moral law, as Kant says, or more generally to stick to our best judgment in the face of temptation. And if we neglect to practice virtue, it will wither away: "If it is not rising, [it] is unavoidably sinking."[16] So our willpower needs constant exercise to build its strength and not weaken—sound familiar? (Take a little extra time if you need it, Mr. Gardner, no hurry.)

The Muscle in the Mind

In a flashback to the death of Abin Sur (the Green Lantern who passed his ring and battery to Hal Jordan), we are told that "the will is very like a muscle. In Abin Sur, that muscle was once extraordinarily strong—so strong that the Guardians of the Universe made him custodian of a battery of power, an amplifier of the will . . . and of a power ring, a device to focus that amplified will."[17] So is this comparison of willpower to a muscle just a fanciful metaphor, or is there more to it? Contemporary philosopher Richard Holton has argued that willpower is indeed much like a muscle.[18] To make his case, Holton draws on groundbreaking research by psychologist Roy Baumeister and his colleagues into the factors that influence willpower—or, in their terms, self-control or self-regulation.

For instance, Baumeister and Mark Muraven write that "controlling one's own behavior requires the expenditure of some inner, limited resource that is depleted afterward" and that this self-control also "shows long-term improvement, just as a muscle gets stronger through exercise . . . gaining strength with practice."[19] We see lots of examples of the limitations of willpower in the Green Lantern stories. Hal will often say things such as that an effort "took lots of will-power. That—and escaping from the energy net—has left me exhausted. I need to regain my strength."[20] We also often see the Green Lanterns—especially the human ones—sweating profusely when straining to exert their willpower through the ring, such as when Hal had to use his ring to move an entire planet, thinking "I know my ring's got limitless power—but it is powered by my willpower. Have I got the strength neces-sary to make this work?"[21] He didn't, as it turned out, which confirms the limitations of willpower—even the willpower of a Green Lantern—but he also acknowledges that it can develop with practice, saying, "Willpower's like a muscle, and I've got-ten better with it year after year!"[22]

Perhaps the most dramatic example showing the sheer effort required to use the ring was provided by Hal's best friend, Green Arrow (Oliver Queen), and Hal's successor, Kyle Rayner, in *Green Lantern: Rebirth*. After using the ring and being astounded at how difficult it was, Ollie says to Kyle, "I don't know . . . if I could've used this thing again. Feels like I haven't slept in days, hard to think. . . . I'm . . . exhausted. Forcing your willpower into the ring. Asking it to give your thoughts . . . life . . . is that what it's like?" Kyle replies, "Every time," to which Ollie simply says, "Damn."[23] If using the ring is truly that taxing, Green Lanterns must have not only incredible willpower, but also tremendous abilities to regenerate it.[24]

Another finding Baumeister and his colleagues report is that "many patterns of self-regulation break down when people are under stress."[25] There are many examples of this in the Green Lantern stories. For instance, when Hal was rescuing a man from a burning building after getting whacked on the head by a falling beam, he thought, "That knock on the head . . . left me dazed . . . hard to concentrate—hard to focus my will through the ring."[26] And stress can take the form of simple exhaustion, as when Hal struggled to hold a building together while completely wiped out: "Can't take much more of this. I've been up all night trying to find the alien. . . . I'm exhausted. . . . Keeping this building together is taking all my concentration . . . all my will!"[27] And let's not forget how much Hal likes to beat Sinestro senseless so the villain can't use his own ring: "Finding it hard to concentrate, aren't you? With me hitting you, I mean! And unless you can focus your willpower, your ring can't work!"[28] Since whatever resource we draw upon to maintain willpower is also used for other mental tasks, anything that uses that scarce "energy" will impair willpower—and therefore a Green Lantern's main weapon.

The Rainbow Connection: Willpower and Emotions

Will and willpower have been central to Green Lantern stories since Hal Jordan's debut in 1959's *Showcase* #22, when Hal said to himself, "I can do anything I want with this ring . . . anything I will to happen . . . I can make happen!" and "All I have to do is use my willpower—and the beam does the rest!"[29] But starting with 2005's *Green Lantern: Rebirth*, writer Geoff Johns further defined the role of the concepts in the Green Lantern mythos, starting with the relationship between willpower and emotion. In that miniseries, Kyle explains the nature of the green energy:

> The Central Battery the Guardians made. It contains willpower for every living being in the universe. Raw emotional willpower converted into energy. . . . There's an emotional electromagnetic spectrum out there that can be harnessed and used. Green willpower is the most pure.[30]

This theme was developed further in Johns's subsequent run in *Green Lantern*, including two crossover events: the Sinestro Corps War, in which the Green Lanterns' willpower-driven energy faced Sinestro's fear-based corps, and the Blackest Night, in which the rest of the "emotional spectrum" was brought to the fore.[31] As Johns explained, in this scheme, the Green Lanterns are "the fulcrum. So if you look at ROY G BIV [a mnemonic for the colors of the spectrum] on a line and it's balancing on the tip of a pin, swaying a little bit—green is the center that doesn't move."[32] Willpower is the balancing force between rage (red), avarice (orange), and fear (yellow) on one side, and hope (blue), compassion (indigo), and love (violet) on the other, with the emotions growing more intense as they move farther from the middle.[33]

Willpower is sometimes described by characters in these stories as an emotion in itself, but it is much better understood as strength in the face of overwhelming emotion. As Johns explained: "You look at emotions of rage and love, these really extreme emotions that can make you do things you never thought you'd do. They're the edges of the spectrum, but as you get into the center, that's where willpower is."[34] Willpower exerts its strength over the emotions so that they can be channeled in the appropriate ways. For instance, during

John Stewart's time on Oa when it hosted a "mosaic" of various alien races (including humans from Earth) the Guardians
had transplanted there, he had to use his ring—and his
willpower—to maintain walls between the different communities to stop them from fighting. Stewart thought to himself, "It
is only a matter of will. To maintain the power of the ring to
glue together the stones and earth that make the walls. Only
a matter of will. To control my own concentration. To harden
my own resolve. To suppress my own terrors."[35] John had to
use his will not only to keep the walls steady, but also to do
so in the face of his fear and other emotions—not to eradi-
cate them completely, but only to "suppress" them when they
didn't serve the greater purpose.

Willpower: The Ultimate Strength

In the final issue of the original run of his book, Hal proudly
proclaims, during a fight with Sinestro, that "in a battle of
willpower, the real strength isn't in power . . . it's in will! My
will has always been the strongest!"[36] That's also true in a
more general sense—a person may be weak physically, but very
strong in terms of willpower and resolve. And it is strength in
this sense that we admire and value in a person's character—
not physical strength, and not even intelligence. No one ever
accused Hal of being the smartest person in the room—unless
he's alone with Guy Gardner—but there's no one else you'd
want at your side when the chips are down.[37]

As Kant wrote, "Strength of any kind can be recognized
only by the obstacles it can overcome," and one such obstacle
is weakness itself.[38] Perhaps Hal said it best when trapped in
the Arctic with a powerless ring:

The measure of a man isn't taken at his strongest. It's
got to be when he's all but down! And when he refuses to
stay down! Even when his body can no longer move . . .

even when all hope has seemingly fled. The measure of man is one who can accept his weaknesses—and make them his strengths.[39]

To recognize the strength in people's characters is to recognize the potential in each of us to be better, to improve ourselves, and to live according to the values we hold dear. Whatever your oath may be, willpower is essential to fulfilling it, and you don't have to be a Green Lantern to do that.

NOTES

1. *Green Lantern: Rebirth #5* (April 2005), reprinted in *Green Lantern: Rebirth* (2005).

2. René Descartes, *Meditations on First Philosophy*, 3rd ed., trans. Donald A. Cress (Indianapolis: Hackett Publishing Inc., 1641/1993); see also E. J. Lowe, *An Introduction to Philosophy of Mind* (Cambridge, UK: Cambridge University Press, 2000), chapter 2, on the topic of dualism.

3. Gilbert Ryle, *The Concept of Mind* (Chicago: University of Chicago Press, 1949/2000), 15–16.

4. See Lowe, *Introduction to Philosophy of Mind*, chapter 8, on the analogy of the mind and brain to computers and artificial intelligence.

5. As the philosopher George Berkeley (1685–1753) is supposed to have said: "What is mind? No matter. What is matter? Never mind." This has been often repeated, but never so memorably as when it was stated by Homer Simpson in the very first *The Simpsons* short in 1987.

6. For more on weakness of will, see Sarah Stroud and Christine Tappolet, eds., *Weakness of Will and Practical Irrationality* (Oxford, UK: Oxford University Press, 2003), especially the introduction by the editors.

7. R. Jay Wallace, *Normativity and the Will: Selected Essays on Moral Psychology and Practical Reason* (Oxford: Oxford University Press, 2006), 174.

8. J. David Velleman, "What Happens When Someone Acts?" *Mind* 101 (1992): 461–481.

9. Wallace, *Normativity and the Will*, 83.

10. John Searle, *Rationality in Action* (Cambridge, MA: MIT Press, 2001), 17.

11. See his *Grounding for the Metaphysics of Morals*, trans. J. W. Ellington (Indianapolis: Hackett Publishing Co., Inc., 1785/1993).

12. Immanuel Kant, *The Metaphysics of Morals*, trans. Mary Gregor (Cambridge, UK: Cambridge University Press, 1797/1996), 397 (emphasis in original).

13. Kant, *Metaphysics of Morals*, 405.

14. Ibid.

15. Ibid., 397 (emphasis in original—Kant liked italics).

16. Ibid., 409.

17. *Action Comics Weekly* #642 (June 1989).

18. Richard Holton, *Willing, Wanting, Waiting* (Oxford, UK: Oxford University Press, 2009), particularly chapter 6.

19. Mark Muraven and Roy F. Baumeister, "Self-Regulation and Depletion of Limited Resources: Does Self-Control Resemble a Muscle?" *Psychological Bulletin* 126 (2000): 247–259, at 247, 254.

20. *Action Comics Weekly* #625 (December 1988).

21. *Green Lantern*, vol. 2, #149 (February 1982). However, in *Green Lantern*, vol. 4, #26 (February 2008; reprinted in *Green Lantern: Rage of the Red Lanterns*, 2009), John Stewart uses his ring to reconstruct the planet of Xanshi (which was destroyed due to his arrogance during 1988's *Cosmic Odyssey* miniseries), and his ring says, "Warning. Willpower exceeding power ring capabilities."

22. *Green Lantern*, vol. 2, #200 (May 1986).

23. *Green Lantern: Rebirth* #4 (March 2005). Obviously, Ollie should have read *Green Lantern*, vol. 2, #135 (December 1980), in which Hal wills his ring back from Dr. Polaris; as the narration box tells us, "The emerald gladiator grits his teeth in agonizing desperation!" (Maybe Ollie was too hurt from being kicked out of the book not long before.)

24. Or maybe Ollie's just a big whiner—after all, his history with women does cast doubt on the extent of his willpower and resolve!

25. Roy F. Baumeister and Todd F. Heatherton, "Self-Regulation Failure: An Overview," *Psychological Inquiry* 7 (1996): 1–15, at 4.

26. *Green Lantern*, vol. 2, #79 (September 1970), reprinted in *Green Lantern/Green Arrow Volume One* (2004).

27. *Action Comics Weekly* #628 (January 1989).

28. *Green Lantern*, vol. 2, #124 (January 1980).

29. *Showcase* #22 (September/October 1959), reprinted in black and white in *Showcase Presents Green Lantern Volume One* (2005) and in color in *The Green Lantern Chronicles Volume One* (2009).

30. *Green Lantern: Rebirth* #3 (February 2005).

31. Both have been collected in a number of trade paperbacks under their respective names.

32. Kiel Phegley, "Q&A: Geoff Johns Prepares for 'Blackest Night,'" *Publishers Weekly*, June 2, 2009 (http://www.publishersweekly.com/pw/by-topic/book-news/comics/article/16267-q-amp-a-geoff-johns-prepares-for-blackest-night-.html).

33. For more on the various Corps connected with each color, see the chapter by Southworth in this volume.

34. Laura Hudson, "Geoff Johns Explores the Emotional Core of 'Blackest Night,'" *Comics Alliance*, August 6, 2009 (http://www.comicsalliance.com/2009/08/06/geoff-johns-explores-the-emotional-corps-of-blackest-night/). However, this should not be taken to deny an important role for emotion in decision-making; see the chapter by Donovan and Richardson in this volume regarding the interaction of emotion and reason.

35. *Green Lantern*, vol. 3, #16 (September 1991); see *Green Lantern*, vol. 3, #14–17 (1991) and the *Green Lantern: Mosaic* series (1992–1993) for more on the Mosaic World.

36. *Green Lantern Corps*, vol. 1, #224 (May 1988). (The second volume of *Green Lantern* was retitled *Green Lantern Corps* starting with #201 and lasting through its final issue, #224.)

37. Of course, the Ch'p is down—R.I.P., honored Green Lantern of Sector 1014 (*Green Lantern: Mosaic* #2, July 1992). Lest you think Ch'p is a joke, make sure you read his solo adventures from the early 1980s, reprinted in *Tales of the Green Lantern Corps Volume One* (2009) and *Volume Two* (2010). (You might be thinking of G'nort—he was a joke.)

38. Kant, *Metaphysics of Morals*, 394.

39. *Green Lantern*, vol. 2, #134 (November 1980).

WOMEN ARE FROM ZAMARON, MEN ARE FROM OA

Sarah K. Donovan and Nicholas P. Richardson

The creators and overseers of the Green Lantern Corps, the Guardians of the Universe, long ago chose to shun emotions and live according to reason alone. Using the Green Lantern Corps to enforce order and fight evil in the universe, they believe that emotion is the root of disorder and evil. By contrast, the Zamarons, originally members of the same race as the Guardians, argue that it is a mistake to stress reason to the neglect of emotion. In this chapter we will use the conflict between the Guardians—until recently, exclusively male—and the Zamarons—all female—as a way to study the classic philosophical argument that reason is superior to emotion, as well as the traditional association of reason with men and emotion with women.[1]

Is Reason Unreasonable?

In philosophy, reason is privileged over sensation or emotion. Reason is supposed to be the most important faculty of the mind, and consequently reason has been traditionally used as a litmus test for who counts as human and is thereby deserving of rights. Trademarks of the discipline of philosophy include abstract thinking and logical argumentation—both activities associated with reason.

In a study of René Descartes (1596–1650), Benedict de Spinoza (1632–1677), and Gottfried Leibniz (1646–1716), contemporary philosopher Moira Gatens shows the way reason has traditionally been seen as abstract and entirely disconnected from culture or history.[2] Even though we need bodies—at least brains—in order to think, traditional ideas of reason assume disembodied knowers. Further, this tradition of reason assumes that the more our reason is disconnected from our everyday lived experience, as people with bodies and feelings, the more it is able to access the truth.[3] A famous example of this is found in Descartes' *Meditations on First Philosophy*. Descartes wants to find the first principles upon which all knowledge is grounded. Rather than explore the world around him, he shuts himself in his study and uses his reason to look within his own mind for answers.

Critics of this view wonder if it is possible or even desirable to weed out the context of our lives as we search our own minds for truths about our world. Even if we were to grant that it is possible for a person's reason to tap into an abstract, timeless truth (that exists, somehow, "out there"), we would still wonder whether that person was able to correctly interpret that truth and accurately convey it to the rest of us. Feminist philosophers are critical of the idealization of the faculty of reason, and question whether a person can use reason correctly in isolation from his or her experiences.[4]

Feminists have also pointed out that the Western tradition aligns men with the mind, reason, and knowledge, and women with the emotions and the body. Against the background of these associations, many feminists have criticized the privileged role of reason in philosophy. While not discounting the value of reason altogether, feminists have extended the discussion in order to explore the value of emotion, both in itself and in relation to reason.

One influential, albeit controversial, example of valuing emotion is found in Carol Gilligan's book *In a Different Voice*. Gilligan is a psychologist who was alarmed by the outcomes of Lawrence Kolhberg's psychological study, which demonstrated that women do not achieve the same level of maturity in moral reasoning as men. Gilligan refused to believe this interpretation of the data and wondered if women achieved moral maturity in a way that would not have been measured by an experiment that employed traditional, masculine categories about what it means to exhibit mature moral reasoning. She argued that women are as sophisticated in moral reasoning as men, but that they reason differently. According to Gilligan, men are predominantly guided by reason and women are predominantly guided by emotion—neither position is superior to the other.

Breaking Up Is Hard to Do

The Guardians' rigid focus on reason over emotion and the Zamarons' devotion to the emotion of love underscore a split between reason and emotion that falls out along gender lines. For instance, the Guardians shun emotion for the purpose of maintaining order in the universe. Naturally, they are predominantly male, and they reside at the center of the universe on the planet Oa, underscoring the central status given to reason over emotion. In "Mystery of the Star Sapphire," from *Wanted: Hal Jordan* (2007), we learn the story of how the Guardians formed the Green Lantern Corps to protect the universe. Since the Guardians place a high value on reason and see emotion as the source of conflict, they devised a set of rules, contained within the Book of Oa, that are intended to help them (and their Green Lantern Corps) police the universe and maintain order. "The Book of Oa will protect us. We can never become victims of the emotional spectrum that has been born out of life's sentience."[5] The Guardians thus protect against any intrusion of emotion, implying that only reason, uncorrupted by emotion, is consistent with their conception of order.[6]

In *Wanted: Hal Jordan*, we learn about the history of the split within the race of Maltusians that resulted in the Oans (who became Guardians) and the Zamarons. Many millennia ago, a group of female Maltusians disagreed with the rejection of emotion dictated by the males and decided to leave the planet. During this period, one woman says about the laws contained in the Book of Oa that "the laws within the book you all have written demand we cleanse ourselves of emotion . . . but life without love or compassion or hope is blasphemy." Collectively, the women who leave Oa in disagreement say, "What you abandon, we shall gather. Beginning with love." On the planet Zamaron, the defectors find two skeletons embracing and a violet light emanating from the skeletons. The women proclaim that "their dying love has given birth to the violet light. We shall shed love's light across the universe," and thereby become the Zamarons.[7]

The Guardians and the Zamarons exemplify a hierarchical relationship between reason and emotion where reason is viewed as superior. Even though the Zamarons were originally Guardians, when they left they became a marginal group that did not significantly rival the Guardians in power or importance in the universe. Through this power imbalance, we can see the relationship between the Guardians and Zamarons as representing the traditional association of men with what is higher (reason) and women with what is lower (emotion).

In her book *The Man of Reason*, contemporary philosopher Genevieve Lloyd examines the historical origins of the imbalance between reason and emotion.[8] Lloyd searches for the roots of reason as a privileged faculty that is both disassociated from the body and associated with men, beginning with the Pythagorean table of opposites. Pythagoras (570–490 BCE) and his followers believed that numbers and mathematics were the key to understanding the world around them. The Pythagorean table broadly categorizes the world in terms of what limits and what is unlimited.[9] As recounted in a testimony by Aristotle (384–322 BCE), "There are ten principles, which they arrange in co-ordinate pairs: limit and unlimited; odd and even; unity and multiplicity; right and left; male and female; still and moving; straight and bent; light and darkness; good and bad; square and oblong."[10] Since these early thinkers place the highest value on rationality, everything on the left side of the table is associated with reason and goodness (male), while that which is on the right is bad and undesirable (female). Lloyd begins with the Pythagorean table in order to explore the persistence of these ideas throughout Western intellectual history. She demonstrates that the very faculty that philosophers believe to have privileged access to the world, reason— untainted by considerations of gender, race, or class—is not in fact neutral but is culturally determined. It follows that assuming the priority of reason perpetuates a legacy of gender inequality throughout history.

In *Sins of the Star Sapphire* (2009), we learn more about the Zamarons' devotion to emotion and witness them in the present day beginning to challenge the Guardians in power and importance. This kind of challenge mirrors what we see in some feminist works (like those of Gilligan and Lloyd). We learn that the Zamarons have become so powerful that the Guardians feel threatened. During a diplomatic meeting on Zamaron, the Guardians and the Zamarons rehash old points of contention about the value of reason and emotion. A Guardian says, "Emotions are like a cancer—they metastasize—love is not a constant—it evolves—it mutates—it's always under internal and external attack." The Queen of the Zamarons, Aga'po, responds, "You have abandoned emotions. And though you deny it, all it's brought you is grief and fear."[11] The Zamarons admit that they plan to continue to accumulate power in order to spread love throughout the universe, and it is clear that the Guardians are concerned.

This developing story line exemplifies Lloyd's point about the reason/emotion divide, and it demonstrates how the split between reason and emotion has been steadily eroding in contemporary times. In the same way that the Zamarons have gained power to rival the Guardians, emotions have gained a more central place of importance in Western culture. For example, traditional expectations of men and women have changed such that men are praised for being nurturing parents and women are praised for excelling in the workplace. Furthermore, the divide between reason and emotions is being challenged. In addition to the expectations about sensitivity in males, politicians (whether male or female) are expected to be politically and emotionally savvy in the sense that we want them to be both strong leaders and people with whom we would enjoy drinking a beer at our local watering hole. Of course, these examples are not without problems, and we are not claiming that the Western world has completely overcome gender bias. But there has been some progress.

Who's Afraid of the Zamarons?

Lloyd's analysis of the philosopher Georg Wilhelm Friedrich Hegel (1770–1831) in *The Man of Reason* helps us to think through at least some of the reasons the Guardians fear the Zamarons (and emotions in general), and it provides us with at least one example of the cultural anxiety that the reason/emotion split creates. According to Hegel, the proper domain of women is the private sphere of the family. Only men belong in the public sphere of politics and government. Women ought to have no role as either active officers or voting members of society because women can only threaten the social and political order. This view is clearly sexist, but let's look deeper and see what it can tell us about opinions from both Hegel's time and the larger intellectual tradition that continues to this day. Hegel's reasoning is as follows: If the proper domain of women is the protection of the family, as associated with the body and emotions, then women cannot, and should not, act in the interests of the state, because the interests of the state are often at odds with those of the family. For example, when there is a military draft, it is in the interest of the state that every eligible citizen register. However, an individual family may not want its children to be drafted and may act in a way to ensure that they are not. According to Hegel and other traditional philosophers, women are not only moderately dangerous to the proper functioning of a state, they possess the power to unravel it. But Hegel is just one example of an intellectual who has internalized the gender norms of his time. His views on women, while in need of critique, reflect a gender framework that both precedes and succeeds him.

Emotions, as associated with women, are portrayed in the *Sins of the Star Sapphire* as threatening to the social and political order. When the Guardians feel as though the Zamarons are gaining too much power, they embark on a diplomatic mission to Zamaron. However, many feminists would argue that the Guardians and Zamarons themselves are trapped in an either/ or mentality (called a false dichotomy) and therefore cannot entertain the possibility that they would all benefit from an alternate way of viewing reason, emotion, and the relationship between them. In her classic book, *Feminist Politics and Human Nature*, Alison Jaggar explores the relationship among reason, emotion, gender, and politics along these lines.[12] One of her premises is that we cannot truly understand political states and social institutions until we have examined the theories of human nature that underlie them. This task is complicated by the fact that human nature has often been viewed as determined by something beyond human control and as monolithic, rather than shaped by culture. Like Lloyd, Jaggar argues that there is no ahistorical position from which to understand the world or human nature. By exploring how the views of human nature that underlie political theories, such as liberalism and Marxism, are culturally influenced, Jaggar underscores the gender bias in traditional political theories.

The *Green Lantern* comics are particularly useful for illustrating aspects of Jaggar's views on liberal feminism. Liberal feminism is based on the traditional, Western, philosophical, liberal political ideals of the Enlightenment (roughly beginning in the mid-seventeenth century) that all rational beings are entitled to autonomy, rationality, independence, and freedom. Liberal feminists accept the foundations of philosophical liberalism as valid—that rational beings are entitled to certain natural rights—but argue that more people (namely, women) need to be included in who counts as rational.[13] Further, they argue that the beings entitled to these rights are not disembodied minds, but human beings whose emotional and embodied needs must be met as well. Traditional liberal political theory fails to recognize this because of its insistence on ahistorical reason.

As with the ideals that underlie liberalism, the Book of Oa is founded on the belief that rules should be written and instituted under the influence of reason only. In other words, emotions ought to play a minimal role in questions of justice and fairness. Jaggar explores the criticisms of liberalism's presentation of itself as somehow exempt from a historical situation. While it prides itself on fairness, this blind spot is the locus of injustice and unfairness. According to liberal feminism, liberalism's emphasis on the ahistorical nature of reason prevents it from seeing the exclusions created by it.

For example, in the United States, prior to the Pregnancy Discrimination Act, women were not protected in the workplace from discrimination if they became pregnant. Pregnancy was seen as pertaining only to women and, therefore, outside of the purview of the law, which was intent only on treating people as equals. In not recognizing a difference that affected justice, the law allowed for injustices.

Likewise with the Guardians: The central goal of the laws in the Book of Oa is to preserve order and justice in the universe. In *Sins of the Star Sapphire* the Guardians add a new rule to the Book of Oa, ruling that "physical relationships and love between Green Lanterns is forbidden within the Corps."[14] This rule intends to protect Green Lantern members whose loved ones would become more vulnerable to violence if they were also members of the Green Lantern Corps, given the Sinestro Corps' refusal to separate their opponents' personal lives from their roles as "soldiers." The goal of the law is to help preserve order and justice in the universe and protect the Green Lantern Corps members. Unfortunately, however, it creates injustice to the extent that it limits who can love whom. The Green Lantern Corps members have not, like the Guardians, forsworn emotions, which are seen by many as central to a full and flourishing life. By imposing this law, the Guardians will unjustly prevent Green Lanterns from having meaningful relationships with each other. After all, if anyone can bear the risk of a dangerous relationship, it's a Green Lantern!

Regardless of how we understand the potential political implications of the split between the Guardians and the Zamarons, it reflects a cultural tradition that men are guided by reason, and women by emotion. The Guardians swear to uphold the principles in the Book of Oa, while the Zamarons defect in order to protect the emotions that the book would suppress. These two groups exemplify a classic, historical dichotomy of mind/body, reason/emotion, and man/woman that contemporary feminist philosophers wish to challenge.

What's a Zamaron to Do?

Feminists such as Lloyd are clear that the final goal of their argument that the reason/emotion split creates a false dichotomy is to allow us to have better philosophical conversations about some of our deepest beliefs. However, some philosophers worry that questioning the privileged status of reason amounts to a rejection of rationality. If reason is no longer privileged, that might seem to be an endorsement of irrationality, and irrationality is often associated with emotion. As we can clearly see, the Guardians provide a fine example of this concern.

Feminists who support positions such as Lloyd's are not suggesting that Western philosophy jettison reason, but that it should move beyond the false dichotomy involved in choosing either reason or emotion. Feminists would say that philosophers who panic at the mere mention of a critique of reason (Immanuel Kant aside!) reflect a general cultural anxiety about women's relationship to reason (or alleged lack thereof), and a stereotype that masculine men are more determined by their minds or reason and feminine women are determined by their bodies or emotions. This is an example of the false dichotomy that feminists are challenging.

Contemporary feminist philosopher Luce Irigaray helps us to think through these questions from a psychoanalytic perspective. Acknowledging that in contemporary Western culture women are typically associated with the (unthinking) body and men with the mind, she argues that this stereotype about women actually disguises their important role as the unacknowledged support and foundation for the rational activities of men. For example, if politics is the proper sphere of men, the traditional politician's career is often made possible by a woman at home who cares for his physical, psychological, spiritual, and intellectual needs. Her role is seen as supporting and not central. For Irigaray, the goal of feminism is not to suggest that women should take over as the dominant sex, but to explore the ways in which women are supporting rationality and to suggest that women may have their own ways of living and defining rationality that may fall outside traditional definitions of that concept. This is not the same as promoting irrationality—to do so would be to attempt to merely argue that the wrong side of the either/or has been dominant.

The struggle between the Zamarons and Guardians exemplifies this kind of wrong-headed battle. If the Zamarons became dominant then they would simply reverse the hierarchy. This would institute a new system of exclusion and oppression on two levels. First, originally the Zamarons only believe that one emotion is important—love. This narrow and limiting view of emotion proves damaging when it overpowers the people who try to harness its power. Second, the goal of overcoming this kind of power hierarchy typically is to move beyond it. In other words, the goal is not a reversal of power, but a rethinking of a power relationship in terms of true equality. This requires both the Zamarons and the Guardians to move to a common ground that does not overemphasize either reason or emotion—some new relationship must emerge.

The *Green Lantern* comics themselves also suggest that thinking in terms of false dichotomies (either/or) is a narrow way of understanding the universe. In fact, this possibility is even written into the Book of Oa as the prophecy of the Blackest Night.[15] It states that there will be an increase in the number of Corps (and thus an increase in the representation of the emotional spectrum) and that this will result in a war. The feared outcome of the war is that light will be extinguished from the universe and everything and everyone will die. Some of the Guardians fear it themselves; they acknowledge it but try to downplay its significance. However, the renegade Guardian Sayd (one of the few female Guardians) demonstrates that she understands it when she says, "The greatest powers in the universe are manifest from emotion. Our power comes from the willpower of sentient life."[16] The concern about emotion in the *Green Lantern* comics extends beyond the relationship between the Guardians and the Zamarons. While still underscoring a philosophical distrust of emotion, it moves beyond associating emotion only with women.

Can't We All Just Get Along?

As the *Blackest Night* story line and its "War of Light" develops, so do the number of Corps associated with the spectrum of emotions, including the Red Lantern Corps, Agent Orange, and the Indigo Tribe.[17] Both the Zamarons and the Guardians begin to rethink their commitment to love and reason, respectively. While no group successfully challenges the false dichotomy of reason and emotion, the events in that story line force groups toward more complex thinking about the relationship between reason and emotion. As an example, in *Blackest Night* #3, the Indigo Tribe believes that the unification of the seven Corps will be able to overcome the Black Lantern Corps. In the cosmology of the series, darkness filled the universe before light appeared; white light, representing life, then dominated until darkness fought back against it and fractured it into the spectrum of colors representing the various emotions. As a member of the Indigo Tribe says, "Every sentient being born from the light now contributes to its emotion spectrum." She indicates that the emotional spectrum must be unified again if they are to successfully combat the darkness, saying, "That is why we have come to you, Green Lantern. Together, the seven corps can replicate the white light of creation. Together we will be capable of locating and destroying the source of the black rings."[18] While we cannot predict how the relationship between reason and emotion will resolve itself, we can see that neither the Zamarons nor the Guardians can survive if they maintain the position of defending only love or only reason, respectively. Both groups arrive at an awareness of this, although we do not yet know exactly what it will mean for them.

At the end of *Wanted: Hal Jordan*, the Zamarons themselves start to see that it is problematic to focus on only one emotion, although they still focus exclusively on emotion in general. After the power of the sapphire takes over their queen and they are unable to control her, they say, "We have been obsessed with the study of one emotion for so long, we have done what the Guardians have. We abandoned emotions."[19] The Zamarons conclude that they need to focus on other emotions besides just love. In fact, they argue that in order to combat the prophecy of the Blackest Night, they must collect all of the emotions. While this does not bridge the gap between reason and emotion, it at least moves along the eventual confrontation between them.

In *The Sinestro Corps War* and the *Blackest Night* story lines, the Guardians also begin to question their exclusive emphasis on reason, culminating in the repeal of the third law (prohibiting relationships between Lanterns). In *The Sinestro Corps War*, two Guardians, Ganthet and Sayd, challenge the rejection of emotions. While they are expelled from Oa for their rebellion, they foreshadow that the Guardians must come to grips with the unrealistic position that reason can be emphasized to the exclusion of emotion; the prophecy of the Blackest Night is being fulfilled.

In *Green Lantern Corps* #47 (June 2010), Lanterns Guy Gardner, Kyle Rayner, and Arisia confront the Guardians about the death of fellow Lantern Sodam Yat. As the Guardians defend themselves by blaming the death on a corrupt Guardian, Scar, the Lanterns argue that the Guardians' rejection of emotion still makes them culpable for many other wrongs done to the Lanterns. Rayner reminds them of the experienced Lanterns who left the Corps because of their disagreement with the third law. He implores them to consider the error of their overly rigid emphasis on reason when he says,

With respect, cold, emotionless logic didn't win this war of light and beat back the Blackest Night prophecy.

Lanterns with heart did. Lanterns with soul did. And Lanterns with will won it and saved the universe. When you all finally realize—and embrace that fact—that's when this Corps will fully be on the right track.[20]

As *Green Lantern Corps* #47 progresses, we learn that the Guardians were swayed by Rayner's plea: the third law is repealed. With this act, the Guardians entered into unchartered territory; they have willingly blurred the line between reason and emotion, and the consequences of this will surely be told in future stories.

The Things We Do for Love

While the relationship between the Guardians and the Zamarons represents the stereotype and not an alternative to the reason/emotion duality, the *Green Lantern* comics grapple with questions that concern contemporary feminist philosophers: Is there a third way besides the confining either/or of reason/emotion? Is there a way for Western thinking to evolve past dualistic thinking in general? Or are we doomed to live out one-sided existences as either "minds" or "bodies?" Will we always be limited by either/or thinking? The *Green Lantern* comics, and the *Blackest Night* story line in particular, can help us to think through these important philosophical questions. If the Guardians and all of the Lantern Corps band together against the Black Lantern Corps, then we will see an example of a third way outside of the either/or of emotion/reason. Regardless of how the story line plays out, the Zamarons have already discovered that they cannot exclusively focus on love as the only emotion of importance, and the Guardians have realized that they must rethink their relationship to emotion if they are to survive. We can only assume that the developments in the *Blackest Night* story line, and the threat imposed by the Black Lantern Corps, will continue to force both the

Zamarons and the Guardians to rethink the relationship between reason and emotion, and to displace them from their entrenched, polarized positions. This is truly a project for our times.

NOTES

1. Here we use the language of "men" and "women" in part because it reflects the language with which reason/emotion divide has traditionally been framed. However, it is important to note that the feminist movement that began in the 1960s helped to articulate the important insight that gender (defined as socially determined behavior) is not causally determined by one's sex or anatomy. For example, just because a person is anatomically female, she does not have to act feminine. While the sex/gender distinction was revolutionary, it is now considered oversimplified. Current discussions of identity now consider the complexities of transgendered and intersexed identities, to name a few.

2. Moira Gatens, "Modern Rationalism," in Alison Jaggar and Iris Marion Young, eds., *A Companion to Feminist Philosophy* (New York: Wiley-Blackwell, 2000), 21–29.

3. Gatens's "Modern Rationalism" glosses key feminist critiques, from a variety of perspectives, of the traditional definition of rationality. For example, with regard to Descartes in particular, she discusses Genevieve Lloyd's philosophical critique and Susan Bordo's psychoanalytic critique.

4. Of course, feminist philosophers are not the only philosophers to initiate these kinds of challenges. Many other philosophers who may not directly identify as feminist are still engaged in deconstruction of the traditional model of knowing, such as Friedrich Nietzsche (1844–1900) and Michel Foucault (1926–1984).

5. *Green Lantern*, vol. 4, #19 (June 2007), reprinted in *Green Lantern: Wanted: Hal Jordan* (2007).

6. Another example that further emphasizes the extent to which the Guardians reject emotion deals with two Guardians, Sayd and Ganthet, who are chastised for allowing emotion to influence them. They are told by another Guardian, "The two of you are charged with the ultimate betrayal—acting on emotion—and are hereby banished from this council" (*Green Lantern*, vol. 4, #23, November 2007, reprinted in *Green Lantern: The Sinestro Corps War Volume 1*, 2008). Emotion is given no positive value among the Guardians.

7. *Green Lantern*, vol. 4, #19. (This is the latest version of the story of the Zamarons, which newly refers to the violet light of love, consistent with the recent emphasis on the "emotional spectrum" introduced to the Green Lantern mythos by Geoff Johns in *Green Lantern: Rebirth*.)

8. Genevieve Lloyd, *The Man of Reason: "Male" and "Female" in Western Philosophy* (New York: Taylor & Francis, 1993).

9. See *The First Philosophers: The Presocratics and the Sophists*, translated with commentary by Robin Waterfield (New York: Oxford University Press, 2000). Waterfield describes Pythagoras as dividing the world into objects that are either "limiters" or "unlimited" (91).

10. Ibid., 103.

11. *Green Lantern Corps*, vol. 2, #30 (January 2009), reprinted in *Green Lantern Corps: Sins of the Star Sapphire* (2009).

12. Alison Jaggar, *Feminist Politics and Human Nature* (New York: Rowman and Littlefield, 1983).

13. Some liberal feminists also support androgyny, which is the belief that both men and women should embrace the best characteristics of masculinity and femininity.

14. *Green Lantern Corps*, vol. 2, #30.

15. *Green Lantern*, vol. 4, #21 (September 2007), reprinted in *Green Lantern: The Sinestro Corps War Volume 1*.

16. *Green Lantern: Sinestro Corps Special* (August 2007), reprinted in *Green Lantern: The Sinestro Corps War Volume 1*.

17. *Blackest Night* (2009–2010) and the lead-in story lines in *Green Lantern* and *Green Lantern Corps*.

18. *Blackest Night* #3 (November 2009).

19. *Green Lantern*, vol. 4, #20 (July 2007), reprinted in *Green Lantern: Wanted: Hal Jordan*.

20. *Green Lantern Corps*, vol. 2, #47 (June 2010).

PART TWO

EMERALD ETHICS: IT'S NOT ALL BLACK AND WHITE

WILL THEY LET JUST ANYBODY JOIN?: TESTING FOR MORAL JUDGMENT IN THE GREEN LANTERN CORPS

Andrew Terjesen

If you're expecting this chapter to be a lengthy diatribe against G'nort, then you will be severely disappointed. I'm not interested in questioning the competence of anyone who is chosen to bear the emerald standard of a Green Lantern.[1] Instead, I want to look at how someone like Sinestro or Universo ever got into the Corps in the first place. Given the awesome might wielded by each power ring, you would think that the Guardians of the Universe would have more safeguards in place than just a weakness against yellow and a twenty-four-hour charge.

When Hal Jordan is given the ring of Abin Sur, he is selected because he is "entirely without fear" and honest.[2] But it is never explained why these are the only two criteria for being a Green Lantern. In fact, at times the Guardians of the Universe even seem whimsical when they pass on a power ring. Charlie Vicker, an actor who plays Green Lantern in a movie, is given a power ring on Hal's say-so without any formal test.[3] And when Kyle Rayner is given the last power ring after a crazed Hal Jordan destroys the Central Power Battery, the Guardian Ganthet says, "You will have to do."[4] It seems like Kyle was chosen just because he was the first person Ganthet ran into.[5]

With such a lax attitude toward their own standards, it is no surprise that there were some individuals who ended up washing out of the Corps or being disciplined for abuses of power. About the only questionable choice the Guardians can't be blamed for is Guy Gardner, since he suffered brain damage after being selected as Hal's backup in Sector 2814.[6] As we'll see, trying to understand the difficulty that the Guardians have in eliminating bad apples from the Corps requires looking at some long-standing debates in ethics concerning the nature of morality and moral judgment.

Sinestro: Evil Is in the Eye of the Beholder?

Perhaps the greatest traitor to the Corps was (and still is) Sinestro. This Korugarian was called the "greatest Green Lantern" until his lust for power led him to abuse his ring, earning him the distinction of being the first Green Lantern to be booted out of the Corps. (The next Lantern to be kicked out was Universo about a thousand years later, which leads one to think the Guardians needed an additional requirement for being a Green Lantern: that your name not end in "o.") Given the ability of the Guardians to read minds, this seems like a serious breakdown of the recruitment system. Sinestro is not simply power-hungry, however. His fall from grace is a direct result of the qualities that made him the greatest Green Lantern long before Hal Jordan took that title.

In his first appearance Sinestro is described as someone who, due to a "psychological quirk," did not have enough resistance to the "virus of power" that infected him when he began to wield a power ring.[7] He eventually establishes himself as dictator on his home planet until he is stripped of his ring by the Guardians. Afterward, Sinestro becomes dedicated to gaining power and getting revenge on the Guardians. The idea that the "wise" Guardians could have failed to notice such a "psychological quirk" seems pretty implausible. In recent retellings of his origin, Sinestro is no longer power-hungry, but rather is someone whose particular interpretation of "evil" is a little out of sync with that of the Guardians.

Now, Sinestro is presented as someone who is obsessed with order.[8] He regards the people of Korugar as "Like children. Basically good, but they need to be watched." In the name of order, he establishes a surveillance state and suppresses all dissent. When the rebels finally overcome Sinestro (with Hal's help), Sinestro insists, "I did the right thing" and is worried that the Guardians will misunderstand his "best intentions."[9] When the Guardians finally strip him of his ring and send him into exile, he insists that the Guardians have become agents of chaos. In Sinestro's mind, he is the only one who realizes what needs to be done to bring about what is best for the universe. During the recent Sinestro Corps War, Sinestro claims that he was only acting in order to push the Guardians to embrace methods that are more effective in dealing with universal chaos and the coming Blackest Night.[10]

Sinestro may be in denial, but his explanation of his actions is plausible.[11] When the Guardians are finally confronted with evidence that Sinestro had exceeded his authority as a Green Lantern, they recognize that their mental probing could eliminate only the "corruptible and self-interested." Sinestro is neither of those; he hasn't been corrupted. Sinestro sticks to his ideals. He's not acting out of his own self-interest, but (in his mind) for the good of his people and the universe.

The case of Sinestro exposes a fundamental problem with the system for selecting Green Lanterns: the Guardians do not choose recruits based on the content of their beliefs. To be fair, this problem arises because the Corps is an intergalactic police force, and the members of the Corps represent a very diverse set of ethical beliefs. If the Guardians were to try to enforce specific morals, they would undoubtedly find themselves in conflict with many of the beings they are trying to protect. Instead, the Guardians have identified character traits that they think are crucial for being successful Green Lanterns and presumably good people. Honesty (or "honor," as it is sometimes described in the comics) seems a pretty straightforward choice. Presumably being "without fear" is connected to bravery or integrity. The Guardians are not concerned with what Sinestro thinks is the best way to create order, but whether he would stick by his principles and not have any ulterior motives for his actions.

One response to moral disagreement is to embrace *moral relativism* and claim that there are no objective moral values. Most of us, however, recognize that relativism has its limits—not every course of action is morally permissible. Even Sinestro and the Red Lantern Atrocitus recognize that allowing the demon Nekron to destroy all life in the universe during the Blackest Night was unacceptable. And just because one rejects moral relativism does not mean one must be a *moral absolutist* who thinks that there is only one answer to the question: What is the right thing to do?

In between relativism and absolutism is *moral pluralism*, the belief that there are different conceptions of the good, but not an infinite number of possibilities. So a moral pluralist could condemn Sinestro's "morality" without feeling the need to decide between the very different moral codes of, say, Hal Jordan and Guy Gardner. What is distinct about the Guardians' moral pluralism is that they believe there are universal moral rules as represented by their two-prong test of honesty and fearlessness.[12] However, as pluralists they recognize that these rules are not the sum total of morality, and so the two-prong test must be vague enough to let different moral codes through. Sometimes that means letting in someone with a bad code of conduct that sounds good—like Sinestro's "I want to create order in the universe."

Jack T. Chance: Doing What Needs to Be Done?

Just because the Guardians believe in the existence of universal moral rules does not mean that they think every situation can be resolved by appeal to any one fixed rule. At the same time, just because one thinks that there is no one moral rule to appeal to does not mean that there isn't a right and a wrong thing to do in any given situation. The Guardians' moral pluralism enables them to recognize that there can be ways of being moral other than the specific way of life that they have chosen. In fact, in some situations their way of life and moral code might not be as well-suited to the circumstances as another. The Guardians seem to recognize this. Just consider the recruitment of Jack T. Chance.

Jack lives in the absolutely worst sector of the universe, on a planet that has become known as "Hellhole." Any Green Lantern who tries to clean up the sector is quickly killed. After the latest Green Lantern appointed to that sector meets the usual fate, the power ring selects Jack as its new bearer and charges him with enforcing justice on Hellhole. But Jack is not your typical Green Lantern. He has a wild, indulgent lifestyle. Indeed, he does not mind committing a number of crimes, and seems to have little regard for sentient life—other than his own. Still, he thinks it would be fun to use his power ring to take down the really awful inhabitants of Hellhole, and so he goes along with his new assignment. When the Guardians confront him, he points out, "You sent a good man to clean up a bad sector. Good men are going to get killed here. What you need is a good bad man. Someone as mean and as nasty as the people he's going up against. . . . You may know order and all that frap. . . . But you don't know the gutter. I do."[13]

Jack's reasoning convinces the Guardians to let him keep his ring. As one of the Guardians notes, "He is honest. Nowhere do the requirements say he must be a nice sentient."[14] But there are limits to the Guardians' moral pluralism: Jack cannot leave Hellhole, and he is still forbidden to kill. The Guardians' approach to this situation suggests that the prerequisites for being a Green Lantern are intentionally few in order to allow for some situational flexibility. While their moral pluralism enables them to recognize that many aspects of their moral code are not well-suited to life on Hellhole, they also recognize that Hellhole is a unique environment. The conception of good that Jack developed on Hellhole is different from the conception of good in the rest of the universe. Guy Gardner gives a similar explanation for why he was selected to be a Green Lantern: "Worthiness means one thing when things are stable . . . and somethin' else when things are fallin' apart."[15] Still, until recently the Guardians refused to budge on the prohibition of killing, which indicates that they think that it is a universal component of all moralities. Even though they're moral pluralists, the Guardians still believe in some pretty strong constraints on what counts as moral behavior.

In recent years the Guardians have taken various actions that show that they are willing to be even more flexible, if the circumstances warrant it. Most notably, they have suspended their own rules against killing on a number of occasions. To begin with, a specially sanctioned black ops group known as the "Corpse," led by unofficial Green Lantern Von Daggle, is used to deal with threats that the Guardians need eliminated but for one reason or another cannot be dealt with by the regular Corps.[16] The Corpse had been operating for a long time using power from the Central Power Battery channeled through a special device so that it did not appear to be the emerald energy of the Corps. Disturbingly, Guy Gardner—yes, *that* Guy Gardner—is deemed too moral to be a member of the Corpse (after he refuses to kill a prisoner). In order to keep the Corpse as the Guardians' dirty little secret, Guy's memory of that mission is erased. Clearly, this is not the behavior of a group that is dedicated to honesty.

It's not clear how much the Guardians will need the Corpse after the Sinestro Corps War and the Blackest Night. During those events, the Guardians removed the prohibition on killing, and rank-and-file Green Lanterns were now allowed to kill members of the Sinestro Corps. This major rewriting of the Book of Oa was followed by a new rule permitting lethal force to be used against any individual who was an enemy of the Green Lantern Corps and for the execution of prisoners. The Guardians licensed the use of lethal force because they thought that the current galactic situation required a more drastic approach to "law enforcement." However, after the Blackest Night, the Guardians did not repeal these new laws, suggesting that they have adopted a new moral code, as opposed to merely suspending the old one. The new moral code is still consistent with their two-prong test, which makes sense from a moral pluralist standpoint. And there are still some constraints: the new rules do not license the use of lethal force against just anyone, and lethal force is still viewed as a last resort.

Laira: The Strength of One's Convictions?

Laira is presented as a Green Lantern candidate who has a very intricate sense of honor instilled in her by her father, himself a former Green Lantern. Laira's final test is to confront a threat on her home planet of Jayd, which turns out to be her long-lost father, Kentor Omoto (proving, once again, the wisdom of the "no names ending in 'o'" rule). Her father had been appalled that Jayd was moving away from the "time-honored customs" he had taught his daughter, and he used his power ring to influence government officials so that they would end the societal reforms they had implemented. When the Guardians discovered what he had done, they stripped him of his ring and made up a story to hide his fate from his daughter Laira.[17]

Yet again, this does not seem to be the work of an organization dedicated to honesty, another possible instance of hypocrisy on the part of the Guardians. To show that this is not necessarily a double standard, we need to examine more closely Laira and her father's concept of honesty—or honor, as the Guardians often call it. Honor is an example of a *thick* ethical concept, which requires a cultural and social context in order to have meaning.[18] A person cannot be honorable unless there is an established code of honor to follow. In contrast, a *thin* ethical concept can be defined without reference to those contexts. For example, "right" is a thin ethical concept that is understood as "doing whatever the morality you follow says you ought to do."

But there is more to a thick ethical concept than just context, otherwise honor would just be a slightly more complex thin concept, implying that one should act according to the rules of the society that one was born into. Honor doesn't specify the rules themselves, because it would be impossible to specify a rule for every situation. Instead, being honorable is about knowing which societal rules to follow, what rules can be broken, and how to interpret vague rules like "Respect your elders." This allows some leeway in application. So even though both Laira and her father are acting according to the social rules of Jayd, they end up taking very different actions. A thick ethical concept requires a tradition to help an individual fill in the gaps in the inevitably incomplete definition of that concept.

Honesty is also a thick ethical concept (although it is not clear that the Guardians recognize this) because an honest person is not simply someone who always tells the truth. For instance, Hal would still be an honest person even if he told Carol Ferris that her latest Star Sapphire uniform was not degrading! In some cases, honesty might even require a lie to protect some greater truth, such as when the Guardians cover up Kentor's actions and the existence of the Corpse. This is not to say that the Guardians' deceptions are necessarily morally justified, but rather that whether they are depends upon a robust definition of honesty that cannot be reduced to simple rules (as happens with thin ethical concepts).

Much like a young Anakin Skywalker, Laira's emotions proved her undoing. When her friend Ke'haan and his family were killed by Amon Sur of the Sinestro Corps (and is also the son of Abin Sur), she finally "snapped" and killed Sur after he surrendered. It gets worse: after she was stripped of her ring and sent for punishment, her anger at her situation led her to be inducted into the rage-fueled Red Lantern Corps.[19] At this point her emotions became so intense that she was in a state of constant rage, without any conscious thought, and took out her aggression on whatever target Atrocitus, the leader of the Red Lantern Corps, pointed to. In the end, she died at the hands of Sinestro after she tried to kill Hal Jordan.[20]

Laira's rage drove her out of control, but as she saw it, the Guardians had treated her very unfairly. At her trial, she claimed that her actions fell within the rules that the Guardians had set. The Guardians had approved the use of lethal force against all Sinestro Corps members, but they never specified that the Corps members had to be engaged in active combat. In addition, she argued that the threat posed by Amon Sur (who was engaging in terrorist actions against the Green Lantern Corps) would not end unless he was killed.[21] During Laira's trial, the Guardians considered the circumstances to determine if she had acted wrongly or rightly, which implies that they viewed murder as a thick ethical concept. In the end, Laira thought the threat that Amon Sur posed was relevant, but the Guardians disagreed.

The conflict between the Guardians and Laira over her actions highlights one of the great concerns about thick ethical concepts: How can we determine who has made a correct moral judgment? Laira and the Guardians looked at the same particular situation and made different judgments about it. The Guardians thought it was "obvious" that lethal force was a last resort for Green Lanterns, even though there is nothing in the new laws that gives guidance as to when something is a last resort. Presumably they would argue that their judgment is better because it is not clouded by grief, anger, or a desire for vengeance. One problem with that argument is that it begs the question against Laira, because it assumes that emotions cannot be a part of the moral perception of a situation. After all, why must rage automatically be excluded from moral consideration? Words seem to fail to capture the horrendous nature of Amon Sur's actions, but rage can really encapsulate our gut reaction to such slaughter. Besides, the Guardians' own change in policy seemed to be motivated by fear and a desire to keep the Corps going. And if Laira's judgment based on emotion must be discounted, then so should their later judgments.

Even among the Green Lanterns there was disagreement concerning whether Laira had acted inappropriately.[22] One Lantern, Sir Deeter, thought that the recorded footage of Laira's encounter with Amon Sur showed that she acted within the strict code of the Corps, whereas another Green Lantern, Varix, thought that Deeter's judgment was colored by the medieval world he lives on. Varix was in turn chided by yet another Lantern, Kraken, because on Varix's world a murderer is only sentenced to two years. The Green Lantern Corps consists of 7,200 sentient beings who have very different judgments about the moral particulars of a situation, which is not surprising when it comes to such thick ethical concepts. However, if there can be such a sharp divergence of opinion concerning Laira's actions, it would seem that the Corps could easily contain individuals who under the right circumstances would view the other members as "evil."

The Alpha Lanterns: Who Gets to Enforce "Justice"?

As we've seen, the Guardians' moral pluralism seems to include the belief that there are at least some universal ethical concepts. By definition these concepts would need to be thin ethical concepts, because thick ethical concepts would be dependent on cultural context and how this context is used to interpret ethical rules. The need for thin ethical concepts probably explains why one of the requirements for the Corps is fearlessness as opposed to bravery or courage, which are both thick ethical concepts. What it means to be courageous cannot be specified without attention to context; under the right circumstances, discretion is the better part of valor. In fact, it seems so hard to determine when one is obligated to retreat that each culture comes up with its own understanding of the distinction between reckless-ness and courage.

The idea that no moral judgments can be made without relying on some thick ethical concepts is known as *moral particularism*.[23] A person can be both a moral pluralist *and* a moral particularist, in which case that person believes there are several different sets of thick ethical concepts (or several different interpretations of the same set of thick ethical concepts) that are equally valid—the pluralist aspect—and which are necessary to make moral judgments—the particularist aspect. Practically speaking, being a moral particularist poses an important problem for the Green Lantern Corps. Given the sheer number of Corps members, the size of their jurisdictions, the large number of cultural contexts that could influence their understanding of thick ethical concepts like honesty, and the myriad ways in which slight changes in circumstances might be relevant, it is practically impossible to determine whether any given

Green Lantern has necessarily done the "right" thing. A moral particularist would say that what matters isn't whether we can know for sure that someone acted morally, but what would make the judgment right (even if no one ever knew it was the right judgment). However, the Guardians depend upon the belief that Green Lanterns act honorably to preserve camaraderie within the Corps and to maintain the public faith that they are impartial arbiters of the peace. Given how important this is to the Corps, it is worth considering whether it is possible to create a working ethical code without relying on thick ethical concepts.

The Alpha Lanterns were created by the Guardians after Laira's trial to serve as internal affairs officers for the Corps. Presumably, the Alpha Lanterns can look at a situation and see it more clearly and objectively than the normal Lanterns involved. But the real problem posed by moral particularism is that it is not clear how to decide between two different assessments of a situation because of the reliance upon thick ethical concepts. So the Alpha Lanterns would need to have some special quality that would distinguish their judgment from that of the other Lanterns. If any Lantern could be an Alpha Lantern, then the Alpha Lanterns are just another level of bureaucracy; they do not have superior judgment. In fact, Lanterns are chosen to join the Alpha Lanterns because they have "the ability to enforce justice."[24] "Justice" is usually thought of as a thin ethical concept, understood as a fair application of the rules to ensure that everyone is treated equally. Although regular Corps members are still relying on the thick ethical concepts that they learned as a part of their upbringing, Alpha Lanterns would have an understanding of the moral principles that govern all of our thick ethical concepts.

But a problem arises because there are good reasons for doubting that justice is really a thin ethical concept. To start with, how is "fairness" to be understood? Does "fair" mean that the rules are applied without any attention to particular circumstances? In that case, the fair way to pick a Green Lantern would be by random lottery. Does "fair" mean that everyone gets the same outcome? The same starting point? I could go on (don't tempt me). Similarly, treating everyone equally seems to be an idea that comes out of a certain cultural tradition. Even in our world today, not everyone agrees with the universal equality of all humans. And in our world the idea that other species are equal to humans is a minority view. The Corps, though, is composed of thousands of species (not all of whom regard one another as equals). It just doesn't seem possible to have a moral code that is completely divorced from thick ethical concepts.

The Green Lantern Kraken became an Alpha Lantern so that she would have even more power to use in her fight against Darkseid, the evil New God of Apokolips. Since Darkseid is such a bad guy (to put it mildly), this does not really seem an immoral motivation. But it does show that Kraken is not necessarily as dedicated to universal justice for all as the Guardians want her to be. She may really be concerned only with what it takes to bring about just results on her home world. What this shows is that even though there may be some thin ethical concepts, we need thick ethical concepts to move us to act as moral agents. (And again, the Guardians' two-prong test contains at least one thick ethical concept.) This means that the Alpha Lanterns can't really address the underlying problem posed by moral particularism. They don't know or represent a set of moral principles that are independent of social context and cultural tradition. At best, the Alpha Lanterns would be imposing the moral code of the Guardians' culture (whatever that might be—Oanism?) with its interpretation of justice, honesty, integrity, and so on.[25] In reality, though—at least the DC Universe reality—every Alpha Lantern seems to be like Kraken, with his or her own particularist interpretation of the Corps' moral code.

The Thin and Thick of It

As our tour through some of the more questionable choices for Green Lanterns has shown, it is not easy to run an intergalactic organization that relies upon its agents to "do the right thing." To begin with, the Guardians must embrace pluralistic conceptions of morality if it is going to work at all, and that means sometimes admitting that someone else's way of life is more appropriate to particular circumstances. After all, that's the only reason Jack T. Chance got the job. At the same time, pluralism is not a license to practice just any morality. Sinestro's conception of what is good for the universe goes too far. The Guardians probably hoped that by relying on certain universal ethical concepts they would be able to weed out the "bad moralities" like Sinestro's. But they should not ignore the fact that even their two-prong test is dependent upon thick ethical concepts. "Do your duty" or "Do what is just" are empty platitudes if we think of "duty" and "justice" as thin ethical concepts. To understand what is just or our duty, we need some idea of what our goals in life should be and what to do when the rules are vague or in conflict. Since there is no single way that everyone should live their life, it is only by situating these concepts into a particular social and cultural context that specifies particular goals that these words have any meaning. And since it is unlikely that there is only one way to resolve a moral dilemma, there will be more than one tradition that could be relied on to give sound guidance in the matter. But that means there will be disagreements, like the one between Laira and the Guardians, that cannot be resolved because there is no undisputed authority to settle the matter. And no Alpha Lantern employing a thin conception of morality will change that.

NOTES

1. It's pretty clear in G'nort's first appearance (*Justice League International* #10, February 1988) that he was intended to cast doubt on the idea that the Guardians always selected candidates based on their merit. He claimed to be a Green Lantern due to his uncle's influence. However, in "A Guy and His G'nort" (*Green Lantern*, vol. 3, #9–13, 1991), it was revealed that G'nort's Green Lantern status was a hoax perpetrated by the Weaponers of Qward (or at least that is the short version of a very complicated retcon designed to reestablish the legitimacy of the Corps). Still, at the end of the adventure, the bumbling G'nort is rewarded for his bravery and honesty with membership in the *true* Green Lantern Corps, so those qualities seem to matter more than competence at one's job.

2. *Showcase* #22 (September–October 1959), reprinted in black and white in *Showcase Presents Green Lantern Volume One* (2005) and in color in *The Green Lantern Chronicles Volume One* (2009).

3. *Green Lantern*, vol. 2, #55–56 (September–October 1967), reprinted in *Showcase Presents Green Lantern Volume Three* (2008). In *Green Lantern*, vol. 2, #157–158 (October–November 1982), a backup story reveals that Charlie does his job, but does not have much respect for the aliens he protects. This is probably why getting a ring usually requires more than a recommendation.

4. *Green Lantern*, vol. 3, #50 (March 1994), reprinted in *Green Lantern: Emerald Twilight/New Dawn* (2003).

5. It was revealed later that Ganthet first sought out Guy Gardner, who refused the ring (*Green Lantern Secret Files* #1, July 1998).

6. Diagnosed in *Green Lantern*, vol. 2, #123 (December 1979). Admittedly, the arrogant, power-mad, brain-damaged Guy was made a Green Lantern by a rogue faction within the Guardians (as detailed in *Green Lantern*, vol. 2, #194–200, 1985–1986) to deal with the Crisis on Infinite Earths. But even after it had passed, the remaining Guardians allowed Guy to remain in the Corps because he had been selected by Guardians according to the traditional criteria. Why those criteria would allow someone like Guy to slip through is what will be explored in this chapter.

7. *Green Lantern*, vol. 2, #7 (July–August 1961), reprinted in black and white in *Showcase Presents Green Lantern Volume One* and in color in *The Green Lantern Chronicles Volume Two* (2009).

8. As depicted in the 1991 *Emerald Dawn II* miniseries that relates the story of how Sinestro trained Hal, and how Hal exposed Sinestro's crimes.

9. Ibid.

10. See *Green Lantern: The Sinestro Corps War Volume 1* and *Volume 2* (both 2009).

11. See the chapter by Dryden in this volume titled "The Greatest Green Lantern" for more on the morality of Sinestro's motivation.

12. The best example of the Guardians' moral pluralism is *Green Lantern*, vol. 2, #154–155 (July–August 1982) in a story titled "Rotten to the Corps." Hal meets Dalor, the Green Lantern of neighboring Sector 2813, who accepts rewards from the people he helps. Hal reports this to the Guardians as a violation of the Corps' rules. Hal learns that all of Dalor's people do good deeds in exchange for rewards (including a mother taking care of her child) and recognizes that he has been too narrow in his moral view. It is strongly suggested that the Guardians arranged Hal's encounter with Dalor in order to teach Hal to respect other conceptions of morality. However, Dalor leaves his encounter with the realization that good deeds do not require rewards and wants to spread that message to his people. Since this is also the result of the Guardians' machinations, it is evidence that the Guardians think that certain moral ideals ought to be a part of every culture.

13. *Green Lantern Corps Quarterly* #1 (Summer 1992).

14. Ibid.

15. *Green Lantern*, vol. 2, #197 (February 1986).

16. The existence of the Corpse is revealed when Guy Gardner joins them for a mission in *Green Lantern Corps*, vol. 2, #7–9 (2007), reprinted in *Green Lantern Corps: The Dark Side of Green* (2008).

17. *Green Lantern Corps Quarterly* #6 (Autumn 1993).

18. Although it is hard to determine who first coined the usage of "thick" and "thin" to describe ethical concepts, credit for popularizing this way of thinking about ethics goes to Bernard Williams (1929–2003) and his book *Ethics and the Limits of Philosophy* (Cambridge, MA: Harvard University Press, 1986).

19. Laira's fall is detailed in *Green Lantern*, vol. 4, #26–28 (2008), reprinted in *Green Lantern: Rage of the Red Lanterns* (2009). (See also the chapter in this volume by White titled "Crying for Justice" for more on Laira's trial.)

20. *Green Lantern*, vol. 4, #37 (January 2009), reprinted in *Green Lantern: Rage of the Red Lanterns* (2009).

21. At the time, the Guardians were still opposed to executing their prisoners, but after the Blackest Night started they rewrote the Book of Oa to permit capital punishment.

22. *Green Lantern*, vol. 4, #27 (March 2008).

23. The most notable moral particularist is the contemporary philosopher Jonathan Dancy, who has even presented his views on *The Late Late Show with Craig Ferguson*; see Dancy's *Ethics without Principles* (Oxford, UK: Oxford University Press, 2004).

24. *Green Lantern*, vol. 4, #27.

25. I have been reluctant to address directly what the morality of the Guardians might be. Recent depictions of the Guardians have emphasized their reliance upon logic (as opposed to emotion) in making moral judgments; see the chapter in this volume by Donovan and Richardson for more on this. Also, see my other chapter in this volume, on moral sentimentalism and moral rationalism, for a fuller discussion of why the Guardians' morality could not simply be reduced to logic. After the Blackest Night, even the Guardians have admitted that a purely utilitarian calculus is inadequate.

THE GREATEST GREEN LANTERN: AESTHETIC ADMIRATION AND THE PRAISEWORTHY HERO

Jane Dryden

Hal Jordan and Sinestro have each been called "the greatest Green Lantern." What makes them so great? And why doesn't Kyle Rayner get the "greatest Green Lantern" adulation, despite his stint as Torchbearer? While Hal and Kyle are both, generally speaking, the "good guys," with Sinestro as a mustachioed "bad guy," Hal and Sinestro have a certain aesthetic quality in common: a larger-than-life quality that commands our admiration, which Kyle simply lacks.

Despite all his faults, we can't help but stand back and admire Hal, however grudgingly. Similarly, despite his being technically a villain, we can also see something admirable in Sinestro, especially in the retellings of his life story in *Emerald*

Dawn II (1991) and the more recent *Secret Origin* (2008). Kyle, by contrast, is likeable and gains the respect of the public, the Corps, the Guardians, and the Justice League, but is never "the greatest Green Lantern," even when he is, in fact, the only Green Lantern. This isn't necessarily a bad thing, however. Ultimately, Kyle is probably the better for it.

The One-Sided Hero of Bold Action

Green Lanterns are known for their willpower. But when a person is focused on what they are willing, they may be blind to alternate possibilities, to compromise. Alternatives are pushed aside by the force of pure will. The hero might do something that he or she may regret later, but since the action is so boldly and decisively undertaken, we can't help but be impressed. We may even find ourselves awed by the magnificence of an action that is ethically abhorrent.

This fits the pattern the philosopher G. W. F. Hegel (1770–1831) described in his analysis of tragedy and tragic heroes. Taking as examples the Sophoclean plays *Oedipus Rex* and *Antigone*, Hegel argues that the problem with the tragic hero is not that she acts in a morally blameworthy fashion, but that she acts from her own moral compass, without attempting to fit in with the communal ethics of the group. Hegel describes this as acting in a one-sided way. Meanwhile, the hero's antagonist is also acting for reasons that to him seem morally justifiable, but in a similarly one-sided way. The moral imperative of the hero is justified, but it is expressed in such black and white terms that the hero can't recognize the possibility that alternatives might also be justifiable. The two are destined to clash and the hero is doomed to destruction, not for acting immorally, but for his or her individualism and one-sidedness. Oddly, while the hero is more or less bringing about her own destruction, and failing to act within the ethical parameters of the group, we do not generally wish to morally censure the hero. While the hero is blameworthy in her neglect of communal ethical norms, we still recognize her attempt to pursue what she believed to be the right thing to do. We are caught up in admiration of her embodiment of an aesthetic ideal: bold, magnificent action in service of true commitment to a moral ideal. (Just to be clear: when Hegel describes the hero as aesthetically admirable, this is not a reflection on the hero's good looks but rather on the larger-than-life quality of the hero's actions.)

This pattern clarifies the limits of looking to heroes for moral or ethical guidance. When we look at the behavior of heroes, we are not just judging them for acting correctly, we are also judging them on the aesthetic qualities of being larger-than-life or awe-inspiring. No one wants a boring, goody-two-shoes hero (sorry, Superman).

The Normal and Extraordinary Practices of Superheroes

Hegel's insight is that we can admire the hero aesthetically while disapproving of his or her actions ethically. In order to understand how this works, we need to realize that for Hegel, ethics and morality are two different things. Morality consists of the principles and rules that emerge from our (usually) independent reasoning about the good. These principles and rules are important, but by themselves they are too abstract to be meaningful. We don't reason in a vacuum—our sense of the good is informed by the values and norms of our society.

This is where ethics comes in. The rules we think of as part of morality are contextualized by our culture, our upbringing, and our societal habits. These create a set of ethical norms that we use to guide our day-to-day actions and help shape our sense of what we hold dear. The cluster of ethical norms that guides us in this way is what Hegel calls "ethical life." Ultimately our actions should be guided both by our free reasoning about the good and by the norms of our culture.

Our reason will help us to determine if certain cultural norms are unjust, but Hegel argues that we can never step outside our cultural upbringing to obtain any kind of utterly pure moral standpoint. The attempt to do so will only lead to absurdity, since it would involve denying everything about ourselves that makes us who we are—namely, our determinate position within our cultural and historical context.

It is easy enough to extend Hegel's ideas about communal norms in nations and states to groups such as the Green Lantern Corps or the Justice League. Sometimes a hero will break out of the group norms of ethical life to follow her conscience and do what she believes to be the right thing. In such cases we clearly see the difference between morality and ethical life. The hero is morally justified: reason tells the hero that her actions are correct and justified. However, the hero's actions are at odds with the community. The hero experiences this as a struggle, and the community may experience it as a betrayal. We, the audience of the tragedy or the readers of the comic, are in turn awed by the courage of the hero, yet at the same time we have a sinking feeling about the ultimate consequences.

Hal Jordan, the Rash and Resourceful

Hal Jordan is a loyal Green Lantern who serves the Guardians and the Corps for years, and as one of the founding members of the JLA, he recognizes the importance of working together with others. Still, he does not follow orders or directives blindly. When Sinestro and Hal first meet, Sinestro tells him not to question a superior officer, and Hal stubbornly and characteristically replies, "Um . . . yeah. That's not gonna work for me."[1] In *Emerald Twilight* we are told: "Hal Jordan was, by most accounts, the best of the Green Lantern Corps. He served the Guardians with distinction, if not always perfect obedience."[2] This is what Hal is known for. More recently, he challenged the Justice League on their mission and priorities, preferring to pursue his own conception of the good. "You want a League," he tells the Justice League, "I want justice."[3] As Green Lantern for sector 2814, he sees that it is his task to "step up" and ensure the protection of Earth, Justice League or no Justice League. Clearly, he is not concerned with obeying Superman or Wonder Woman.

This is part of why we like Hal. He would not be the greatest Green Lantern if he were more strictly obedient. (We can see this belief in the importance of challenging authority in John Stewart and Guy Gardner as well, also excellent Green Lanterns.) We know, of course, that Hal often acts before he thinks. In *Rebirth*, Batman criticizes Hal, saying that he never worried, never prepared, acted rashly; John Stewart points out that this is because Hal is the man with no fear.[4]

Indeed, Hal has no fear, and he questions authority. He acts to do what is right, regardless of what others might say to hold him back. He's a hero—he's Hal Jordan! And, as Hegel would have predicted, this is exactly how Hal goes wrong. Just like Oedipus, in his search for truth at all costs, so too is Hal destroyed by his search for justice. As a tragic hero, Hal is so sure that he knows the right thing to do that he goes forward on his own in a one-sided manner to right wrongs, without compromise.

We see Hal doing this at least twice: in *Emerald Twilight*, when he tries to restore Coast City after Mongul's destruction and ends up destroying the Corps, and in *Zero Hour*, when he tries to restore the universe by destroying it.

Of course, Hal does both of these things while under the power of the Parallax entity. Consequently, it could be argued that it's not really Hal acting (and certainly this is the tone of some of the events in the comics—much of the end of *Rebirth* and some of the events in the *Sinestro Corps War* seem largely intended to make it look like a person is utterly powerless under Parallax's influence). But if we look at Hal's actions, he really is stubborn and individualistic. As Flash points out in *Blackest Night* #4 (December 2009), unlike the other members of the Justice League, Hal's not concerned about trying to fit in: "He let the rest of the world fit in around *him.*"

Hal has a vision of what is right. He wants to fix the world and doesn't usually listen to others' counsel. Other than the "destroying the world" thing, *Zero Hour* is not that unlike him. If anything, it's Parallax's ability to make a detailed plan that seems unlike rash Hal Jordan, rather than the belief that he knows what is right. And Hal's reunion with Parallax in the *Blackest Night* storyline, for the purpose of defeating the Black Lantern version of the Spectre, is another illustration of Hal's single-mindedly pursuing what he deems to be the right course of action without really consulting those around him.[5] As he says, "I made a vow. No fear. Never again." These words do not bode well in our Hegelian tragic context.

Sinestro, Fallen from Heroic Stature

Sinestro started off, in the early years of the Silver Age *Green Lantern* comics, as a simple villain, a "relentlessly evil" renegade Lantern, power-hungry and with a "super-evil mind."[6] Just being evil for evil's sake, however, is not really all that interesting aesthetically. It is a rather limited motivation, with little scope for exploration. Consequently, in the 1991 story *Emerald Dawn II*, his character is broadened. Sinestro is described not as seeking power or craving evil, but as trying to establish and maintain order on his home planet Korugar. While this particular story (which includes Hal being locked up for a DUI but regularly escaping prison to train as a Green Lantern) is now of doubtful canonicity, Sinestro's desire for order, rather than evil for its own sake, has been repeated regularly and is now fairly established. Notably, in 2005's *Secret Origin* story, Sinestro proclaims that "Korugar will *never* embrace chaos. Not as long as I am around to instill *order.*"[7]

In and of itself, this would seem a morally praiseworthy goal. We can understand Sinestro's desire, especially since as a Green Lantern he would be familiar with the chaotic possibilities of the universe. Disorder and chaos can create injustice and suffering in a political state. The philosopher Johann Gottlieb Fichte (1762–1814), a contemporary of Hegel's, wrote:

> The sole source of every evil in our makeshift states is *disorder* and the impossibility of bringing about order in them. In our states the only reason why finding a guilty party often involves such great and insurmountable difficulties, is that there are so many people the state fails to care for, and who have no determinate status within it.[8]

According to Fichte, in a perfectly ordered state, no one would be homeless; everyone would have a trade and a recognized position within society; and there would be no crime. No one would go hungry, and "in a state where everything is ordered and runs according to plan, the police will observe any unusual activity and take notice immediately; and so . . . [n]either the crime [n]or the criminal can remain hidden."[9] To bring about such order Fichte would require everyone to carry identity cards, register their job and their address with the government, and report any travel or change of address immediately. Hegel mocked this proposal as involving too much micromanagement for a philosopher to be engaged with, and said that Fichte's idea of community was really tyranny.[10] Sinestro, however, would probably have quite liked Fichte's plan for political order.

Of course, it all goes horribly awry. Sinestro's one-sided quest for order—rooted in a firmly held moral conviction of what would be good for Korugar—means that he acts without regard for the wishes and desires of the Korugarians as a whole. He acts on his own, outside of the ethical norms and customs of Korugar, and so the people do not see him as acting for the good at all. The Korugarians see him as wicked, and Sinestro's Green Lantern ring is described by Korugarian Soranik Natu as "a symbol of oppression and pain."[11]

Sinestro is great not for his one-sided ways but for his inner convictions and quest for rightness. In a Corps that is strong by virtue of its members' willpower, Sinestro stands out through the strength of his force of will. And it is this strength of will, this sense that he knows the good, that makes him one-sided. The one-sidedness is a consequence, therefore, of the same qualities that make him so great.

Getting along with the Corps didn't come easily to Sinestro. He tells Hal, "I am an individualistic thinker, as you are. I'd never belonged to a group like the Corps before. So I had never learned how to trust the beings around me. In part, that's where my questioning came from. He [Abin Sur] helped me to learn to trust my fellow Corpsman. Thankfully, it didn't change my drive to seek the truth or my determination to argue against the theologies I disagree with."[12]

Sinestro is an interesting villain within the Green Lantern mythos precisely because of the way his character has developed into one we can respect, even while fearing his actions. His development within the *Blackest Night* and *Brightest Day* story lines in particular reveals his continued pursuit of his own individual conscience: he still believes he can be the greatest Green Lantern, taking on the living light entity. "I am alive to lead us out of the blackest night!" he cries.[13]

Kyle: Graphic Artist and "Corps Conscience"[14]

What about young Kyle Rayner, then? Is he not heroic? He tends never to be called the "greatest Green Lantern," except perhaps during that period in which he was the only Green Lantern—but even then, he was usually in Hal's shadow or working alongside John. When Kyle is at his best, he is still not the self-assured character that Hal and Sinestro tend to be. Kyle was selected as a Green Lantern not because of his immense strength of will, but through the circumstances of Ganthet's desperation. Kyle is a different kind of Green Lantern, and so might be capable of a different kind of strength, but it also means that we're not in awe of him as we can be of the others.

For a long time, he doubts his abilities as a Green Lantern, in a way that we never see Hal do. Kyle's self-doubt is explored in *Circle of Fire*, when a facet of Kyle's personality—his "sorrow, anger, self-doubt, and fear"[15]—becomes embodied as Oblivion and takes on the Justice League. He is finally able to face Oblivion and fight him off, but he recognizes that Oblivion will never be fully defeated. Rather than destroying his fears, Kyle must "grow up" and acknowledge that they are a part of him.

Dream of the Endless (a character from Neil Gaiman's *Sandman* in DC's Vertigo imprint, who sometimes crosses over to the DC Universe) recognizes that Kyle doubts himself. Noting that Kyle's thoughts and actions seem to be overshadowed by his predecessor, Hal Jordan, Dream states that Kyle will surpass Hal: "You already know what he could never learn." After Kyle wonders what that could possibly be, Dream responds, his right eye gleaming: "Fear. You will surpass him."[16] In *Rebirth* this theme reoccurs: Kyle is noted as being special among Green Lanterns for knowing fear.[17]

This is what saves Kyle from falling into Hegel's pattern of the tragic hero: He is capable of feeling fear and doubt, and so cannot act with a one-sided conviction of the rightness of his actions. Consequently, it is not his own actions that bring about his downfall. Certainly, horrific things occur to Kyle, but they are brought about by external forces. We are frequently given reason to believe that Hal's own actions and character are inextricably bound up with Parallax (especially in the recent *Blackest Night* story line and his deliberate decision to reunite with the parasite[18]). But Parallax's possession of

Kyle is presented as being an attack by an external force. Parallax is separate from who Kyle really is, and he is not presented as ultimately responsible for it: "Parallax is calling the shots, and I'm just along for the ride. It's like being a passenger in an airplane. I have no control over what the pilot is doing."[19] (Kyle's possession by the Ion entity is similarly presented as external to who Kyle really is: "You were never truly intended to be the Ion bearer. But we needed a temporary vessel," says one of the Guardians.[20]) The death of his girlfriend Alex occurs shortly after Kyle becomes a Green Lantern, but it is not the result of Kyle's particular actions—her killer, Major Force, would have turned on anyone who had donned the Green Lantern ring.[21] Similarly, the death of Kyle's mother, first thought to be a natural death and then alleged to possibly be the work of Despotellis, a virus member of the Sinestro Corps,[22] was part of a wholesale assault on the Green Lantern Corps.

Not only does Kyle's ability to feel fear and doubt mean that he doesn't fall prey to the problems of a Hegelian tragic hero, it also causes him to be more sensitive to the dynamics of the groups to which he belongs. He is concerned with how he fits into groups—both the Justice League and the Green Lantern Corps—in a very different way than Hal. He is concerned with determining and promoting the values of the group. He is concerned, in other words, with the ethical life of the group, in a sense that Hegel would be proud of.

This doesn't mean that Kyle blindly follows the decree of the group; far from it. However, it does mean that when he criticizes the actions of the group, or members of the group, it is not on the basis of his own individually held sense of the moral good, but on the basis of what the group's shared values are. The most recent example of this might be when he and Guy Gardner stop the secret executions by the Alpha Lanterns of the prisoners of war in the "Prelude to Blackest Night" story line.[23] Kyle appeals to the Alpha Lanterns, not on the basis of his personal ideals, but their shared ideals, saying, "It's about preserving an ideal, damn it! . . . You know in your hearts this is against everything we've believed in and fought for."

Not "the Greatest," but a Pretty Damn Good Green Lantern

Kyle is thus a good "corps conscience," a key member of the Green Lantern Honor Guard, and a worthy recipient of ethical admiration. But Kyle is far less *aesthetically admirable* than Hal and Sinestro. Kyle is not magnificent or awe-inspiring. He can be good, and he can be brave and strong, but he does not have the single-mindedness of the tragic hero whose pursuit of the good leads to his own downfall. Kyle won't be called "the greatest Green Lantern," but the role he plays is vital. And if we are looking to the members of the Green Lantern Corps as role models, we are much better off following Kyle than Hal.

At the same time, it can hardly be denied that there is something magnificent about going off on one's own. Perhaps this is why not just Hal, but also Sinestro, keep drawing us in over and over again.

NOTES

1. *Green Lantern*, vol. 4, #32 (August 2008), reprinted in *Green Lantern: Secret Origin* (2008).

2. *Green Lantern*, vol. 3, #49 (February 1994), reprinted in *Green Lantern: Emerald Twilight/New Dawn* (2003).

3. *Justice League: Cry for Justice* #1 (September 2009).

4. *Green Lantern: Rebirth* #1 (December 2004), reprinted in *Green Lantern: Rebirth* (2005).

5. *Green Lantern*, vol. 4, #50 (March 2010), reprinted in *Blackest Night: Green Lantern* (2010).

6. *Green Lantern*, vol. 1, #9 (November–December 1961), reprinted in black and white in *Showcase Presents Green Lantern Volume One* (2005) and in color in *The Green Lantern Chronicles Volume Two* (2009). Sinestro's first appearance was two issues previously (#7, July–August 1961, also reprinted in both volumes).

7. *Green Lantern*, vol. 4, #35 (November 2008), reprinted in *Green Lantern: Secret Origin*.

8. Johann Gottlieb Fichte, *Foundations of Natural Right*, trans. Michael Baur (Cambridge, UK: Cambridge University Press, 2000), 302.

9. Ibid.

10. G. W. F. Hegel, *The Difference Between Fichte's and Schelling's System of Philosophy*, trans. H. S. Harris and Walter Cerf (Albany: State University of New York Press, 1977), 145–147.

11. *Green Lantern Corps: Recharge* #1 (November 2005), reprinted in *Green Lantern Corps: Recharge* (2005).

12. *Green Lantern*, vol. 4, #33 (September 2008), reprinted in *Green Lantern: Secret Origin*.

13. *Blackest Night* #7 (April 2010).

14. *Blackest Night* #1 (September 2009).

15. *Green Lantern: Circle of Fire* #2 (October 2000), reprinted in *Green Lantern: Circle of Fire* (2002).

16. *JLA* #22 (September 1998), reprinted in *JLA: Strength in Numbers* (1998).

17. *Green Lantern: Rebirth* #1 and 3 (2004–2005), reprinted in *Green Lantern: Rebirth*.

18. *Green Lantern*, vol. 4, #50 (March 2010), reprinted in *Blackest Night: Green Lantern* (2010).

19. *Tales of the Sinestro Corps: Parallax* (November 2007), reprinted in *Green Lantern: Tales of the Sinestro Corps* (2008).

20. *Tales of the Sinestro Corps: Ion* (January 2008), reprinted in *Green Lantern: Tales of the Sinestro Corps*.

21. *Green Lantern*, vol. 3, #54 (August 1994), reprinted in *Green Lantern: Emerald Twilight/New Dawn*.

22. *Ion* #12 (May 2007), reprinted in *Ion, Guardian of the Universe: The Dying Flame* (2007).

23. *Green Lantern Corps*, vol. 2, #38 (September 2009), reprinted in *Green Lantern Corps: Emerald Eclipse* (2009).

THERE SHOULD BE NO FORGIVENESS FOR HAL JORDAN

Nicolas Michaud

Let me be direct: I believe that Hal Jordan, widely considered the "greatest" Green Lantern of them all, is a murderer. Burning green fury through friends, comrades, and his own teachers, Hal killed almost every member of the Green Lantern Corps to exact retribution on the Guardians of the Universe for trying to revoke his power.[1] Hal's misdeeds occur after Superman's epic, fatal battle with Doomsday.[2] The Cyborg Superman—one of the contenders for the throne after Superman's death—shows his true colors by destroying Coast City, Hal Jordan's hometown.[3] After the Cyborg's defeat, in his grief Hal uses his ring to re-create the city for a short time before the Guardians tell him that he must return to Oa in order to be punished for using his ring for selfish reasons. Hal loses control and decides to gather as much power to himself as is necessary to re-create his home for good. All that stands in the way is the Green Lantern Corps, but given Hal's immeasurable pain and unbeatable will, the Corps is unable to withstand his onslaught. With each needless death Hal becomes more brutal, only stopping to strip the rings from their broken bodies.

Hal knows no remorse, no regret, and no mercy. Eventually, his apparent choice to enact vengeance against the Guardians leads him to become the supervillain Parallax. What is Hal's excuse? Later we find out that Hal's actions were the result of his possession by an alien parasite (itself called Parallax), which fed Hal's fears and hatreds. Hal's actions were supposedly not his own. I think we're forgiving Hal too easily if we accept this explanation. I don't believe we can ever trust Hal Jordan again—and as we'll see, I'm in good company.

To determine who is right about Hal, we need to figure out if Hal is responsible for the actions that he committed while under the parasite's influence. As we will see, Batman, at least, is reluctant to exonerate Hal after he is separated from Parallax. Given Hal's "unbeatable" strength of will, how and why did he succumb? After all, Hal eventually found the strength within himself to suppress the parasite and save Earth from destruction, so perhaps he could have resisted the parasite earlier. Could it have been because the parasite was pushing Hal to commit acts that he really wanted to commit?

Action theory is a branch of philosophy that, among other things, addresses the problem of moral responsibility. Under what circumstances does it make sense to praise or blame a person for what he has done? Recently, action theory has been deeply influenced by contemporary philosopher John Martin Fischer. Fischer's work with fellow philosopher Mark Ravizza supports my claim that even though Hal did not have total control over his actions, he is still morally responsible for those actions.

The Destruction of the Green Lantern Corps

First, let's recap briefly the events that led to Hal's actions. Coast City, Hal's home, was left as nothing more than a crater by the Cyborg, killing all seven million residents. Hal could not handle the fact that his failure resulted in the deaths of those he loved and had sworn to protect, so he attempted to use his power to re-create Coast City and bring the dead back to life. Since he was using the power of his ring for purely selfish purposes, the Guardians chose to revoke his power and bring him to Oa to face their judgment. Instead, Hal took the power that he needed to re-create Coast City by force and set out for vengeance upon the heartless Guardians who could not forgive Hal for a moment's weakness. As he burned toward Oa to take the power he needed, his colleagues and friends in the Corps tried to stop him. He defeated all of them and left them without their rings in space, lying near death. Then, after killing his former mentor and greatest foe, Sinestro, and his friend and teacher, Kilowog, Hal absorbed all of the power in the Guardians' Central Power Battery and destroyed it, killing most of the Guardians and leaving the Corps members drifting in space without the power to survive.

Why might we absolve Hal of responsibility for these acts? The main reason is that his actions were revealed to be the result of his infection by the alien parasite Parallax—fear incarnate, and the original yellow impurity in the Central Power Battery. This entity fed on Hal's insecurities and fueled them, and when Coast City was destroyed, Parallax saw its chance and pushed Hal over the edge. Once Hal killed Sinestro and flew into the Battery, Hal gave himself over to the fear and became a combination of Hal Jordan and Parallax, adopting the name of the impurity itself. It is important to note that Hal's will was not completely taken over by Parallax. After failing to change time itself to bring Coast City back in *Zero Hour*

(1994), Hal later gave his life to save Earth by restarting the sun in *Final Night* (1996). Eventually, Hal was brought back to life when he was bonded to the Spectre in the *Day of Judgment* miniseries (1999). Hal still struggled both with his nature as the Spectre and with Parallax until *Green Lantern: Rebirth* (2004–2005), when he was truly resurrected and purged of Parallax's corruption.[4]

Even though the Corps accepts him back, as does most of the Justice League of America, Batman does not trust him. We can see why. When Hal begins his rebirth, Batman says to J'onn J'onzz, "I don't think Hal Jordan *ever* changed, J'onn. Hal always had an ego. He never worried when things came crashing down. He never prepared. He just flew in— damn the consequences. We should've known back then a man like him couldn't be trusted."[5] Batman thinks we should not forgive Hal so easily, and he may be correct: although Parallax pushed Hal over the edge, it was unclear whether Hal's consciousness and will were completely subdued. Hal's successor, Kyle Rayner, said that Parallax "warped his sense of right and wrong," implying that while Parallax certainly influenced him, Hal was still in control to some extent.[6] And he still had sufficient control, even as Parallax, to choose to save Earth to prevent the Final Night. We are also told that Parallax first began to turn Hal by influencing Hal mentally—by taking advantage of Hal's fear after seeing Coast City destroyed. This fear isn't sufficient to absolve Hal of the fact that he chose to let that fear drive him (even with a push from Parallax). In life we are driven, pushed, and pulled by emotional forces, but it is up to us to handle those forces in determining our actions.

Did Hal *Want* to Kill His Friends?

According to John Martin Fischer and Mark Ravizza, the fundamental issue we must face when we want to praise or blame someone is control. In contemporary action theory, most conversations about moral responsibility have turned on whether a person was free "to do otherwise." The assumption has been that if a person couldn't have done otherwise, then that person cannot be held responsible. Fischer and Ravizza, however, have a different idea. In *Responsibility and Control*, they argue that what actually matters when we praise or blame someone is not the ability to have done otherwise, but how much control the person had over the act.[7] So what we really need to figure out is how much control Hal had over his actions when he was infected by Parallax.

Fischer and Ravizza provided this new account of responsibility because the problems in explaining what makes someone blameworthy had become extremely complex due to another contemporary philosopher, Harry Frankfurt. There was already substantial disagreement in philosophy regarding whether it is the consequences of our actions or our intentions that really matter when assigning responsibility or blame. Imagine the philosophical argument that would result if one person argued that all that matters is the fact that Hal destroyed the Corps, and the other argued that all that matters is the fact that Hal didn't intend that to happen. It seems like a near-impossible problem to solve. The consequences of our actions seem very important, but we can't necessarily foresee all of them. Similarly, our intentions seem important, but how much are good intentions worth if our actions don't follow through? What philosophers in both camps agreed on was that if a person could not have done otherwise than he did, that person could not rationally be blamed for his actions. It seems intuitively true to say that if I cannot do anything to prevent an event from occurring, then I should not be blamed for the event. Then Frankfurt sneakily developed a series of example cases in which it actually does seem reasonable to blame a person for an event, even though the person had no other options.[8] And the mess of moral responsibility was made far worse (even more so than Hal's recent history!).

Consider the following example: Imagine that, say, an evil parasite called Larappax takes control of your body and can make you do whatever it wants. Suppose Larappax decides that it will make you rob the nearest bank. But, much to the parasite's surprise, you're a supervillain and you were already planning to rob the bank. Larappax doesn't have to do anything to make you do it; it just sits back in your mind and watches you commit the robbery. But had you decided *not* to rob the bank, the parasite would have forced you to do so against your will. As it happened, though, Larappax doesn't have to use any force at all. Are you still responsible for robbing the bank even though you were going to rob the bank in any case, regardless of your will? Frankfurt's point is that you are still blameworthy because even though the parasite would have forced you, it didn't have to—you chose to rob the bank because you wanted to.

So, what matters is not the fact that you are under the control of a mind-controlling parasite and thereby have no legitimate choices; what matters is whether the parasite is using its ability to control you. Admittedly, Hal's case is a little more complex than this. Parallax influences and pushes him in some ways, but then again, Hal demonstrates the ability to fight the parasite's influences, so he did have at least some control. According to Frankfurt, Hal's guilt would be clear. If Hal had no choice but to destroy the Corps, even though he would have done it anyway under his own free will, he would still be responsible for it. Frankfurt's argument shook the philosophical world. Paper after paper was written in an attempt to resolve the issue, and then Fischer and Ravizza brought the problem into a new light, demonstrating that what we really need to worry about is how much control the person had over the action.

Hal Had Control, but Did He Have the Will?

So can we figure out if someone like Hal is blameworthy? According to Fischer and Ravizza, a *particular* kind of control is what matters. There are two kinds of control that we have over our actions. Normally, the kind of control that we talk about is what they term "regulative control," the control that we need to choose to take one path or another. But there is another kind of control that Fischer and Ravizza believe is more essential to responsibility—"guidance control," the kind of control that results from a person having ownership of the action, even if he could not do anything else. Having ownership of an action means that the action is one that resulted from our conscious mental deliberation over the action—we thought about it, and in our process of thinking about it we were capable of responding to reasons to do it or not. (This capability, oddly enough, is known as being "reasons-responsive," but more on that later.) Fischer and Ravizza argue that sometimes we should be forgiven for our actions because they were not really ours, as in the case of mind control. But in other cases, when the actions were our own, we can be blameworthy—even if we had no other choice.

Let's give Hal the benefit of the doubt and say that he really didn't have a choice in his actions during his time with Parallax. The parasite was going to force him into certain actions whether or not Hal agreed to perform them. If Fischer and Ravizza are correct, then even though Hal may not have had a choice to perform certain actions as Parallax, he could still be blameworthy for those actions. What we really need to know is this: Was Hal's action his own while under Parallax's influence, or did it actually "belong" to Parallax?

The core of the question is about the kind of control that Hal had. We can probably agree that Hal did not really have regulative control. Hal's fans argue that once Parallax took hold of him after Coast City was destroyed, Hal no longer had sufficient control to be blamed for his actions as Parallax. Even if it was Hal's body and mind performing the actions, Parallax was buried too deep for Hal to resist. But notice that lack of options does not necessarily absolve Hal. The question is whether Hal really tried to fight Parallax, or if he even wanted to. Hal actually admits that he could have tried harder to fight Parallax's influence: "But whatever Parallax pushed me to do—it was still my hand that did it. He got me from the inside. I was cocky. Overconfident. Should've been able to fight it off."[9] Perhaps Hal is simply beating himself up for being too weak, or perhaps Hal believes that he *let* Parallax push him to act as he did. If this is true, then even if he lacks regulative control, Hal is guilty because he has guidance control—the action was his own.

To have guidance control, all we need to have is ownership of our action—it was not done against our wills—and our action must be what Fischer and Ravizza call "moderately reasons-responsive." "Reasons-responsive" means that we have the capability, at least in theory, to respond to reasons, which means that we have the ability to weigh, measure, and determine the relevance of a reason to our decision-making process. So, first of all, to be reasons-responsive, you can't be completely insane or unable to understand what you are doing. What matters is that whatever act we commit is one we commit for our reasons. Hal is reasons-responsive: he shows the ability to make choices that Parallax does not want him to make. And Hal cannot say that he takes the main battery's power only because of Parallax's reasons. Although Hal's fear was amplified by Parallax's manipulations, Hal's reasons for acting were his own: they came from his own reasons-responsive mechanism. Parallax did not destroy Hal's ability to think of, develop, and consider his options. Hal's actions, although encouraged and fostered by Parallax, still started with Hal's wants and desires. Even before he was largely overwhelmed by Parallax, when Parallax was only goading and fueling his fears, Hal destroyed the Corps and the battery. And he *was* Parallax when he sacrificed himself to save Earth, so clearly Hal's reasoning can shine through despite Parallax's indirect influence or direct control.

Hal shows virtually no hesitation as he fights and defeats his comrades. He does not seem to take a moment to consider whether what he is doing is right or wrong until the end of his rampage. Before he destroys the battery and takes its power for himself, he does take a moment to consider if this is what he actually wants to do—and then chooses to destroy the Corps. He was not forced to make this decision kicking and screaming. Quite the contrary, he wanted the power he needed to bring back Coast City. It might well be that Hal's self-loathing and self-doubt were caused by Parallax, feelings that resulted in his selfishly using his power to try to restore Coast City, but it is Hal's reasons, wants, and desires that result in him taking the power from the Guardians. It is Hal's desire to restore Coast City at any cost that results in his choice to destroy the Corps. It certainly seems that Hal had guidance control.

Hal's Greatest Failure: The Triumph of Fear over Control

Fischer and Ravizza reframe the problem of moral responsibility in a way that makes it easier to solve. What we realize through this investigation is that Hal isn't just a little blameworthy—he is a lot blameworthy. When we think about it, we realize that Hal wanted to steal the Corps' power, regardless of the consequences, so his actions were his own and Parallax's influence did not force him to act. So, according to Fischer and Ravizza, Hal is already blameworthy.

But I think the situation is worse than this. I don't think it is true that Hal lacked regulative control. His actions in saving Earth suggest that he could have resisted Parallax's control from the beginning, even if it was difficult. In other words, had he fought back hard enough, he might not have destroyed the Corps—his actions were not inevitable with respect to his will. So not only did he have guidance control, he also had regulative control. This is something that Batman knows; he probably intuitively recognizes how easily we give up our regulative control and try to absolve ourselves "because we didn't have control." While most of us absolve ourselves of our own mistakes because we argue that we just didn't have the ability to make any other choice—like when we can't resist spending too much money on comic books—Batman knows that if we tried hard enough, we could have done otherwise. He would never excuse his own weaknesses, nor ours, and definitely not Hal's.

Kyle Rayner defends Hal's actions, but even in defending him, he acknowledges that Hal had a choice:

> Parallax made Jordan afraid. Afraid of what might happen tomorrow. Jordan tried to recreate Coast City and was reprimanded by the guardians. He was threatened. Told he may be stripped of his power because he used it for personal gain. So he did what anyone desperate and terrified would do—he fought back. And the truth is I don't entirely blame him.[10]

This is not an explanation given for the actions of a man who is controlled, powerless to act of his own will. Instead, this explanation is given by Kyle to help us *understand* why Hal acted as he did. Parallax's fear was coercive and powerful, and, yes, it changed Hal significantly. But it could not have done so if Hal had not wanted to bring Coast City back, nor could it have done so if Hal had not let fear and anger drive him to commit atrocities. Why is it that Kyle doesn't "entirely blame him"? It is not due to a lack of choice, but because Kyle understands why someone terrified and desperate would fight back. Kyle understands why a person would *choose* to fight back given that fear, because he, unique among Green Lanterns, knows fear.

Kyle, however, is perhaps overly kind. Failure to use regulative control is especially inexcusable in Hal's case. Remember that Hal has developed more mastery over his ring than any other wielder—because of willpower. The ring is capable of almost anything the bearer can will, and Hal has demonstrated over and over again that he is unstoppable as a Green Lantern *because of his will.* I doubt that Hal lacked the willpower to stop himself from destroying the Corps, even at Parallax's prompting. Hal gave himself over to his fear, and even in the face of killing those who trusted, admired, and needed him the most, he allowed himself to do the unthinkable. We do Hal Jordan a sincere disservice when we absolve him of his crime. By doing so, we treat him as if he lacked the will necessary to overcome Parallax. Instead, we should blame him, and accept his action for what it really was—the result of a broken man's pain, rage, fear, and hate. Even superheroes can fail; the problem is, when they fail, they fail *big.*

NOTES

1. *Green Lantern*, vol. 3, #48–50 (January–March 1994), reprinted in *Green Lantern: Emerald Twilight/New Dawn* (2003).

2. *Superman*, vol. 2, #75 (January 1993), reprinted in *The Death of Superman* (1993).

3. *Superman*, vol. 2, #80 (August 1993), reprinted in *The Return of Superman* (1993).

4. Of course, Hal being Hal, a few years later he willingly bonded with the Parallax entity again when he thought it would give him a chance to defeat Nekron during the Blackest Night (*Green Lantern*, vol. 4, #50, March 2010, reprinted in *Blackest Night: Green Lantern*, 2010). At least this time he didn't kill anybody.

5. *Green Lantern: Rebirth* #1 (December 2004), reprinted in *Green Lantern: Rebirth* (2005).

6. *Green Lantern: Rebirth* #3 (February 2005).

7. Martin Fischer and Mark Ravizza, *Responsibility and Control: A Theory of Moral Responsibility* (Cambridge, UK: Cambridge University Press, 1999).

8. Harry G. Frankfurt, "Alternate Possibilities and Moral Responsibility," *Journal of Philosophy* 66 (1969), 829–839.

9. *Green Lantern: Rebirth* #5 (April 2005).

10. *Green Lantern: Rebirth* #2 (January 2005).

MORALITY, ATONEMENT, AND GUILT: HAL JORDAN'S SHIFTING MOTIVATIONS

Joseph J. Darowski

Why Do Heroes Do What They Do?

Good superhero origin stories not only tell you how a character becomes a superhero, they also explain *why* that character becomes a superhero, selflessly doing good rather than evil. After all, when characters receive superpowers, there are many avenues their lives could take. They could become superstar athletes or famous performers, ignore their powers to lead normal lives, or become supervillains. The best origin stories include an explanation, even a simple one, of why the character chooses the particular path he or she does.

For example, Superman gained his powers due to the environmental differences between Krypton and Earth, but the superhero he became was inspired by the moral values he learned in Smallville. Bruce Wayne drove himself to become an almost perfect physical and mental specimen after a random act of crime took his parents from him. He was motivated by a personal quest for revenge—not revenge against a single criminal, but against crime itself. Peter Parker gained spider-like powers after an irradiated spider bit him, and at first he pursued fame and fortune, not the life of the hero. But after his actions inadvertently led to the murder of his uncle, guilt caused Peter to abandon his pursuit of wealth for a selfless mission to protect the innocent as Spider-Man.

In Hal Jordan's origin story, first told in 1959's *Showcase* #22, we see that his motivations for becoming a hero are very similar to Superman's, involving honor and respect for the ideals of justice, honesty, and integrity, as passed down from an authority figure. Some elements of the story may seem corny to a modern audience (including Jordan's reaction upon entering an alien ship and seeing its occupant: "Good gosh! A spaceman."). But the story ably establishes how Jordan is chosen by the dying Abin Sur's ring to be his successor as the Green Lantern of that space sector, and it further establishes that the ring and battery are "to be used as a weapon against forces of evil and injustice." Accepting the ring and battery, Jordan then "vowed that I would carry out my new responsibilities to the best of my abilities."[1] There is no tragic incident that sparked his quest for justice (though Hal is haunted by the death of his father in a jet accident years before), but rather a simple desire to do good. Is this really as simple a motivation as it seems, however?

Over the past half-century, many changes have occurred to Hal Jordan. In the 1994 stories *Emerald Twilight* and *Zero Hour*, he stops acting selflessly and heroically when he becomes the megalomaniacal villain Parallax. Following his death at the end of *Zero Hour*, Jordan's soul is bonded with the Spectre, God's spirit of vengeance, who, as the description implies, carries out vengeance against the guilty. And in 2005's *Green Lantern: Rebirth*, Hal Jordan came back from the dead and once again assumed his role as a Green Lantern. This rebirth is intriguing. Whereas Jordan originally was motivated by moral values alone, at times after his rebirth he is also motivated by guilt over his former actions as a villain. To some extent, he is performing his duties to absolve himself of the sins of his past, as well as to serve justice. So at different times throughout his narrative history, Jordan has been driven by moral duty, megalomania, vengeance, and guilt, with his motivations becoming more complex as the character develops.

Lantern Be Good

Hal Jordan is a hero because he is honest and fearless and gave his word to do the right thing. Philosophers have debated morality as a motivation for action for centuries, and with good reason. As explained by contemporary philosopher Connie Rosati, "Morality is widely believed to conflict, frequently and sometimes severely, with what an agent most values or most prefers to do."[2] But how can morality motivate us to act against our own desires?

In his origin story, Hal Jordan is given a ring that responds to his willpower: it can project his thoughts into physical shapes, allow him to fly (even in space), and (for the most part) protects him from harm. Jordan is asked to take the ring and join an intergalactic peacekeeping force, and he gives his word that he will. From that moment on Jordan selflessly becomes a hero because he believes it to be the right thing to do. But what are the alternatives?

For one, he could have satisfied any of his own material desires with the ring. With the power he now possessed he could have obtained riches by many means, legal and illegal. Also, given his womanizing tendencies, he could have used the power ring to impress women. But instead he chose to romance his boss Carol Ferris as Hal Jordan, test pilot (while she was infatuated with his alter ego). There is, though, an even greater personal interest that Jordan is setting aside by choosing to become a hero: self-preservation. Jordan constantly puts himself in mortal danger—even a Green Lantern ring isn't perfect—with no potential for reward, which conflicts with one of the most basic human instincts.

Some philosophers argue that people do not have to choose between morality and self-interest, and therefore Hal's actions are not as unusual as we might think. Plato (circa 428–348 BCE) argued that knowing the good is sufficient for doing the good. For instance, doing evil will lead to harm to those around us, which Plato thinks will then harm us in turn. Consequently, it is in our best interests not to do evil, and once we have proper knowledge of good and evil, we will, for our own benefit, do the good. For Plato, wrongdoing is the result of failing to have properly understood the good—our self-interest in being rational or moral pushes us to act well. If this were the case, then Green Lantern may not have made a choice between his own self-interests and his moral values, because they would be the same thing by definition. If he had a true understanding of "the good," then it is only natural that he would perform heroically, since using his powers for good ultimately serves to promote his own self-interest.

On Plato's account, knowledge of the good and one's own self-interest are tied together. We thus have an overwhelming motivation to act morally, one that overrides lingering inclinations to pursue baser interests. If this were the case, then not only would it be natural that Green Lantern behaved heroically, but we couldn't even praise him for doing so—we would say that he had no choice.

Plato's view doesn't fly, however, among moral philosophers today, who are deeply suspicious of the idea that "a grasp of morality's requirements would produce overriding motivation to act accordingly."[3] Morality doesn't seem to provide the same sort of compulsion as, say, intense hunger or having Sinestro's minions attacking your family. Not everyone feels the urge to uphold moral values—consequently, doing so seems to be a choice. Consequently, Hal Jordan did make a choice between selflessly serving others and pursuing his own self-interests, and this choice itself can be interpreted as heroic (as opposed to being compelled to do the right thing). Since it was a choice, it was also open to him to act differently and choose instead to pursue his own selfish desires. In other words, even though it is in Hal's self-interest to behave morally, morality itself doesn't provide sufficient reason to do so: it isn't the only thing that appeals to our self-interest. With Green Lantern's powers the simple route would be to do whatever he wanted, and in one pivotal story line, he did just that.

Fallen from Grace

In 1993, as part of *The Reign of the Supermen* story line, which followed *The Death of Superman*, Hal Jordan's home-town, Coast City, was destroyed by an alien named Mongul. Understandably, Jordan reacted rather poorly. Becoming emotionally unstable, he planned to rebuild Coast City and to get more power. He thus went on a quest to collect as many power rings as possible, in the process murdering many of the other Green Lanterns and Guardians. Eventually, in the *Zero Hour* story line, realizing that his plan would not work, he teamed up with a villain named Extant, who had powers over time. Now calling himself Parallax, Jordan worked with Extant to attempt to rewrite the history of the DC Universe so that Coast City never would have been destroyed. But Parallax was defeated by a collection of heroes (including his best friend Green Arrow and new Lantern Kyle Rayner).

The actions Jordan took during this time simultaneously showed the breadth of the power he could access and the dangers of acting selfishly with it. Jordan's moral compass had previously led him to act as a hero rather than in his own self-interest. The destruction of his hometown caused his moral compass to lose its bearing, and his motivations shifted from his moral beliefs to his selfish desires. Morality by itself failed to be sufficient motivation to prevent Hal, as Parallax, from trying to make the world over as he saw fit.

As Parallax, Hal Jordan explained what drove him to this course of action: "I had never asked for anything. The one time I did, I was denied."[4] Therefore he decided to use force to take what had been denied him. During the 1996 event *Final Night*, he acts to redeem himself as a hero, sacrificing his life to save Earth's sun. Eventually, in 1999's *Day of Judgment*, his soul is bonded with the Spectre, God's spirit of vengeance in the DC Universe who pursues and punishes the guilty. This status would prove to be temporary, lasting just over two dozen issues of *The Spectre* from 2001 to 2003 (as well as some appearances in books like *JLA* and *Green Lantern*). And, as we'll see, though Jordan would soon be reborn as a Green Lantern, his motivations would sometimes veer from the purely heroic.

Turn to the Dark Side

Adding a dark past and a guilty conscience to Hal Jordan's character mirrors several trends in the comic book industry during the late 1980s and early 1990s. Many industry observers cite Alan Moore and Dave Gibbons's 1986–1987 *Watchmen* and Frank Miller's 1986 *The Dark Knight Returns* as comic books that changed the tone of storytelling in superhero comics in a darker, grittier direction. Journalist Dave Itzkoff discussed *Watchmen*'s influence on the industry in the *New York Times*:

> "Watchmen" has another legacy, one that Moore almost certainly never intended, whose DNA is encoded in the increasingly black inks and bleak storylines that have

become the essential elements of the contemporary superhero comic book—a domain he has largely ceded to writers and artists who share his fascination with brutality but not his interest in its consequences, his eagerness to tear down old boundaries but not his drive to find new ones.[5]

As Itzkoff notes, *Watchmen* introduced a brutality, some would say reality, to superhero comic books that was not common before its publication. The superhero comics of the 1990s, in efforts to capture the critical and commercial success of *Watchmen* and *The Dark Knight Returns*, featured excessive grittiness both in artistic styles and narrative content: Superman killed three Kryptonian villains; Batman had his back broken by the villain Bane and was succeeded by an out-of-control vigilante; Black Canary was raped and tortured; Kyle Rayner's girlfriend was killed and stuffed in a refrigerator simply as a strike against him.[6] During this period, in the *Emerald Dawn* miniseries (1989–1990), Jordan's origin was revised to include drunk driving well before he became Parallax.

In 1999's *Day of Judgment*, Geoff Johns had Golden Age Green Lantern Alan Scott suggest that the deceased Hal Jordan assume the role of the Spectre's human host in a search for redemption and atonement. Always the skeptic, Batman questions Alan's judgment, but Hal answers, "Parallax is gone, Batman. This is my chance. Hal Jordan's second chance. To make up for the mistakes I've made."[7] As he prepares to merge with the Spectre, Hal says, "This is what I've been waiting—praying for. A chance to make it up to you—all of you. I can't bring you back—but I can answer for my sins."[8] Hal would struggle against the Spectre's endless quest for vengeance through their time together, but it was always about redemption for Jordan: "I've fought so long and hard for redemption."[9]

In 2004–2005 writer Geoff Johns set out to revive Hal Jordan once more in *Green Lantern: Rebirth*, this time as a

Green Lantern, by not only bringing him back to life but, more importantly, explaining that Jordan's actions as Parallax were not his own. Following the destruction of Coast City, Hal's emotional devastation allowed a fear entity called Parallax, retroactively understood (or "retconned") to be the yellow impurity in the Central Power Battery, to take control of him.

Nonetheless, in *Rebirth*, Jordan expresses some personal responsibility for Parallax's actions, claiming that "whatever Parallax pushed me to do—it was still my hand that did it. He got me from the inside. I was cocky. Overconfident. Should've been able to fight it off. I'm stronger than the impurity. I have to be. I will be."[10] Parallax overpowered Jordan and then nearly destroyed the universe. While Jordan does not accept total responsibility for the actions Parallax took, nonetheless he does feel guilt for allowing Parallax to overpower him because of his weakness. Since his murderous rampage as Parallax, the weight of guilt has hung on Jordan, and he has been fulfilling his duties, especially as the Spectre but also as Green Lantern, not just out of moral duty but also to atone for his past. Upon his return in *Rebirth*, Jordan continues to be motivated by a desire to prove to his former friends and allies that he is a hero once more. There is obvious distrust from some of the heroes on Earth—most notably Batman—and also the members of the reformed Green Lantern Corps, many of whom knew Lanterns killed by Parallax and many of whom hold Jordan responsible.[11]

One of Jordan's first adventures after his return is a quest to recover the Lost Lanterns, a group of Green Lanterns who were attacked by Parallax and left for dead in space (but survived after being captured by another villain). Jordan goes on a rescue mission (against the Guardians' wishes), not just to save his fallen comrades, but also to atone for his actions while influenced by Parallax. As he tells Guy Gardner, "I have to try to find them. I have to bring them home. I have to figure out some way to set things right."[12] To make matters even more complicated, after their captor attacks Arisia, a Green Lantern—and, more importantly, Hal's former girlfriend—Jordan announces, "This was about atonement. Now it's about something else," implying that threatening Arisia roused Hal's protective instincts as well.[13] So whereas for most of his early career as a hero Jordan acted for purely selfless reasons, since his rebirths as Spectre and Green Lantern, he has been driven also by desires to atone for his past, prove himself to others, and protect his friends.

Questioning our Heroes

Hal Jordan's motivations have changed from a simplistic, black-and-white heroism to a vicious quest for self-interest to a search for atonement and vengeance and finally to a combination of many purposes. These significant shifts get at the heart of philosophical issues such as morality, belief, and desire. Identifying these shifts does not mean that the discussion is at an end, however. Recognizing these changes in the character should lead to new discussions. Is Jordan's new motivation less moral than his original? If motivations are laid out on some imaginary morality scale, where does the desire for atonement fall in relation to selflessness? Is one nobler than the other? What standards should we hold our heroes to? If a hero stumbles but tries to correct the error, is he or she less of a hero than they were before? How do these standards translate to our real-world heroes? What moral standard do we hold ourselves to? The long histories and narrative twists and turns of comic book superheroes have entertained readers for decades, but if we let them, they can also make us think deeply about some of the standards and ideas that frame our perceptions of the world around us.

NOTES

1. *Showcase* #22 (September–October 1959), reprinted in black and white in *Showcase Presents Green Lantern Volume One* (2005), and in color in *The Green Lantern Chronicles Volume 1* (2009).

2. Connie S. Rosati, "Moral Motivation," *Stanford Encyclopedia of Philosophy* (http://plato.stanford.edu/archives/fall2008/entries/moral-motivation/).

3. Ibid.

4. *Zero Hour* #0 (September 1994).

5. Dave Itzkoff, "Behind the Mask," *The New York Times*, November 20, 2005 (http://www.nytimes.com/2005/11/20/books/review/20itzkoff.html).

6. This led Gail Simone, before her rise as a fan-favorite comics writer herself, to coin the term "Girl-in-the-Refrigerator" to describe graphic depictions of senseless violence against a woman motivated only by animus against her (male) superhero love (see http://www.unheardtaunts.com/wir/index.html).

7. *Day of Judgment* #3 (November 1999).

8. *Day of Judgment* #4 (November 1999; this was a weekly miniseries, all issues cover-dated November.)

9. *JLA/Spectre: Soul War* #1 (January 2003).

10. *Green Lantern: Rebirth* #5 (April 2005), reprinted in *Green Lantern: Rebirth* (2005).

11. See the fight on Oa, in which Guy Gardner and Hal take on many resentful Lanterns, in *Green Lantern*, vol. 4, #11 (June 2006), reprinted in *Green Lantern: Revenge of the Green Lanterns* (2006).

12. Ibid.

13. *Green Lantern*, vol. 4, #13 (August 2006), reprinted in *Green Lantern: Revenge of the Green Lanterns*.

PART THREE

I'M WITH GREEN LANTERN: FRIENDS AND RELATIONSHIPS

HARD-TRAVELING ETHICS: MORAL RATIONALISM VERSUS MORAL SENTIMENTALISM

Andrew Terjesen

Aside from a shared appreciation of the middle of the light spectrum, the only thing that Hal Jordan and Oliver Queen seem to have in common is that they've both come back from the dead. And I don't mean the usual comic book you-never-saw-the-body back from the dead, or the it-was-my-robot-duplicate-or-clone-that-died, plot device, or even the recently popular time-traveler-from-a-second-before-they-died routine. I'm talking about crossing back over after spending some time in the Elysian Fields. Other than those similarities, Hal and Ollie may be the oddest couple on the superhero block: Ollie was a superrich liberal with only his talent with a bow to rely on, while Hal was a working-class test pilot who probably voted for Nixon and has a weapon of mass destruction on his ring finger. But when writer Denny O'Neil, together with penciller Neal Adams, paired them up in the 1970s, he ushered in a new era of social relevance in comics and created something that was much greater than the sum of its parts.

O'Neil juxtaposed the intergalactic cop Green Lantern, with his faith in established authority, and the man of the people Green Arrow, who was all about questioning authority. In many ways this pairing was very much a product of its time, embodying the turbulence of the late 1960s, but their relationship lasted long beyond the time they shared a comic book together. Also, it is about more than just a clash of political views. It is also about contrasting approaches to moral dilemmas. Hal understands right and wrong in terms of the rules that we can discover through rational reflection on the situation, while Ollie acts from the heart and is very comfortable with the idea that morality may not be a system of hard-and-fast rules. In philosophical terms, Hal is a *moral rationalist* and Ollie is a *moral sentimentalist*, a distinction that goes back to debates over ethics in the seventeenth and eighteenth centuries. What is special about Hal and Ollie is that they illustrate the idea that while these two perspectives are opposing views, they can actually complement each other. The lesson to be learned is that we all need a little Hal *and* a little Ollie in our lives.

Hal Jordan and Rational Morality

In the first issue of O'Neil and Adams's run on *Green Lantern*, Hal swoops down to stop a kid from pushing around slumlord Jubal Slade; he uses his ring to send the kid to jail to be booked on assault charges.[1] Hal is surprised when his actions are greeted with a rain of trash from nearby tenement roofs. Before he can use his ring to smoke out the vandals,

Green Arrow shows up to give Hal a personal tour of the buildings owned by Slade. Although Hal appreciates that the people are living in squalid conditions, he still does not think he has done anything wrong in sending the boy off to jail. As he tells Ollie, "He was breaking the law!"

This is the first of many exchanges over the course of their partnership where Hal's strict adherence to the rules collides with Ollie's tendency to bend or even break them. Hal's perspective is shared by his "employers," the Guardians of the Universe, who in that same issue stop Green Lantern from using his ring to punish Jubal Slade, because Slade has committed no crime. The mentality that Hal and the Guardians share is a form of *moral rationalism*. Several moral theories are clear examples of moral rationalism, such as the deontological ethics of Immanuel Kant and the utilitarianism of John Stuart Mill.[2] Although these moral theories differ in their details, they share in common the idea that right and wrong are something we can figure out if we apply our reason correctly to the world in order to discover abstract moral principles. Moral rationalists in the seventeenth century made an analogy between morality and mathematics: the rules of morality were waiting to be discovered in the world, just like the rules of geometry.

Hal's moral rationalism leads him to view situations in terms of fixed and abstract principles, such as "No one person should push another around." Throughout their time together, Hal is uncomfortable with doing anything that violates accepted rules. Even when he and Ollie are saving Black Canary from a mind-controlling child, without an invitation Hal is reluctant to enter the school building where she is being held.[3] Hal's reluctance to challenge authority or circumvent the law could be seen as a lack of moral fortitude, but I would argue that it represents a type of reasoning about the nature of morality that we need to take seriously. For example, when he is partnered with his new backup Green Lantern, John Stewart (an African American), to keep the peace during a demonstration by a racist, rabble-rousing U.S. senator, Hal comments that "such stupidity is the price we pay for free speech!"[4] Hal's attitudes reflect a commitment to abstract principles even when the particulars offend him.

Moral rationalists place great emphasis on strict adherence to the rules because they are concerned about what happens if we start treating everything on a case-by-case basis. Most people would agree that racist speech is bad, but who gets to determine what is racist and what is not? There is a good chance that people's opinions will be affected by their personal interests. It's much better to use objective measures such as "Is the person knowingly saying something false?" instead of more subjective measures such as "Does it offend me?" From Hal's perspective, allowing racist speech (as long as it is not directly inciting violent action) is better than leaving judgments to individual whim—which is what could happen if we don't follow strict, universal, abstract rules.

Why Hal Needed Ollie

Many people criticize moral rationalism for its commitment to abstract principles. When Hal locks that kid up for pushing around Jubal Slade, he pays no attention to the particulars of the situation, nor does he consider that the kid might have had a very good reason for accosting his slumlord. Neither does Hal consider the impact his actions would have on the kid's mother, who was depending on him to get the medicine she needed. Green Arrow reminds Hal of all of these complexities to the situation and in so doing begins the process of getting Hal to rethink his abstract moral principles.

Green Arrow has the gumption to call out the Guardians on their strict adherence to principle, telling them to "Come off your perch! Touch . . . taste . . . laugh . . . and cry! Learn where we're at . . . and why!"[5] The Guardians are persuaded by Ollie's impromptu rhyme and send one of their own to travel the United States in human form with Hal and Ollie in order to better understand humanity. In the course of their travels, the Guardian, who becomes known as "the Old-Timer," begins to comprehend the complexity that is not erased, but only ignored, when we assess the world by abstract principles. A classic example is when Hal has been injured on a boat loaded with hazardous waste.[6] The Old-Timer saves Hal's life even though it means letting the hazardous waste fall into the sea. Another Guardian regards this as a "foolish" action because "one life against billions . . . surely this is no fair exchange."[7] The rest of the Guardians put the Old-Timer on trial for the "mistake" of saving Hal; he pleads guilty and is punished by being stripped of his immortality.

In appealing to the greater good, the Guardians are treating morality as a numbers game. Hal's life is just one life, and it is worth no more or less than the life of each person who would suffer years down the road due to the pollutants of the water, much less all of them. At the very least, what is lacking in Hal's (and the Guardians') moral rationalism is an appreciation for the need to have exceptions and more complicated rules. As Ollie points out to Hal, "You're with me 'cause I specialize in little problems . . . which are often the key to understanding the big ones!"[8] In practice, Hal's moral rationalism had left him viewing the world in a very simple fashion and with black-and-white categories, such as "lawbreaker" and "law-abiding citizen."

Parallax and the Dangers of Moral Rationalism

Let's move up a couple decades, from the 1970s to the 1990s. Hal's eventual downfall after the destruction of his beloved Coast City can be interpreted as the product of his strict moral rationalism (and what happens after too much time away from Ollie's influence). Hal could not accept that the people and city he loved were gone, so he tried to re-create them using his ring, but the result was only temporary.[9] The Guardians, in typical fashion, kept Hal from recharging his ring and tried to punish him for using his ring for "personal gain." Instead of being sensitive to the circumstances surrounding Hal's life at that point, they simply enforced an abstract set of rules. The result was that Hal cracked and began dismantling the Green Lantern Corps and the Guardians themselves in a quest to amass the power necessary to fulfill his wishes. Ultimately, as we know, he was transformed into the villain Parallax.

Why do I say that this was caused by his moral rationalism, as opposed to the yellow fear entity (also named Parallax) that supposedly possessed him (as "revealed" retroactively in 2005's *Green Lantern: Rebirth*)? To start with, Hal's dedication to abstract principles left him in a lurch when he found himself in a situation where principles seemed to conflict. On the one hand, he wanted to "save" Coast City, but on the other hand, he was supposed to reject doing so because it would be acting for "personal gain." In the end, his inability to reconcile these two unyielding principles shattered his faith in the system overall. If all of his years faithfully serving the Guardians would stand in the way of a happy life, then what's the point? As Ganthet, the only Guardian who would survive Hal's rampage, points out, "Unwavering adherence to our edicts, prevented the slightest compassion."[10] Moral rationalism encourages us to think in terms of decision-making procedures that can be applied uniformly to every situation and discourages flexibility about circumstances.

A second way in which his strict moral rationalism worked against Hal is that it led him to view everything in very basic terms: you were either someone who followed the moral rules or you weren't. As clear rational principles, these moral rules did not allow for any gray areas; once you crossed the line, that was it. Hal says as much after he kills his old friend and trainer, Kilowog. In Hal's mind, he had already crossed that line when he killed his archenemy Sinestro, so his only recourse is to kill Kilowog and use the power of the Central Power Battery to set everything right again. The same strict moral rationalism that leads the Guardians to refuse Hal any special allowances in his time of need causes Hal to give up on the idea that he can still be a good person after his first fall from grace.

Hal's time as Parallax is typified by a kind of twisted moral rationalism. It is hard to believe that Parallax was acting on moral truths that he discovered by reason—after all, Hal seemed crazier than the Joker after he destroyed the Corps, and reason wasn't very welcome in his life at that point. However, he still acted with the mentality of someone who *thinks* that they are rationally determining moral principles. In 1994's *Zero Hour* event, Parallax decides to go back to the beginning of time and start the universe all over again, using his power to make sure that everything goes the "right" way this time. The logic that he needed to start over because everything is now irreparably broken (including himself) is typical of the extreme mentality discussed in the previous paragraph. In Hal's mind, the universe had to be perfectly good, with no bad elements, or else it was no good at all. In addition, the idea that he can figure out what is the best of all possible worlds indicates a belief that there is some sort of algorithm that he could implement that would produce the right world. In the end, appropriately, it is his old friend Green Arrow who has to take the kill shot that puts an end to Parallax's madness (for the time being, at least).

If Green Arrow's only point was that Hal needed to be sensitive to the particulars of a situation or willing to suspend a rule on occasion, then Ollie would not be challenging moral rationalism as a whole, but merely pointing out flaws in particular versions of it. There are moral rationalists who think that reason can be used to discover what we ought to do when confronted with a moral dilemma, but do not think that reason will give us abstract principles that can be used to guide our action.[11] And there are other moral rationalists who think that morality has its limits, what is usually called an *agent-centered prerogative*, which says it is okay to place one's relationships or personal projects outside or above the judgment of morality. The agent-centered view is based on the belief that it is not realistic to expect people to pursue morality for morality's sake or to assume that all morality is universal and abstract and that therefore personal relationships and goals are immoral (or at least nonmoral or amoral).

There are other ways that moral rationalists could respond to concerns about flexibility and circumstances, but Ollie's point seems to go deeper. It's not just that Hal is using his reason inflexibly, it's that reason alone can't yield good moral judgments on a regular basis. Focusing on the particulars is a means to an end for Green Arrow because the particulars are what engage his emotions, and his emotions—his gut—tells him right from wrong. A great example of how sentiment can see what reason can't or won't is found in Green Arrow's response to the supervillain Prometheus's threat to blow up every major city in the United States unless he is released from custody. (He even devastates Ollie's own Star City—killing his "granddaughter" Lian in the process—to prove he is serious.[12]) Hal, and the rest of the Justice League, take the rationalist "we don't negotiate with terrorists" approach, but Ollie makes an impassioned speech asking them to "think of the living," and convinces the rest of the Justice League to let Prometheus go (though, as we'll see, he doesn't get far).

Oliver Queen and the Moral Sentiments

Hal's experience of being overwhelmed by his emotions after the destruction of Coast City embodies the argument against moral rationalism made by the philosopher David Hume (1711–1776). According to the English philosopher William Wollaston (1659–1724), right and wrong are a matter of reason, and emotion seems only to get in the way. (In fact, the

Guardian who traveled with Hal and Ollie usually described his own rule-breaking as "emotional" outbursts.) Since Hal was used to ignoring his emotions when he was dealing with moral dilemmas, he was not prepared to handle strong emotional reactions that conflicted with his moral principles. Hal's rage and grief simply overwhelmed what moral framework he had, and there was nothing to push back against the onslaught of his emotions.

None of this would be a surprise to Hume, who is famous for the expression "Reason is and ought only to be the slave of the passions." This quote comes from his magnum opus, *A Treatise of Human Nature*, in which he argues that reason—by which he means the sort of "mathematical" moral reasoning described earlier—is unable to stop a passion from taking hold of us. For example, when Hal is upset that the Guardians will not help him restore Coast City, no amount of explanation of the consequences or principles of fairness will bring Hal's rampage to an end. Kilowog tries to reason with Hal by pointing out that if he destroys the Central Power Battery, he will kill any Green Lanterns who are using their rings at that moment to fly, to hold a weight over their heads, or to do anything else that is keeping them out of danger. But Hal is unmoved by this, and the only way that he would have been moved by Kilowog's reasoning, according to Hume, would be if he cared more about the lives of his fellow Lanterns than he did about the loss of Coast City. In that case, it would be another passion, not reason, that would stop him. In the past Hal's disagreement with the Guardians had been moderated by Hal's passion for law and order, but even that was not strong enough to counteract his grief during the "Emerald Twilight."

Hume builds upon this idea to draw conclusions about the nature of morality, arguing that

> Since morals, therefore, have an influence on the actions and affections, it follows, that they cannot be derived

from reason; and that because reason alone, as we have already proved, can never have any such influence. Morals excite passions, and produce or prevent actions. Reason of itself is utterly impotent in this particular. The rules of morality, therefore, are not conclusions of our reason.[13]

Given that morality is about how we ought to act, it must be derived from sentiments. When Green Arrow is moved to take action against the fat cats in his city, it's not because he has rationally determined that they are hurting the community— it's because it upsets him that they are doing so.

Moral sentimentalists may differ in their conclusions regarding right and wrong. In fact, because emotions are so complex, people can take very nuanced positions that are not easily accounted for in terms of rules. During the *Identity Crisis* miniseries (2004–2005), it was revealed that the Justice League of America (of which both Green Lantern and Green Arrow were members at the time) had collectively decided to alter the memories (and eventually the personalities) of criminals they defeated. Ollie approves of altering the villains' memories (to erase knowledge of the heroes' secret identities), but draws the line at altering their personalities (to make them less danger- ous). When he is outvoted, however, he goes along with the group and even votes to alter Batman's memories when he discovers what the rest of the Justice League are doing. Any attempt to describe Ollie's position in terms of a rule will face difficulties: for example, the rule "Only do it to villains" is trumped by the situation with Batman.

What really determines Ollie's moral positions are the emo- tions that the situation evokes in him. All moral sentimentalists agree that something is morally good if it evokes a positive reac- tion and morally bad if it evokes a negative reaction, with the strength of the reaction helping to determine the thing's rela- tive goodness or badness. However, moral sentimentalists don't think that every emotional reaction is a moral judgment, and moral sentimentalists are distinguished by which emotions they think serve as the basis for our moral attitudes. For instance, Hume thought it was the pleasure as expressed in love and pride that determined what was good. Ollie seems to be more concerned with our emotional responses to seeing people suffering and being treated unfairly. He also places a lot of weight on the emotional bond between friends. When the Old-Timer saves Hal instead of stopping the hazardous waste from falling into the sea, Ollie thinks that he took the only morally acceptable course of action: "Saving his friend . . . was [ironically, for a Guardian] the only human thing to do!"[14] The feeling of kinship with humanity seems to be an important emotion for Green Arrow, which also makes it a central moral sentiment for him.

One of the appeals of moral sentimentalism is that it explains how morality can motivate us to action (assuming that only emotion, not reason, can do so), but that's not the only argument given in its favor. Moral sentimentalists also point out that emotions often convey information that is not easily translated into words. For instance, the racist senator mentioned earlier seemed to make John Stewart feel ill; that sort of revulsion might better capture what is wrong with racist speech than saying that it's factually false or stupid. Stupidity is pretty broad, covering the kinds of things that often come out of Guy Gardner's mouth, but racist speech is on a different level altogether. John Stewart's reaction comes from experiencing personally how racist speech can condone and encourage racist acts. Context matters, so racist speech might be regarded differently if it is uttered in a situation where people can still remember witnessing a lynching as opposed to one where someone utters racist opinions about Kryptonians. Hal's inability to feel what is wrong with the senator's words, or to consider John's feelings, suggests that perhaps he can't truly appreciate how wrong it is, though presumably he can understand it on a rational level.

Your Ward Is a Junkie: The Problem with Our Sentiments

As much as Ollie is a poster boy for relying on the moral sentiments, he also serves as a cautionary tale for this approach. Green Arrow is not just passionate about the "little people" and standing up to those who take advantage of the system—he's passionate, period. And in some cases his passions get the better of him—especially when his on-and-off lover Black Canary is involved. When Ollie finds a guy with Black Canary's bike, he opens up a family-size can of whoopass on him, and has to be pulled off by Hal. Ollie seems to be in a murderous rage, shouting "He hurt her! He doesn't deserve to live!"[15] The fact that he was close to killing somebody (and seemed to think he was justified in doing so) because the guy might have harmed (not even killed) his girlfriend seems a bit much.

Our sentiments can vary widely when our own interests are involved, and any sentimentalist theory of morality has to address that variability. One response would be to simply accept that morality varies from person to person, but that would mean that from Ollie's perspective, he was right to try to kill the biker, and from the *biker's* perspective, he was *not* right to try to kill the biker—both at the same time. If morality yields contradictory judgments, then it yields no real judgments at all, lapsing into moral relativism. So perhaps we should consider alternatives that recognize the variability of sentiment while maintaining the objectivity of morality.

Hume and his good friend Adam Smith (1723–1790) were moral sentimentalists who nonetheless maintained that morality was absolute. Both insisted that we can filter our sentiments through an impartial point of view, eliminating personal biases that could influence our judgment of a situation. Smith's filter was what he called the "impartial spectator." To judge our behavior, we should imagine how an impartial spectator would feel if he or she tried to imagine being in our situation. If we don't think that the impartial spectator would share our feelings, then these feelings shouldn't be used in making a moral judgment. Smith was not very clear on how we learned what an impartial spectator would feel, but he seemed to think that most of us learn through our experiences with other people in our society. At the very core of the impartial spectator concept is avoiding being self-centered to the point of disregarding others' feelings, which is definitely where Ollie has a problem.

Adopting an impartial point of view would not only help Ollie rein in his rampant emotions, it would also bring out emotional responses that he suppressed or ignored. Ollie's greatest moral failure is contained in the most famous story from the O'Neil-Adams run, which reveals that Green Arrow's teenage ward Roy Harper—also his original sidekick, Speedy—is a heroin junkie.[16] To begin with, Ollie has been neglecting Roy to focus on his relationship with Black Canary. Then, when confronted with evidence suggesting that Roy has a drug problem, Ollie tries to rationalize it, assuming that Speedy is working undercover in a drug den. In the end, however, Roy's heroin addiction is undeniable, and Ollie responds by kicking him out of his apartment. In anger at having his failings as an adoptive father exposed, Ollie turns his back on Roy. Had Ollie only taken a step back and imagined his situation through the eyes of an impartial spectator, he would have dismissed his own hangups and realized that Roy was a young man hurting and in need of some guidance (which it was left to Canary and Hal to give).[17]

Why Ollie Still Needs Hal

Ironically, Hal helps Roy kick his habit because he sees a person in need (as an impartial spectator would). He doesn't see someone who has let him down or whose addiction is a sign of bad parenting. Although sentiments can be a valuable source of moral judgments, they need to be guided by rules and principles, or at least by an impartial perspective that constrains them. If we always wanted and desired the right thing, we wouldn't even need to talk about morality. But in order to keep a check on the excessive passions and egoism of someone like Green Arrow, a moral point of view is necessary.

Despite Hal's "squareness," there are times when his cooler head is crucial in making sure that Green Arrow's actions actually yield a morally desirable result. When Hal and Ollie come across a man who appears to be stealing land from a local Native American tribe, Ollie's response is to advocate violent resistance.[18] In a questionable move, he even dresses up as the spirit of a tribal chief in order to inspire the locals. Hal refuses to condone such lawbreaking: "If a law is unjust, I had to do whatever possible to change it, not disobey it." Hal's desire to work within the system leads him to try to track down the original deed to the land. When he fails to find it, he convinces a congressman to meet with the tribe and discuss legal means for reasserting their claim. Although Hal's approach is slower, it avoids the bloodshed and cycle of violence that would ensue as each side fought to gain control of the land.

Not every moral sentimentalist appreciates this, but reason and principle do have roles to play in our determinations of right and wrong. After all, Hume never said that reason is irrelevant to morality, only that it will be effective only insofar as it serves a sentiment. Hal's concern for humanity—his sentiment—directs his reason to find the most effective and peaceful means for settling the dispute. Ollie does not bother to use his reason to consider the consequences of the violent action his passion leads him to. He is so steamed at the treatment of the tribe that he does not consider what a dangerous precedent is set by disregarding laws concerning property and assault. Hal's method does not guarantee success, but sometimes an honorable loss is better than victory at all costs. Ollie doesn't realize that just because you can take action doesn't always mean you should.

As we have already seen, Ollie has a serious problem keeping things in perspective when it comes to Black Canary. For instance, he approves of the mind-wipes during *Identity Crisis* because he fears for her safety (which is pretty ridiculous if you know anything about Black Canary). Instead of helping him to see the moral complexities of the situation more clearly, his emotions seem to oversimplify the matter and blind him to what is really wrong with it. Some of Ollie's overreactions can be astounding: much later, after accidently killing a criminal, Ollie destroys all of his equipment and leaves it all behind to join an ashram.[19] Then, after Canary is injured, it's up to Hal to find Ollie and remind him about all the things he left behind when he acted so hastily. Ollie crossed the most important line recently when he hunted down Prometheus and shot him in cold blood, ostensibly from a "cry for justice" but clearly in retaliation for the death of Lian (Roy Harper's daughter) during the destruction of Star City.[20] His actions forced his teammates to hunt him down and force him to fight everyone—including Black Canary.

What Is This, *Green Arrow and Philosophy*?

It would be great if we could conclude that moral rationalism and moral sentimentalism just need to work together like Hal and Ollie, but the two views do express contrary ideas about the nature of morality. It's not possible for the source of morality to be emotion *and* reason—like superheroes, morality can't have two origins at the same time. What can be true, and what can be gleaned from Ollie and Hal's bromance, is that morality is based in our sentiments, but we must use reason to make sure that those sentiments are based upon a full appreciation of the situation and all the possible consequences of action. When Ollie is acquitted of the murder of Prometheus, even he recognizes that the jury let "their anger trump morality."[21] We also need reason to identify when our sentiments are being overly influenced by our own interests. Ollie is the heart of compassion, but he needs Hal's ability to step back from a situation in order to identify when his compassion is being appropriately directed (an ability that failed Hal when he was Parallax).

Green Arrow's hunt for Prometheus's henchmen nicely illustrates the balance that can be struck between sentiment and reason in making moral judgments. Right before he was going to kill Prometheus's trigger man, Electrocutioner, Ollie stopped because he saw his murderous rage reflected in the eyes of Mia Dearden (the current Speedy).[22] He was willing to cross the line himself, but he couldn't let someone he cared about do the same. Ollie's judgment can veer wildly at times, but when his sentiments are properly applied and viewed from outside his individual point of view, he clearly knows right from wrong. I can't help but think that Ollie's time with Hal made him more cognizant of what happens when he goes off the handle. Of course, Hal's advice is effective only if Ollie desires to maintain their friendship, showing that sentiment still has the upper hand—and in this case the hand is pulling back the string on a boxing-glove arrow.

NOTES

1. *Green Lantern*, vol. 2, #76 (April 1970). The entire O'Neil-Adams run of *Green Lantern* has been reprinted several times, most recently in two trade paperbacks: *Green Lantern/Green Arrow Volume 1* (2004) reprints *Green Lantern*, vol. 1, #76–82 (1970–1971), and *Volume 2* (2004) reprints *Green Lantern*, vol. 1, #83–87 and 89, plus the Green Lantern backup stories from *Flash*, vol. 1, #217–219, 226 (collectively 1971–1974). All references to this run will be given by the original issue number (without dates); refer to this note for the appropriate volume of the trade collection.

2. For more on utilitarianism and deontology, see any introductory ethics book, such as James Rachels's *The Elements of Moral Philosophy* (sixth edition by Stuart Rachels; New York: McGraw-Hill, 2009).

3. *Green Lantern*, vol. 2, #83.

4. *Green Lantern*, vol. 2, #87.

5. *Green Lantern*, vol. 2, #76.

6. *Green Lantern*, vol. 2, #80.

7. *Green Lantern*, vol. 2, #81.

8. *Green Lantern*, vol. 2, #111 (December 1978).

9. As chronicled in the "Emerald Twilight" story line in *Green Lantern*, vol. 3, #48–50 (January–March 1994), reprinted in *Green Lantern: Emerald Twilight/New Dawn* (2003).

10. *Green Lantern*, vol. 3, #50 (March 1994).

11. See my other chapter in this volume, "Will They Let Just Anybody Join?", for a discussion of moral particularism.

12. *Justice League: Cry for Justice* #7 (April 2010).

13. David Hume, *A Treatise of Human Nature*, ed. David Fate Norton and Mary J. Norton (Oxford, UK: Oxford University Press, 2000), Book III, Part I, Section 1.

14. *Green Lantern*, vol. 2, #80.

15. *Green Lantern*, vol. 2, #78.

16. *Green Lantern*, vol. 2, #85–86.

17. Nor does the emotional Ollie learn his lesson. After Prometheus tears Roy's arm off in the 2009–2010 *Justice League: Cry for Justice* miniseries, Ollie is once again emotionally distant and runs off to help total strangers in Star City and to hunt down Prometheus's henchmen, again leaving Black Canary to console Roy.

18. *Green Lantern*, vol. 2, #79.

19. *Flash*, vol. 2, #217–219 (1972–1973), reprinted in *Green Lantern/Green Arrow Volume 2*.

20. *Justice League: Cry for Justice* #7. In *Justice League: Rise and Fall* (May 2010), it is suggested that Ollie convinced the heroes to let Prometheus go because he was planning to kill him later.

21. *Green Arrow*, vol. 4, #32 (June 2010).

22. Ibid.

"I DESPISE MESSINESS": THE PLATO-ARISTOTLE DEBATE IN THE TROUBLED FRIENDSHIP OF GREEN LANTERN AND GREEN ARROW

Brett Chandler Patterson

In *Green Lantern*, vol. 2, #83 (May 1971), the villain Grandy, who has hypnotized and enslaved a large group of children, describes himself in the following manner: "You can say that I'm a person who wants order! I despise messiness . . . and nothing is so disordered as the average school."[1] This sentiment reflects the context of writer Denny O'Neil and penciller Neal Adams's groundbreaking run with *Green Lantern* in the early 1970s. Together with editor Julius Schwartz, O'Neil and Adams revitalized the fading Green Lantern comic series, first by teaming the character with Green Arrow, and second by transforming the comic into a medium for social commentary. Despite pressure from the Comics Code Authority (established in the 1950s), which frowned on the inclusion of certain questionable topics, this creative team dared to take on such issues as drug abuse, environmental decay, and racism.

The conflict between the Comics Code and DC Comics' efforts to be more "relevant" resembles a dispute that took place many centuries ago between Plato (428–348 BCE) and Aristotle (384–322 BCE). In the *Republic*, Plato presented the dangers of theatrical drama, arguing that young people would imitate vices portrayed onstage and that fiction generally produced an "escapism" that did not contribute to the building of an ideal state. On the other hand, Aristotle argued for the benefits of imitation. According to Aristotle, there is a human need for identifying with characters, and such identification can sometimes lead to catharsis, a release of emotions that contribute to social ills. The concerns of the Comics Code Authority are reminiscent of Plato's endorsement of censorship. Meanwhile, DC Comics and the O'Neil-Adams team represent the spirit of Aristotle, redefining both heroism and the domain of comics storytelling for a new generation.

Some Monsters Are Human

When the Green Lantern series was struggling in the late 1960s, O'Neil and Adams seized the opportunity to experiment with the comic art form. They wanted to do something radically different, something that would show that comic books were not just escapist literature for male adolescents. In his 1983 introduction to the original trade collection, O'Neil wrote that he believed that this run of *Green Lantern* drew from the spirit of the 1960s, the era of social consciousness, change, and anti-establishment feeling. He wondered if he could emulate in comic book form the "New Journalism" of such writers as Tom Wolfe, Norman Mailer, and others; O'Neil had worked for a bit as a reporter before going into writing fiction, and he had longed to be a part of the social activism of his time in some way.[2]

Studying the characters in the series that Schwartz handed him, O'Neil quickly saw Green Lantern as a representative of "the establishment" (in particular, the Guardians of the Universe), essentially serving as a police officer, charged with enforcing the social standard of order. To provide dialogue in the series, O'Neil would need a counterpoint. Thus Green Arrow became a modern-day Robin Hood, someone who would break the rules to see that justice was served.[3] Likewise, Green Lantern shunned space in favor of exploring his home planet Earth, joining Green Arrow on the open road to discover America. On their adventures they expose Slapper Soames's unjust mining operation, defend a Native American tribe's claim to land that a developer seeks to seize, deal with Speedy's (Green Arrow's sidekick) addiction to heroin, and more generally stand up to the rigid belief system of the Guardians. By portraying characters who really struggle to find a moral ground in a corrupt world beset by numerous ills that comics weren't "supposed" to address, O'Neil was breaking the rules that had restricted comic writers since the implementation of the Comics Code in the 1950s.

The Comics Code Authority (CCA) was created in 1954 by the comics industry for the purpose of self-regulation. Frederic Wertham's book *The Seduction of the Innocent* (1954) brought popular attention to the violence, drug use, and sexual content in comic books, whose primary audience at the time was children.[4] Because the Senate Subcommittee on Juvenile Delinquency was investigating the industry, several publishers decided to form an organization of their own to regulate content before the government began its own censorship. The resulting Comics Code Authority guidelines would become the standard for years to come. Comic books could not show anyone in the government (including politicians, judges, and police officers) in a negative, anti-establishment light; stories had to clearly portray the victory of good over evil; and certain topics were to be highly regulated, such as kidnapping and firearms, or entirely forbidden, such as gruesome violence, drug use, sexual promiscuity, or monsters that resembled vampires, werewolves, or ghouls.[5]

Although several critics, including Wertham, thought that the CCA guidelines did not go far enough and instead favored age-based ratings like those used for modern movies, many comic book writers and artists found the code too constraining. The code certainly did change the substance of comic books in the following years; even though acceptance and compliance were voluntary, many retailers would not carry books that did not have the CCA stamp on the cover. Many comic book characters changed over this time period, including Superman and Batman, becoming simplistic, goofy, or pedantic. Some creators broke from the leaders in the industry and sought to publish and distribute so-called underground comics, but the major titles in the industry largely worked with the code. No significant challenge to the code arose until the 1970s. In addition to O'Neil and Adams's groundbreaking work on *Green Lantern* at DC Comics, in 1971 Marvel Comics, in coordination with the federal government, addressed the issue of drug abuse in what would become a celebrated Spider-Man story that debuted without the code (and led to revisions in the code itself).[6]

Plato's Vote for Censorship

The debate in the comics industry between those supporting censorship and those pushing for greater creative freedom echoes, in its own way, a much earlier argument between the two greatest Greek philosophers. Most literary theory textbooks begin with selections from Plato's *Republic* and Aristotle's *Poetics*. In fact, one of my teachers, E. D. Hirsch, boldly pronounced in his literary theory graduate course that the ancient debate between Plato and Aristotle set the parameters for all other literary theory since. Whether or not you agree with Professor Hirsch on this issue, you will have to admit that the arguments in the Plato-Aristotle debate have surfaced in many different forums over the centuries and do not show any signs of settling into obscurity. The issues are too important: What value do stories play in our society? Do stories—whether as books, plays, films, or comics—exert any moral or immoral influence over those who experience them? If so, then should we as a society monitor the content of the stories that are distributed to our citizens?

Plato offers one of the earliest recorded voices in support of censorship, going so far as to banish any poetry that is "imitative" from his ideal society. He develops these ideas in the *Republic*, which consists of a fictionalized dialogue between Socrates (Plato's teacher in real life) and some friends, primarily Glaucon and Adeimantus. For the most part, the character of Socrates is used to develop Plato's ideas. The crucial discussion comes in Book X of the *Republic*: in a dialogue with Glaucon, Socrates argues that "all such poetry is likely to corrupt the mind of those of its hearers who do not have the knowledge of what it is really like as a drug to counteract it."[7] In his justification of this statement, Plato (through Socrates) lays out distinctions between a god making a form, a craftsperson making a product, and a painter making an imitation. His example is a table: a god fashions the concept of the table, the carpenter carves a table, and the painter offers a representation of a table. Plato argues that as we move from one to the next in this series, we move further from the truth. Glaucon and Socrates label the artist an "imitator," one who specializes only in appearances, not things "as they are."[8]

Plato continues his criticism through Socrates' words:

> So, imitation is surely far removed from the truth. And
> the reason that it produces everything, it seems, is that
> it grasps only a small part of each thing—and that is
> an illusion. For example, the painter, we say, can paint
> us a cobbler, a carpenter, or any other craftsman, even
> though he knows nothing about these crafts. All the
> same, if he is a good painter, by painting a carpenter
> and displaying him at a distance, he might deceive
> children and foolish adults into thinking it truly is a
> carpenter.[9]

Thus, Plato is accusing the artist of being an illusionist, a
sorcerer, a deceiver, who excels at catching his audience in
an attractive fiction. Socrates laments that many people let
themselves be deceived easily and fail to distinguish between
knowledge and imitation.

Advancing the argument, Plato has Glaucon confirm that
it does not make sense that if someone could make something,
they would devote their time to making an image of it. If I
could make an automobile, why would I not make an automobile rather than a drawing of one? Plato (through Socrates)
questions, "But if he truly had knowledge of what he imitates,
I suppose he would take deeds much more seriously than their
imitations, would try to leave behind many beautiful deeds as
his own memorials, and would be much more eager to be the
subject of a eulogy than the author of one."[10] Plato suggests
that readers of Homer should ask him what cities have been
better governed or what wars have been better fought or what
person has lived more virtuously because of his work. If there
has been no practical application of his work, then it is nothing
but an escapist illusion. For Plato, Homer's imitation of life is
far from the truth of living; it is only a game that we should
not take seriously.

If this argument were not enough to convince skeptics, Plato advances another condemnation of art, focusing on how it manipulates us. The real problem with imitative art is that it "consorts with an element in us that is far from wisdom."[11] Socrates states that this element within us is our emotional side, our passions, which must come under the rule of our reason. But artists typically want to appeal to our passionate side, which is "easier" to imitate. As the poet "arouses and nourishes this element in the soul," he "destroys the rational one."[12] Socrates identifies the danger in giving ourselves over to the lamentation involved in identifying with a suffering character, because we are doing the opposite of what we should be doing in life. To be virtuous, to be complete and truly happy, we must foster self-control and be guided by our rational side. But imitative art promotes indulgent moments of grief, base humor, anger, and sexual appetite, which lead to division, vice, and wretchedness. For these many reasons, Plato has Socrates and Glaucon banish poets from their ideal republic.[13]

Aristotle's Vote for Expression

Aristotle directly challenges these two arguments in his *Poetics*. Embracing the imitative nature of art, Aristotle says, "Imitation is natural to man from childhood, one of his advantages over the lower animals being this, that he is the most imitative creature in the world, and learns at first by imitation."[14] Art is an advanced form of imitation, and such imitation can be done well or badly. Our natural delight in imitation is not an insidious thing, as Plato thinks; instead, we delight that we are learning from the imitation. Indeed, it is easier for us to view painful, traumatic events in art than to experience them directly.

The fragment of the *Poetics* we have today devotes many of its pages to a study of tragedy, highlighting the elements in successful expressions of this art form. Tragedy arouses feelings of pity and fear. Aristotle does not dodge this fact, but instead turns it into a praiseworthy characteristic. Plot, character, and spectacle come together to give us these feelings, and we find pleasure in them: "The tragic pleasure is that of pity and fear, and the poet has to produce it by a work of imitation."[15] Here we come to the concept of *catharsis*. Scholars have debated exactly what Aristotle means by this term, whether a form of *purging* negative emotions or of *purifying* our base emotions into nobler ones. Either way, it works by having us identify with the characters onstage and their feelings. If we see catharsis as purgative, it means that through a tragedy, the poet arouses emotions of pity and fear within us to release them. We experience and learn through these moments, and they do not lead to the corruption of our characters as Plato argued; instead, we learn from our dramatic experiences. Aristotle presents a counterargument that has created a lively debate through the years as various people have lined up on either side, supporting either Plato's censorship or Aristotle's support of art.

Hard-Traveling Heroes—and Comics Creators!

This debate played out again in the 1950s when the Comics Code Authority was created. The arguments that comic books were escapist literature far removed from real life or prurient melodrama corrupting our children, drew on Plato's legacy, while those publishers and creators (like Denny O'Neil) who argued for the creative potential of the art form carried the banner of Aristotle. Furthermore, O'Neil and Adams's run on *Green Lantern* captured the spirit of this debate, especially in the relationship of the two central characters. Green Lantern represented the establishment, the Platonic voice for order and potential censorship, while Green Arrow represented the Aristotelian spirit of creative expression. He was emotional, involved, countercultural, fighting injustice even if it meant opposing the established order.

The friendship between Green Lantern and Green Arrow developed through a number of challenges, which they often approached in radically different ways while retaining a mutual respect. Along their way, these two characters confronted and debated many of the controversial social issues from this era, starting with the first story in the run, "No Evil Shall Escape My Sight!"[16] While on patrol, Green Lantern spots a rough-looking kid grappling with a richly dressed middle-aged man and assumes that the youth shows no respect for "law and order." In order "to teach him a little respect," Green Lantern cages him and sends him off to police headquarters. Promptly, Green Arrow confronts Green Lantern, saying that he has no idea what is going on. The rich man has been seeking the eviction of the poor tenants (including the kid) who live in his building. Ollie (Green Arrow) takes Hal on a tour of the building, showing him the people who are suffering in poverty. Hal tries to defend his action, saying that the kid was breaking the law, and Ollie responds by saying that technically he was, but that there are larger issues at work in that encounter.

The argument builds until one of the tenants, an older African American man, steps forward to ask Green Lantern a question:

> I been readin' about you . . . how you work for the blue skins . . . and how on a planet someplace you helped out the orange skins . . . and you done considerable for the purple skins! Only there's skins you never bother with—the black skins! I want to know . . . how come?! Answer me that, Mr. Green Lantern!

The last panel on the page shows Hal Jordan head bent low, lamenting, "I . . . can't . . ."

When this encounter motivates Green Lantern to confront the rich tenant owner, he loses his temper, at which point the Guardians of the Universe recall him to their home world of Oa for discipline. Green Arrow helps Green Lantern confront the Guardians over their detachment and smug self-righteousness. The Guardians ask what they are supposed to do, and Green Arrow suggests that they come off their thrones to experience human life. In the Guardians, O'Neil represents a rigid establishment; they don't seem able to handle the complications of moral problems, and wish to keep a tight reign over those they watch.

Hal comes away from the experience upset with the willful blindness of the Guardians. His faith has been shaken; future stories in the series speak to his doubt, confusion, and growing awareness of the suffering in the world. When the Guardians actually decide to send a representative to Earth, Hal and Ollie decide to go on a road trip across America in Ollie's old green pickup truck to examine the messy, emotion-laden world of unjust policies and exploitation.

Breaking Up Is the Hardest Thing

The conflict between Hal and Ollie is even more clearly spelled out in "Ulysses Star Is Still Alive!" The story focuses on a lumber company that is angling to cut down trees on land belonging to a Native American tribe.[17] The tribe cannot produce the paperwork to show that the land belongs to them, even though a hundred years earlier Ulysses Star, the chief of the tribe, had made an agreement with the U.S. government for the land. The government's copy was lost, and the local record mysteriously went missing. The tribe's copy went with Ulysses' son Abe Star, who left for the city some twenty years before and then disappeared. Green Lantern believes that their hands are tied: "Then there's nothing we can do to help!" But Green Arrow strongly disagrees: "The heck there isn't! We can stay and fight! We're supposed to be good at fighting—remember?!" Hal lashes back, "I'm getting tired of your lording it over me . . . with your moral superiority routine. If you want to break the law, go ahead! But count me out!" They break off and go their separate ways.

Green Lantern, shaken by his companion's fervor, admits to himself that he was wrong and seeks to track down Abe Star. When he finds Abe, Hal finds his building in flames and soon learns that the legal papers were lost in the blaze. Flying away, Hal is lost in thought:

> I won't give up! There must be another way . . . a way I can help legally! I can't let myself believe Green Arrow was right! My whole life is based on a respect for authority. I've always believed that if a law isn't just, I had to do whatever possible to change it, not disobey it! Maybe I'm wrong, but I won't accept that until I've tried everything.

Hal's point of view arises from a sense of order about the universe, and particularly human society. He believes that he must uphold this order at all costs.

While Green Lantern heads off to speak with his congressman, we learn that someone has been posing as the ghost of the ancient tribal chief Ulysses Star, disrupting the lumber company and giving courage to the Native Americans to fight to defend their land. Green Lantern arrives with the congressman in the midst of the conflict, and a fistfight between Hal and Ulysses reveals that Green Arrow was posing as the tribal hero. The fight ends only when a log rolls down and hits them both in the head. At the end of the story, evidence has arisen implicating the lumber company's leaders in the fire that claimed Abe Star's building. There seems to be no resolution between Hal and Ollie, but the Guardian who is traveling with them confronts them, saying that they should have learned that violence is not the answer to their dispute; rather, they should have mutual respect for each other even in their differences.

In the most celebrated stories of the run, "Snowbirds Don't Fly" and "They Say It'll Kill Me . . . But They Won't Say

When!", O'Neil brought attention to another subject that was taboo under the 1950s Comics Code: drug use.[18] In these stories, Green Lantern and Green Arrow fight against the drug trade in their neighborhood, only to discover that Ollie's ward and crime-fighting sidekick Roy Harper (aka Speedy) has become a heroin addict. When Hal starts questioning him, Roy's response shows the spirit of youth, the suspicion of the established order:

> I had the sermons thrown at me! But Lantern, your generation has been known to lie, dig it? You've told us war is fun . . . skin-color is important . . . a man's worth is the size of his bank account . . . all crocks! So why believe your drug rap?

The story ends with Green Lantern and Green Arrow taking down the drug ring, and with Speedy struggling through the pain of withdrawal and coming clean. The issue also shows someone dying of a drug overdose, in a large, impressionable image, which surely would have inspired criticism in the 1950s. O'Neil and company once again invoked the spirit of Aristotle in their efforts. Instead of conforming to the Comics Code and avoiding any representation of drug use, they chose to portray it, and readers learned more about the horrors of drug use when they were drawn into the story and experienced the pain of Roy's drug problem. Within the story, Green Lantern, and in this case Green Arrow too, learned that fighting the presence of illicit drugs in society was more complicated than just arresting those who trafficked drugs.

A Lasting Legacy

In their classic *Green Lantern* run, Denny O'Neil and Neal Adams created stories that achieved critical acclaim but did not garner high sales, and in the world of publishing that inevitably leads to cancellation. Even though their run was short, the series has been remembered by many since then as a "classic" in the genre. It is a testament to their value that these comics have been republished several times in various formats since they originally appeared in the early 1970s. Their enduring value drives home the idea that comics can be about more than pulp-inspired adventures; they can also address real problems and concerns.

The lasting legacy of these comics owes no small part to their echoing of an older philosophical debate, one that Plato and Aristotle effectively voiced and one that may never find a resolution. Art is imitation, art plays on our emotions, and art involves us in an act of our imaginations. We will always argue about the content of that art, whether it corrupts or whether it teaches as it entertains. We can avoid questionable or messy issues, and like Plato, the Comics Code Authority, the Guardians, or even Hal Jordan early in the run, we might distance ourselves from such issues, not wishing to get our hands dirty. On the other hand, Aristotle, Denny O'Neil, and Green Arrow challenge us to get involved, to face these issues, to come out on the other side with a more nuanced understanding of the world around us. Aristotle and company call us to start our own road trips, to make our own journeys between order and activism, and to decide where we will make our stand.

NOTES

1. Reprinted in *Green Lantern/Green Arrow Volume 2* (2004), the second of two trade paperbacks collecting the O'Neil-Adams run. *Volume 1* (2004) reprints *Green Lantern*, vol. 1, #76–82 (1970–1971), while *Volume 2* reprints *Green Lantern*, vol. 1, #83–87, 89, and the *Green Lantern* backup stories from *Flash*, vol. 1, #217–219, 226 (collectively 1971–1974). All references to this run will be given by the original issue number (without dates); refer to this note for the appropriate volume of the trade collection.

2. *Green Lantern/Green Arrow Volume 1*, 4–7 (from which much of the following background also comes).

3. See *Justice League of America*, vol. 1, #75 (November 1969), which also happened to be the second appearance of the modern Green Arrow costume (and goatee), designed

by none other than Neal Adams for *The Brave and the Bold*, vol. 1, #85 (September 1969).

4. Danny Fingeroth, *Superman on the Couch* (New York: Continuum, 2004), 22.

5. Jamie Coville, "Seduction of the Innocents and the Attack on Comic Books," http://www.psu.edu/dept/inart10_110/inart10/cmbk4cca.html.

6. *Amazing Spider-Man*, vol. 1, #96–98 (May–July 1971).

7. Plato, *Republic*, trans. C. D. C. Reeve (Indianapolis: Hackett Publishing Company, Inc., 2004), 595b4–6.

8. Ibid., 597d10–598a10.

9. Ibid., 598b6–c4.

10. Ibid., 599b3–6.

11. Ibid., 603a10–11.

12. Ibid., 605b2–3.

13. See the chapter by Donovan and Richardson in this volume for more on the debate between reason and emotion.

14. Aristotle, *The Basic Works of Aristotle*, ed. Richard McKeon (New York: Modern Library, 2001), 1448b5–9.

15. Ibid., 1453b12–13.

16. *Green Lantern*, vol. 2, #76.

17. *Green Lantern*, vol. 2, #79.

18. *Green Lantern*, vol. 2, #85–86.

CAN'T LIVE WITH 'EM, CAN'T LIVE WITHOUT 'EM: GREEN LANTERN, RELATIONSHIPS, AND AUTONOMY

Jane Dryden

One of the first things I usually find myself explaining to people when they ask me about Green Lantern—after I show them my collection of *Blackest Night* rings—is that "Green Lantern" is not just the name of one superhero, but a title granted to all the members of the Green Lantern Corps. While other superheroes have shared "legacy" names—the Flash comes immediately to mind—Green Lantern in particular points to a whole community of hard-working heroes operating at the same time. They all rely on one another for support and will go to great lengths to defend each other.

The community involved is further extended when we think of the families and loved ones of each of these Lanterns. These loved ones are sometimes supportive of the Corps (think of Hal's niece and nephew, so excited to see him flying by on his way to an adventure[1]) and sometimes disapproving (think of the reaction of the Korugarians to Katma Tui's joining the Corps, calling her "Katma Tui the Lost"[2]). All of the Green Lanterns bear the influences of these relationships, for good or for ill, as they fly about the universe, even when they go to the most distant galaxies. Neither time nor space severs links like these.

With this in mind, do their relationships to one another and to others outside the Corps help or hinder their service as Green Lanterns? Do they represent weaknesses to be exploited or sources of strength? Fortunately, these sorts of questions have been raised by philosophers working in the field of personal autonomy, so let's turn to that discussion to see if it can help us out.

Doing Your Own Thing

Personal autonomy refers to an individual's capacity for self-determination: in other words, the individual's ownership of his or her actions, decisions, and commitments. If I'm being controlled by, say, a gigantic yellow parasite that forces me to attack a fellow Green Lantern, then I'm not autonomous with respect to that action—my autonomy is impaired.[3] On the other hand, if I've thought about what's really important to me, despite the disapproval of my xenophobic parents on Daxam, and I have made the decision accordingly to accept a Green Lantern ring, then I am autonomous with respect to that decision.[4]

These examples may make it seem as though autonomy is always a matter of acting against the influence of others—as though we are more autonomous the more individualistic we are. Certainly, it might seem as though severing—or at least downplaying—our relationships with others means that we have more control over our lives, since that would limit their influence over us (both directly and in terms of how much we let what happens to them affect us). Along these lines, Epictetus (circa 55–135 CE), a Stoic philosopher, argued that there are some things we can control and other things we can't, and that we should focus only on the former: "Things in our control are by nature free, unrestrained, unhindered; but those not in our control are weak, slavish, restrained, belonging to others."[5] Attachments to others are a source of weakness, restricting our freedom, since we then let our happiness be held hostage by what happens to them. As Epictetus counsels, "If, for example, you are fond of a specific ceramic cup, remind yourself that it is only ceramic cups in general of which you are fond. Then, if it breaks, you will not be disturbed. If you kiss your child, or your wife, say that you only kiss things which are human, and thus you will not be disturbed if either of them dies."[6] In other words, we can appreciate humanity, but we shouldn't be so partial to any specific humans that their loss disturbs us.

This idea may be startling when put this bluntly, but it sort of makes sense, especially when you think about the way in which Green Lanterns have been attacked through their families and loved ones. In addition to the famous example of Kyle's girlfriend Alex, killed by Major Force and stuffed in a refrigerator to demoralize the brand-new Green Lantern,[7] there was also the deliberate attack on family members of Green Lantern recruits by members of the Sinestro Corps.[8] The Green Lanterns are fearless in the face of danger to themselves, but their families are another matter. The first wave of the attack on recruits' families is especially ironic, as it occurs just after Kyle has been telling the new recruits, "Everyone's got a weak spot! Your job is to find it and exploit it to your advantage!"[9] Eyeballs begin to fall from the sky, which are revealed by Soranik Natu's ring to be those of their families. The recruits revolt, demanding to know what is being done to protect their families, and they're not satisfied when told that vengeance "cannot be sanctioned."[10] Faced with the threat to their families, many recruits leave. Family ties, then, seem to undermine the integrity of the Corps. Worry about the safety of loved ones prevents the recruits from determining how to live their own lives and carrying through on their decision to join the Corps. Their attachment to their families means that their actions have been determined by the Sinestro Corps rather than by their own will.

According to Immanuel Kant (1724–1804), the most famous philosopher to write about autonomy, we are autonomous only insofar as we are acting according to what our reason tells us is the morally right thing to do.[11] Our freedom and dignity as human beings are tied up with our ability to reason. When we act according to our inclinations or our emotions, we are being controlled by something other than our own free will—Kant calls this being *heteronomous* as opposed to autonomous.[12] (Kant didn't know about the hormones or neurotransmitters used to explain some of our feelings today, but their effects, such as strong mood swings, would further underscore his point that our feelings can be quite external to our truest, autonomous self.) In the case of the Green Lantern recruits, if their fears for their families are leading them to act against their promised duties to the Corps, they are acting heteronomously—that is, being controlled by their fears (and the Sinestro Corps), not their own wills.

Sins of the Autonomy Corps?

We might ask, however, whether protecting our loved ones shouldn't also be considered an important priority. Aren't the recruits choosing to protect their families because their families are important to them? (And aren't they autonomous with respect to their decision to leave?) A life without attachment seems rather impoverished. While the case of the Sinestro

Corps attack on families might make it seem like families are a weakness, families are often really important, giving many Lanterns a reason to go on and a reason to fight. Even Hal Jordan, often happy to go it alone in the face of danger, realizes the importance of his friends and family. As he tells his brother Jim when counseling him to get away from Coast City during the Sinestro Corps War, "Back when Dad died, I didn't care about what happened to me anymore. I didn't care for a long, long time. But today . . . more than anything right now, I care about what happens to you and your family."[13]

Even more poignant is the case of Kilowog, whose entire species was destroyed by Sinestro. Kilowog's species (the Bolovaxians) strongly valued relationships, since they could join together into a collective mind.[14] It is thus particularly painful for him to be alone, and his relationships with his friends in the Corps are especially important to him. The presence of these friends, especially Arisia, helped him to overcome his loss.[15] His family still lingers within his heart, as we see in the aftermath of the Sinestro Corps War, when he has dinner with energy constructs of his family. As the construct of his dead wife says, "Here's to us having your father back where he belongs. With his wife and children who love him with every essence of their being." Kilowog responds, "I've missed you all more than you can possibly imagine. Here's to my family."[16] Despite the pain of his loss, Kilowog's family is still essential to who he is.

At least one possible Green Lantern turned down the opportunity to join the Corps precisely because of the priority she gave to her family. Back in the 1950s, before Hal Jordan was chosen to be Green Lantern, the Guardians approached Donna Parker, a teacher, widow, and mother of three. The Guardians thought it might be a good idea to find a Green Lantern who wasn't so much of a loner, in order to see "if a being who is a parent might be more willing to temper justice with compassion."[17] Donna asks what would happen to her children if she died, and a Guardian tells her that they would receive shelter and education, though he can't assure her that they would be loved. Donna turns down the ring, arguing that "my children must come first. . . . There must be someone else who could do it. But who else can love my children the way I do?"[18] Similarly, after the Guardians pass a law outlawing relationships between Corps members, married Lanterns Amnee and Matoo Pree give up their rings, saying, "This life is difficult enough—to expect us to simply shut off our love for each other and abide by this. . . . Without a doubt, this is the easiest decision we've ever made."[19] The priorities of Donna Parker, and Amnee and Matoo Pree, are clear: their loved ones come first.

Autonomy Recharge: Having It Both Ways

The ideal of autonomy as removing yourself from external influence came under a great deal of criticism from feminist philosophers in the 1980s. They argued that autonomy is a "noxious concept" that "encourages us to believe that connecting and engaging with others limits us."[20] The alternative, they argued, is that we can find strength in relationships, which give meaning to our lives and are part of who we are.

At the same time, feminists also wanted to argue that autonomy was a good thing, something that people suffering from oppression around the world in fact needed to have more of. It is important to be able to take a reflective look at our society and our relationships, even if this means stepping away for a little while. For example, it is a good thing for Sodam Yat to realize that his family's xenophobic values aren't ones he wants to endorse; and on a smaller scale, we can understand former Justice Leaguer Ice saying to Guy Gardner upon her resurrection that even though she loves him, she needs "to figure out who I really want to be."[21]

But do we need to choose between our ability to run our own lives and our ability to open ourselves to others? Both sides of the autonomy coin have merit, and so it's no surprise that feminist philosophers ultimately tried to bring them together. By the late 1980s, then, the idea of *relational autonomy* was born. Instead of seeing the self as something that has to fight against outside influences in order to be autonomous, relational autonomy theorists argued that relationships with others in fact help us to develop the kind of skills and strengths needed to be able to exercise our autonomy.[22] Further, the values and commitments that guide our decisions and choices are all formed within the context of our society and our relationships. Feminist philosophers see this relational aspect as part of what it means for us to be autonomous.[23] We don't need to separate ourselves from the relationships that give our lives meaning.

Not Quite Star Sapphire

To endorse the idea of relational autonomy is not, however, to suggest that all relationships are good and autonomy-promoting. Feminist philosophers are not Zamarons and do not necessarily think that love will always save the day. Given the reality of problems like domestic violence and child abuse, it is clear that relationships can go horribly awry, and that love alone is not enough to guarantee healthy interactions with other people. Some philosophers of relational autonomy argue that what matters is developing *autonomy competency*: our ability to reflectively negotiate our values, commitments, and relationships in a way that we can take ownership of.[24]

Our relationships can be a source of strength, even though they can also make us fragile. During the Sinestro Corps War, Sinestro taunts Kyle with the revelation that Kyle's mother was killed by Sinestro Corps member Despotellis, a sentient virus, making it yet another death that Kyle must feel responsible for. This revelation, together with Kyle's sense of guilt, leads to his being taken over by the Parallax entity (which once possessed Hal as well).[25] When the entity once again claims Hal, he finds Kyle and reassures him: "For guys like us, overcoming fear is what we do best, but when it comes to guilt, regret . . . loss. Even Green Lanterns struggle with those. But we don't have to do it alone."[26] Grasping hands, they break free of Parallax (who explodes in a gooey, rather unpleasant way). When Kyle opens up to Hal's influence in this instance, it makes him stronger and more able to escape the influence of both Parallax and Sinestro. We can see from this example that self-determination is not a matter of escaping outside influence altogether, but a matter of how we work with these influences and how we manage our relationships. Kyle realizes that accepting Hal's help is better than trying to prove that he can go it alone; it does not detract from his autonomy but rather enhances it.

Relational autonomy differs from some traditional ideas of autonomy in its acknowledgment that our relationships with others can shape who we are even if we would prefer that they didn't. The revelation that Sinestro is her father, for instance, bothers Soranik Natu, as it risks changing her sense of identity by allying her (even just biologically) with someone she despises. But she can't undo the fact any more than she can laser Sinestro's family crest from her cheek.[27]

Natu's inability to remove Sinestro's imprint is analogous to the inability to sever genetic ties with our family members— even ones we may never speak to. Contemporary philosopher and bioethicist Anne Donchin recounts such an example, involving a mother who lies to her estranged daughter about having tested positive for Huntington's disease, pointing out the difficulty of honoring the mother's autonomous decision not to tell against the daughter's right to know about her chances of also developing the disease.[28] The two are connected despite their wishes and will need to learn to carefully negotiate their relationship—the daughter ought to learn the truth. Similarly, like it or not, Soranik Natu needed to learn that Sinestro is her father because she needed the warning that the Red Lanterns might be after her in order to get at him. More generally, she needs to learn to understand how her father plays into who she is.

You Never Walk Alone

Working through the kind of problems that Kyle and Soranik faced is a matter of autonomy competency.[29] We have to learn to navigate our chosen and unchosen relationships in order to make decisions with open eyes. Of course, philosophers working on relational autonomy don't have an easy or predetermined answer to the question of how you should live your life or how you should pick your friends. The point of autonomy, after all, is that you have to figure it out for yourself—but just like Kyle when dealing with Parallax, you don't have to do it alone. Opening up to others and letting our relations with them shape who we are can be frightening, but as Hal says, "Even rookies know a Green Lantern isn't without fear. A Green Lantern overcomes fear. Every time they face it."[30] Even if it opens us to weakness, this is what makes life meaningful in the first place. One of the great strengths of the Green Lanterns is that they do have a Corps, they do have one another—they are not alone.

NOTES

1. "Kick their butts, Uncle Hal!" says his niece Jane (good name!) in *Green Lantern*, vol. 4, #25 (January 2008), reprinted in *Green Lantern: The Sinestro Corps War Volume 2* (2008).

2. *Green Lantern Corps: Recharge* #1 (November 2005), reprinted in *Green Lantern Corps: Recharge* (2006).

3. This particular example might be a tad contentious—see the chapter by Michaud in this volume.

4. See *Green Lantern Corps*, vol. 2, #18 (January 2008; reprinted in *Green Lantern: The Sinestro Corps War Vol. 2*), for Sodam Yat's upbringing, and *Green Lantern Corps*, vol. 2, #35–36 (June–July 2009; reprinted in *Green Lantern Corps: Emerald Eclipse*, 2009) for his return to Daxam, insisting that he hasn't come to help Daxam because it's his home planet, but because Green Lanterns are supposed to help everyone—thus showing the work of his ideals over his upbringing.

5. Epictetus, "The Enchiridion," translated by Elizabeth Carter, available at *The Internet Classics Archive*, http://classics.mit.edu/Epictetus/epicench.html, 1.

6. Ibid., 3.

7. *Green Lantern*, vol. 3, #54 (August 1994), reprinted in *Green Lantern: Emerald Twilight/New Dawn* (2003).

8. *Green Lantern Corps*, vol. 2, #27–28 (October–November 2008), reprinted in *Green Lantern Corps: Sins of the Star Sapphire* (2009).

9. *Green Lantern Corps*, vol. 2, #27.

10. *Green Lantern Corps*, vol. 2, #28.

11. Immanuel Kant, *Groundwork of the Metaphysics of Morals*, trans. Mary Gregor (New York: Cambridge University Press, 1785/1998), 432–440. (All citations to Kant's work use the standard Academy pagination from his collected works, which appears in any reputable edition.)

12. Ibid., 440–444.

13. *Green Lantern*, vol. 4, #25 (January 2008). See also Hal's admission to the Guardians that his love for Carol Ferris interferes with his performance as a Green Lantern before his year's exile in space (*Green Lantern*, vol. 2, #149, February 1982), and his later defense of his attachments as being part of what makes him human (*Green Lantern*, vol. 2, #172, January 1984).

14. *Green Lantern Corps*, vol. 1, #218 (November 1987). See the chapters by Finkelman and Jaissle in this volume for group or communal ideas of mind, and the chapter by White titled "Crying for Justice" for Kilowog's desire for justice.

15. *Green Lantern Corps*, vol. 1, #219 (December 1987).

16. *Green Lantern Corps*, vol. 2, #19 (February 2008), reprinted in *Green Lantern: The Sinestro Corps War Volume 2*.

17. *Green Lantern Corps Quarterly* #4 (Spring 1993).

18. Ibid.

19. *Green Lantern Corps*, vol. 2, #32 (March 2009), reprinted in *Green Lantern Corps: Sins of the Star Sapphire*.

20. Sarah Hoagland, *Lesbian Ethics: Toward New Value* (Palo Alto, California: Institute of Lesbian Studies, 1988), 144. See also Jessica Benjamin, *Bonds of Love: Psychoanalysis, Feminism, and the Problem of Domination* (New York: Pantheon Books, 1988), 197.

21. *Green Lantern Corps*, vol. 2, #29 (December 2008), reprinted in *Green Lantern Corps: Sins of the Star Sapphire*.

22. See Jennifer Nedelsky, "Reconceiving Autonomy: Sources, Thoughts and Possibilities," *Yale Journal of Law and Feminism* 1 (1989): 7–36, and Catriona Mackenzie

and Natalie Stoljar, eds., *Relational Autonomy: Feminist Perspectives on Autonomy, Agency, and the Social Self* (Oxford, UK: Oxford University Press, 2000).

23. This work has been particularly influential in the field of biomedical ethics, where patients' decision-making has a lot to do with the context of their families and larger community.

24. For a discussion of autonomy competency, see Marilyn Friedman, *Autonomy, Gender, Politics* (New York: Oxford University Press, 2003), 13.

25. *Green Lantern: Sinestro Corps Special* (August 2007), reprinted in *Green Lantern: The Sinestro Corps War Volume 1* (2008).

26. *Green Lantern*, vol. 4, #24 (December 2007), reprinted in *Green Lantern: The Sinestro Corps War Volume 2*.

27. *Green Lantern Corps*, vol. 2, #36 (July 2009), reprinted in *Green Lantern Corps: Emerald Eclipse*; Natu's parentage is revealed on the last page of the previous issue. It doesn't help that Sinestro taunts her, asking "Just how far do you think the kimar falls from the tree, hmm?" or that the mark he left on her allows him to always know where she is (she tries to remove it in *Green Lantern Corps*, vol. 2, #38, September 2009, also reprinted in *Green Lantern Corps: Emerald Eclipse*).

28. Anne Donchin, "Autonomy and Interdependence," in Mackenzie and Stoljar, *Relational Autonomy*, 246.

29. Furthermore, they will likely face them together, as they are a couple (as of this writing), which means they will have even more of an opportunity to learn about their relational autonomy.

30. *Green Lantern*, vol. 4, #25.

PART FOUR

WITH THIS RING, I DO SWEAR: POWER, DUTY, AND LAW

THE OATHS OF SORANIK NATU: CAN A DOCTOR BE A GREEN LANTERN?

Ruth Tallman and Jason Southworth

One of the most interesting new members of the Green Lantern Corps is Soranik Natu of Korugar, added since writers Geoff Johns and Dave Gibbons revitalized the franchise. Before being tapped by a power ring to be the next Green Lantern for Space Sector 1417, Natu was a brilliant surgeon.[1] It makes sense that future members of the Corps excel in their chosen professions, as courage and steadfastness in the face of difficulty would serve one well in almost any career. Once becoming Lanterns, however, these individuals must put their careers on the back burner, because their duties as Lanterns trump any responsibility they feel to their professions.

This isn't a big deal for an artist, an architect, a test pilot, or a bar owner. In the worst-case scenario, it takes a little longer for a plane to make it to production, or someone else has to serve the drinks. What makes Natu so interesting is that, like doctors on Earth, she took professional vows when she swore the Hippocratic Oath (or its Korugarian equivalent), and sometimes those vows may conflict with being a Lantern. In this chapter, we will examine the struggles Natu faces and consider whether it is possible to be both a good doctor and a good Green Lantern.

First, Do No Harm

What does it mean to be a good doctor? In the fifth century BCE, Hippocrates (circa 460–377), tried to answer this question by establishing standards within the medical profession: founding a medical school and drafting the first code of professional ethics—the Hippocratic Oath.[2] The oath is amusingly archaic by today's standards; for example, it prohibits doctors from performing surgery (back then, with no way to fight infection, opening up a body was as good as signing a death warrant). Most importantly for our purposes, the oath establishes physicians firmly as healers. When Hippocrates was writing, it was not uncommon to seek suicide at the end of one's life. There were few options by way of cures or pain relief, and Stoic writers such as Epictetus (55–135 CE) counseled the permissibility of taking control of one's own death, writing that one should not be a slave to "the poor body."[3] In a society that viewed suicide as acceptable, many who called themselves doctors saw nothing objectionable about selling lethal drugs to those who sought them. Hippocrates' oath firmly asserted his belief that doctors should not be in the business of aiding death, but only of striving to stave it off: "I will never administer poison to anyone—even when asked to do so."

Today, few physicians recite Hippocrates' original oath; most if not all medical schools use some modernized version. Physicians disagree about how much Hippocrates' original conception of the medical profession should be maintained, especially around the issue of taking life. There is debate regarding the appropriateness of physician involvement in the suicide or voluntary euthanasia of their patients. Some, agreeing with Hippocrates, hold that physicians must restrict their efforts to prolonging life, never to shortening it. Others argue that a physician, as a professional in the art of medicine as well as a patient advocate, is best suited to assist a patient who seeks only to end her pain.

Regardless of one's view regarding physician-assisted suicide or euthanasia, there is little doubt that the modern understanding of a doctor's role includes a duty to heal, not harm, and to not make a patient's medical situation worse. As a doctor, the duty is to treat those who need emergency care, regardless of who they are. This means that physicians might be called upon to treat their enemies or those who have threatened the lives of others. Once that person becomes a patient needing care instead of one who is a threat, a doctor is to do what she can to heal. These are standard rules accepted by physicians, yet clearly, as will be shown in more detail below, they will often result in a conflict for a physician who is also a Green Lantern, who would be disobeying orders and compromising the mission by pausing in the middle of battle to treat fallen enemies.

Welcome to Oa, Poozers

In brightest day, in blackest night, No evil shall escape
 my sight
Let those who worship evil's might,
Beware my power . . . Green Lantern's light!

This is the traditional oath sworn by members of the Green Lantern Corps. As with doctors and the Hippocratic Oath, not every Lantern takes this exact oath. In fact, it has become common for Lanterns to write their own oaths. Arisia Rrab of sector 2815 has been known to use both the standard oath and the following:

> From lantern comes the gift we give
> To shed light's grace on all that live![4]

Tomar-Re of sector 2813 never uses the standard oath, instead choosing to swear:

> And I shall shed my light over dark evil,
> For the dark things cannot stand the light,
> The light of the Green Lantern.[5]

These oaths don't really say anything about the duties of a member of the Green Lantern Corps. Instead, the oaths are understood as affirmations of one's commitment to the Corps. They are pledges to follow the code of conduct for Lanterns set forth by the Guardians in the Book of Oa (in which there are, as of this writing, twenty laws).[6]

The most important duty for a member of Green Lantern Corps is to follow the orders of one's superiors. This stems from the fact that the Corps is an intergalactic military/police organization, and as such has a highly regimented hierarchical structure. Ordinary rank-and-file Lanterns are at the bottom and the Guardians are at the top, with various positions filling in the chain of command in between: Senior Officer Salaak is the highest-ranking Lantern, followed by Kyle Rayner and Guy Gardner, members of the Honor Guard, with the Alpha Lanterns serving as internal affairs officers. Orders from the Guardians must be followed without question, and the penalty for disobeying a direct order can be expulsion from the Corps (Law 2). The standard is slightly less strict for orders that come from fellow Lanterns of higher rank, with the penalty for disobeying varying from probation to extra duties to exile from Oa. Lanterns of an equal position in the hierarchy must respect and cooperate with one another (Law 7).

Lanterns assigned to a space sector must follow strict regulations, as must all other Lanterns visiting those sectors. Foremost among Lanterns' responsibilities in their space sectors is to protect the life and liberty of those living there (Law 1). Indeed, Lanterns are prohibited from taking actions against anyone until they have been shown to be a threat to life and liberty (Law 5). This does not mean that a Lantern must help, or is even allowed to help, those they see suffering. Local customs and political systems must be respected, and all local laws must be obeyed (Laws 3 and 4). This means that loss of life and liberty due to institutional factors (such as slavery, segregation, and the death penalty) must be allowed unless an order from the Guardians calls for intervention. Lanterns must also give priority to the greatest danger in the sector, and this means knowingly leaving people in dangerous situations that may result in injury or death (Law 9). Additionally, lethal force is sanctioned against members of the Sinestro Corps and other enemies of the Green Lantern Corps (Laws 11 and 12), although it must be the option of last resort (Law 8). At these times, a concern for life and liberty takes a back seat as well.

What Should We Do When Our Oaths Conflict?

On the face of it, the Hippocratic Oath and the Green Lanterns' vows look incompatible. Doctors, swearing the Hippocratic Oath, must heal those before them and refrain from harming others. Lanterns must follow the instructions of their superiors, even when that means abandoning those in need, causing bodily harm, or killing. So how can Soranik Natu be both a Lantern and a doctor? What should she do when her duties conflict?

We might reject the idea that oaths have morally binding force. On that view, vows simply serve as useful rules of thumb that govern behavior, but we would not hesitate to break a vow in the name of a greater good. Wonder Woman demonstrated this type of thinking when she broke her personal ban on killing to take down Maxwell Lord when he had control of Superman's mind.[7] She believed his death would save lives, and she was not about to let a vow stand in the way of doing what needed to be done.

Other people feel that oaths are important, but that when oaths conflict, one oath is naturally more important and therefore has to trump the other. The Guardians, and many of the Green Lanterns, seem to think that the Lantern oath is the most important vow they can take, and thus any other commitments will be secondary. Isamot Kol of sector 2682 exhibited this attitude. In order to follow the direct orders of his Corps superior, Isamot Kol broke his vow to Qalyra, the woman with whom he had committed to starting a family. Not only was this the violation of a personal commitment, but Kol also seemed to understand it as a betrayal of his race (choosing a Corps made up of foreigners over the propagation of his own species), a sacrifice that caused him considerable pain, yet one he still felt he must make.[8]

Many physicians, on the other hand, see their Hippocratic vows to heal those before them and refrain from harming others as superseding all other vows. Natu's colleagues at the hospital in Korugar are outraged that she would even think of splitting her commitments between the Corps and her patients. Another superhero physician, Dr. Mid-Nite (Pieter Cross) of the Justice Society of America, refuses to join his teammates in battle when he has patients to attend to. Although he is committed to his team, Dr. Mid-Nite sees his duty to his patients as his primary duty. When a choice must be made he consistently upholds his Hippocratic Oath at the expense of his "super" commitments. For example, in *JSA* #21–22 (2001), Dr. Mid-Nite stays behind while the rest of the team travels to Thanagar to rescue Hawkgirl, because he is caring for Lyta Hall, the wife of Dr. Fate (not a medical doctor!).

Rather than saying that one particular oath always trumps the other in cases of conflict, some people believe that the context of the situation will determine which oath must be upheld. We saw this often when Robin (Dick Grayson) was both Batman's sidekick and the leader of the Teen Titans. Sometimes Dick allowed his commitment to the Titans to trump his commitment to Batman, such as when Starfire needed assistance with a crisis on her home world of Tamaran.[9] At other times, however, Dick temporarily abandoned the Titans in order to follow Bruce, flying halfway around the globe after Ra's al Ghul, for example.[10]

The Dark Side of Green: Natu's Story

From her very first panel, Soranik Natu's story has been about the conflicting duties of a doctor and a Lantern. When her power ring found her, she was in the middle of brain surgery that was not going well; in all likelihood, the patient was going to die. Natu accepted the ring in a desperate attempt to save a patient's life. Once the patient was saved, she felt a strong compulsion to reject the ring, but she allowed it to bring her to Oa to be trained as a Green Lantern. Still feeling conflicted, Natu quit the Corps before the induction ceremony, but kept the power ring to use as her transportation home. On the way, Natu encountered danger that required her to combine the ring's power with her own cunning to cleverly save her own life. She swallowed the ring and commanded it to reduce her bodily functions to the absolute minimum needed to sustain life, thus making it appear that she was already dead. Despite the ingenuity of this plan, Natu required the help of others, as she could not command the ring in her state of hibernation. By the time Guy Gardner and Kyle Rayner managed to find and revive her, the raging emotions that had caused her to flee Oa had subsided, and the two Lanterns (with their patented good-Lantern-bad-Lantern shtick) convinced her to return with them and remain a Lantern.[11]

But Natu's unease with being a Lantern does not end there. She never stops identifying herself as a doctor, and often seems torn, unsure whether her primary duty is to the Corps or to her profession. Rather than remain on Oa, as the Corps prefers, she chooses to spend the time she is not on assignment back on Korugar, using her newfound powers to heal. When she is chased out of the hospital by her fellow doctors, who are angry that she is using her powers to perform medical feats that they could never manage, she continues to heal the sick in the streets. The Lanterns pressure her to focus on her service to the Corps, and her fellow physicians think she should give up the ring and be a full-time healer. Despite the pressure from both sides, Natu insists on retaining her dual roles.

Natu's attempt to balance her two roles, though well-intended, often proves detrimental to one or the other of the causes to which she is committed. As a Lantern, her role is to keep the peace in her sector. Her decision to perform surgeries illegally in the streets of Korugar violated her Lantern's oath, which demands that she adhere to local laws. Indeed, her actions prompted a violent street fight as Korugarian officials attacked her makeshift facility in an anti-Lantern rage.[12] Natu ended up being rescued by an angry Kilowog (not a pleasant sight), with the battle resulting in physical harm to the very people she was trying to heal.[13] Natu's commitment to healing resulted in her failure to promote peace in her sector; her role as a Lantern brought violence to Korugar. By trying to fill the roles of doctor and Green Lantern, she had failed at both.

Is Half a Lantern Better than No Lantern at All?

Unlike Wonder Woman, Natu thinks it's important to try to uphold both her vows at all times; otherwise, she would not exhibit such distress when her oaths conflict. She does not always give priority to her Lantern duties, as Isamot Kol does, nor to her Hippocratic vows, like Dr. Mid-Nite. Neither does she think, like Dick Grayson, that the vow that binds her in any given situation is context-dependent. Rather than reflect on the conflict, Natu seems to act in the moment and regret her action later. Sometimes she is loyal to her physician's oath, and at other times she is true to her power ring. No matter what, she ends up feeling that she has done something wrong. Natu thinks both vows are absolute, and thus she thinks she does something morally wrong each time her actions violate a commitment.

Philosophers describe such a situation as an "irresolvable dilemma," which Rosalind Hursthouse defines as a situation in which a person must act, yet no act open to her is a good one.[14] Hursthouse distinguishes between two ways in which a person might come to be in such a situation. In one case, it is the person's own previous poor decision-making that led to the current dilemma. Hursthouse offers an example of a man who has convinced two women, A and B, to go to bed with him by promising marriage; now both women are pregnant and he cannot keep his promise to both. The man has three options: marry woman A, marry woman B, or marry neither. While there might be good reasons to choose any of these options, Hursthouse holds that even if there is one clearly best option (suppose woman B has a new lover waiting with open arms to marry her and adopt the child), the man does not have any *good* options. The best he can do is choose the least bad option, because no matter what he does, he will be breaking a promise.[15]

Of course, the twice-betrothed man's dilemma stems from his past immoral behavior, and therefore to some extent it is his fault that he is in his present irresolvable dilemma. Hursthouse contrasts this situation with one in which a person finds himself in a dilemma through no fault of his own. To illustrate this type of situation, Hursthouse gives an example from another philosopher, Bernard Williams (1929–2003).[16] One day while vacationing in an unnamed country, a man named Jim stumbles upon a militia preparing to execute twenty people. The militia, excited by Jim's presence, give him a choice: if Jim is willing to take a gun and kill one of the twenty himself, they will let the others go free. Jim stumbled into this situation blamelessly, but either way he leaves with blood on his hands—either direct responsibility for the death of one person or indirect responsibility (through his inaction) for the death of twenty. Both Jim and the double-betrothed man are in irresolvable dilemmas, but Hursthouse describes Jim's case as a tragic dilemma, which is one in which an otherwise good life will be irretrievably marred no matter what action is chosen. If Jim is a good man, as we are told he is, no matter what he does, bearing the responsibility for the death of one or twenty will leave a permanent gash in his life. In the case of a good person, this is a tragedy.

Out of these two examples, Natu more closely resembles the double-betrothed man than she does Jim. Although she does not seem to have acted with bad intent, Natu realized that swearing the Green Lantern oath meant compromising her ability to uphold the Hippocratic Oath just as the double-betrothed man knew as he promised marriage to the two women that he could not follow through on both promises. We might be able to excuse Natu's initial acceptance of the ring. In the flurry of the moment she didn't have time to carefully consider the consequences of accepting, plus she might have been unaware of exactly what being a Green Lantern entailed. When she returned to Oa after her initial decision to quit the Corps, however, such excuses were no longer available to her. She knew what she was getting into, and still she returned. Thus, when she now finds herself in a situation where she cannot act without betraying one of her vows, Natu is in an irresolvable, but not a tragic, dilemma. (It's not tragic because she brought it on herself.)

Natu believes adherence to her vows to be ultimate goods, or goods that are of utmost and primary importance. As both goods are primary for her, there is no way to choose between them. She sees herself as acting immorally anytime she fails to conform to the standards of either of her roles. In fact, this conflict is built into the two jobs, and Natu will continue to experience this conflict and guilt as long as she remains both a Lantern and a doctor. With the recent amendment to the Book of Oa lifting the ban on lethal force, Natu is headed straight for a huge personal crisis. What will she do when a Lantern superior orders her to kill? A conflicted soldier is not an effective soldier, and an ineffective soldier is dangerous to herself and her comrades. In her current situation, Natu does a disservice to her fellow Lanterns as well as to her patients—she gives neither group the full devotion they deserve.

The only way for Natu to resolve this conflict would be to surrender one of her roles. The power ring will always find a person with the ability to overcome great fear. Her resignation would not result in a gap in the Corps. However, if she stops being a physician, there will be a great loss because she is "the best doctor in her sector, possibly in the whole galaxy."[17] If she gives up the medical profession in order to serve the Corps, many whom she could have saved will die. Thus, to resolve the conflict, Natu should turn in her power ring and devote herself to fulfilling the commitments she made when she swore the Hippocratic Oath.

Not a Dream, Not an Imaginary Tale—But a Real-Life Problem

In this chapter, we have argued that given how Soranik Natu understands her duties as a doctor and as a member of the Green Lantern Corps, perhaps she should turn in her power ring. While this conclusion is interesting on its own, suggesting that Natu should be seen as a tragic character who may never find happiness as a member of the Corps, it also has direct parallels with people in the real world. For instance,

Natu is no different from many people who serve as medics in the military. Many of these men and women swear oaths as doctors and nurses, and all of them swear oaths to the armed forces. Just like in the DC Universe, most individuals will see their duties as either a doctor or as a member of the military as trumping all else. All of those individuals who see their duties to the military and as medical professionals as being of equal importance, however, are in Natu's Catch-22 situation—at times they will have to do wrong according to one set of commitments in order to do right by the other.

Leaving aside the specific duties discussed in this chapter, we all must be careful about putting ourselves in the same situation as Natu. Duties inherent to your job may conflict with those you have to your family. Commitments you made to your parents and siblings can conflict with promises you make to your spouse, and so on. For those who see duties in this way, the story of Soranik Natu should be a cautionary tale—think carefully before you commit, because your loyalties may be tested, power ring or no power ring.

NOTES

1. *Green Lantern Corps: Recharge* #5 (March 2006), reprinted in *Green Lantern Corps: Recharge* (2006).

2. See http://www.iep.utm.edu/hippocra/. Some modern scholars believe that Hippocrates himself did not write the oath, but that the document emerged from the school that bears his name.

3. Epictetus, *Discourses*, Book 1, Chapter 25, available at http://www.constitution.org/rom/epicdisc1.htm#1:25.

4. *Green Lantern*, vol. 2, #198 (March 1986).

5. *Green Lantern*, vol. 2, #38 (July 1965), reprinted in *Showcase Presents Green Lantern Volume Two* (2007).

6. The Book of Oa made its first appearance in *Green Lantern*, vol. 2, #188 (May 1985) with ten laws. During the Sinestro Corps War, the Guardians added ten new laws that were slowly revealed in the lead up to the Blackest Night (see *Green Lantern*, vol. 4, #23, November 2007, reprinted in *Green Lantern: The Sinestro Corps War, Volume 1*, 2008). In the name of convenience, all references to the laws of Oa come from the official DC wiki on the Book of Oa found at http://dc.wikia.com/wiki/Book_of_Oa.

7. *Wonder Woman*, vol. 2, #219 (July 2005).

8. *Green Lantern Corps*, vol. 2, #4–5 (2006–2007), reprinted in *Green Lantern Corps: To Be a Lantern* (2007).

9. *New Teen Titans*, vol. 1, #23–25 (September–November 1982).

10. *Batman* #232 (June 1971).

11. *Green Lantern Corps: Recharge*.

12. *Green Lantern Corps*, vol. 2, #10 (May 2007), reprinted in *Green Lantern Corps: The Dark Side of Green* (2007). The people of Korugar haven't had the best of luck with Green Lanterns—the renegade Lantern and current archvillain Sinestro is from Korugar (and is, in fact, Natu's father). When Sinestro was a Lantern he policed the planet in such a way that everyone lived in a constant state of fear of punishment. While the Guardians took away his ring once Hal Jordan informed them of how Sinestro kept the peace, the Korugarians still see the Corps as a symbol of fear and oppression.

13. Ibid.

14. Rosalind Hursthouse, *On Virtue Ethics* (Oxford, UK: Oxford University Press, 1999), 74.

15. Ibid., 46-47.

16. Ibid., 75; the example comes from J. J. C. Smart and Bernard Williams, *Utilitarianism: For and Against* (Cambridge, UK: Cambridge University Press, 1973).

17. *Green Lantern Corps*, vol. 2, #12 (July 2007), reprinted in *Green Lantern Corps: The Dark Side of Green*.

CRYING FOR JUSTICE: RETRIBUTIVISM FOR THOSE WHO WORSHIP EVIL'S MIGHT

Mark D. White

In the beginning of 2008's *Final Crisis* event, a group of supervillains led by the mysterious Libra killed J'onn J'onzz, the Martian Manhunter.[1] Endowed with Superman-level powers (and a gentle soul to boot), J'onn was beloved, admired, and respected by the entire superhero community, so his death hit them particularly hard. Among those affected the most were Green Lantern (Hal Jordan) and Green Arrow (Oliver Queen). Standing over J'onn's body, Hal says, "If the people responsible for J'onn lying here were standing outside the door . . . God help me . . . I'd incinerate them all without a moment's hesitation." Ollie replies, "No you wouldn't. That's why we are who we are and they're who they are."[2]

That's certainly the traditional picture of the superhero—fight the bad guys, catch the bad guys, and then hand the bad guys over to the proper authorities for trial, sentencing, and punishment. But the uncomfortable truth is that even in the DC Universe, with its technologically advanced prisons for metahuman villains, they always get out, return to a life of crime, and often kill innocent people (and, to an increasing extent in recent years, heroes).[3] Understandably, some heroes are getting tired of this—especially Green Lantern. In an effort to become more proactive in seeking out murderous villains and holding them accountable, Hal split from the Justice League of America in the *Justice League: Cry for Justice* miniseries (2009–2010), saying, "You want a league. I want justice."[4]

But is this justice, or merely vengeance? Might they be one and the same? As it happens, the Guardians of the Universe and the Green Lantern Corps have had some experience with these issues as well through the years, since they are no strangers to death at the hands of their enemies. In this chapter, we'll explore these questions by discussing the philosophy of punishment known as *retributivism* or *retributivist justice* and the relationship between retributivism and feelings of revenge or vengeance.

Cry for Definition!

Most generally, retributivism can be defined as the view that wrongdoers (and only wrongdoers—never the innocent) must be punished as a matter of justice, right, or desert.[5] Retributivism is usually contrasted with justifications of punishment such as *deterrence*, which holds that punishment is meant to reduce future crimes, or *rehabilitation*, which is focused more directly on helping criminals reform. These justifications are *consequentialist* in nature because their goal is the promotion of overall well-being or utility through preventing future crimes. Retributivism, by contrast, focuses on crimes that have already been committed, and it demands punishment to right those wrongs. In other words, consequentialist theories of punishment are forward-looking, while retributivism is backward-looking.

The collected members of the Green Lantern Corps discussed the philosophy of punishment during the trial and sentencing of their greatest foe, the Korugarian renegade Sinestro, in *Green Lantern Corps*, vol. 1, #222 (March 1988). After recounting all the deaths across the universe that Sinestro was responsible for—and concluding that his guilt was unquestionable—some of the Green Lanterns wanted to return him to his cell on the Guardians' home world of Oa. But Katma Tui (Sinestro's successor from Korugar) reminded them that the Guardians were never able to keep Sinestro prisoner for long. One Green Lantern argued from deterrence, saying that Sinestro should be killed because "society must protect itself," while Kilowog, whose entire race was wiped out by Sinestro, sought justice or retribution. In the end, the Corps voted to execute him, each member potentially making his, her, or its decision for a different reason, which shows that any punishment—even the death penalty—can be justified (and opposed) in many ways.[6]

It's easy to understand the deterrence rationale for punishment: crime is bad, less crime is better, and therefore anything that deters crime is good. But the reasoning behind retributivism is not as clear, and simply saying (as Kilowog did) that it serves justice doesn't help—it just shifts the question to "What is justice?" If retributivist punishment isn't meant to prevent future crimes, then what does it "do" instead, and what type of justice does it promote?

No Debt Shall Escape My Sight

While some retributivists believe that punishing the guilty is an intrinsic good (one that doesn't lead to some further good but is good in and of itself), most find a justification for punishment in a citizen's obligation to the state and his or her fellow citizens. For instance, according to the concept of "unfair advantage," people who break the law are free-riding on the people who don't. A thief can steal someone else's property with reasonable confidence that it won't be stolen back, because the law prohibits theft and most people obey the law. Likewise, a murderer can kill somebody while enjoying the protection of the law regarding his own life.

In essence, the criminal takes advantage of everybody else's compliance with the law in order to break it himself, and thereby incurs a debt to society that is repaid by punishing him. One of the classic retributivists, G. W. F. Hegel (1770–1831), wrote that to punish a criminal "is to annul the crime, which otherwise would have been held valid, and to restore the right."[7] This explanation of retributivist justice can be traced back to the biblical *lex talionis*, or "an eye for an eye," which not only invokes the idea of repaying debt, but also emphasizes the element of fairness and equality—key elements of justice—in the penalty. As another early retributivist, Immanuel Kant (1724–1804), wrote, "What kind and what amount of punishment is it that public justice makes its principle and measure? None other than the principle of equality. . . . Accordingly, whatever undeserved evil you inflict upon another within the people, that you inflict upon yourself."[8]

The "debt theory" of retributivism seems very intuitive— the Latin meaning of "retribution" is "to pay back," after all—and as such, it appears quite often in Green Lantern stories. When Sinestro once again faces execution following the Sinestro Corps War, Hal tells the Blue Lanterns who want to prevent his death that "Sinestro's going to pay for his crimes—with his life."[9] And when Fatality seeks out a wheel-chair-bound John Stewart to avenge his destruction of her home world, Xanshi, and her entire race, she invokes both his debt and the *lex talionis*: "I am fulfilling my blood oath. This pathetic cripple owes a debt. What do you say on this world, 'an eye for an eye'? You have four billion eyes to account for, Stewart!"[10]

But the debt theory doesn't work as well when you get away from major crimes like murder and theft. For instance, does the woman who runs a red light in the middle of the night, with no cars in sight, "take advantage" of anybody? What about the gambler who places an illegal bet on a football game? True, most people obey laws such as these, but it's hard to see how they are losing anything from a few people breaking them. Most people would still say that such lawbreakers should be punished, though there is no apparent debt to be "settled." Clearly, the debt theory doesn't seem to work with all crimes. So is there a better, more general justification for retributivism?

It's Not about Me—It's about You

Like consequentialist theories of punishment, the debt theory is goal-oriented (or *teleological*) in that it aims toward a resolution or "annulment" of the crime, rebalancing the scales of obligation between citizens. But another understanding of retributivism is more focused on the treatment of the criminal himself, and does not rely on any particular goal of punishment or the nature of the crime. Rather, it is based on the importance of treating criminals, however guilty they may be, always as human beings. For this theory we return to one of the key retributivist philosophers, Immanuel Kant.

Kant's retributivism is consistent with his broader ethical and political philosophy, which is based on the inherent dignity and value of every person. This dignity is an immeasurable and incomparable value that every rational being possesses, and respect for it places limits on what you can do to a person and for what reason. As Kant wrote in one of the versions of his famous *categorical imperative*, you should always "act in such a way that you treat humanity, whether in your own person or in the person of another, always at the same time as an end and never simply as a means."[11] For instance, if Hal lied to Carol Ferris in order to go out with his fellow pilot "Cowgirl," he would be using Carol's trust in him simply as a means to further his own ends, without treating her as an end in herself, as a person with dignity. If that weren't bad enough, he would also be using his own good name, which inspires Carol's trust, as a means to that end. Deceit is one of the most obvious ways one can fail to respect a person's dignity, and Kant is well known for opposing it (often to extremes).[12]

According to Kant's political philosophy, the state must also treat persons as ends and not merely as means—and this includes convicted criminals. He tells us that punishment

> can never be inflicted merely as means to promote some other good for the criminal himself or for civil society. It must always be inflicted upon him only *because he has committed a crime*. For a human being can never be treated merely as a means to the purposes of another.[13]

Note that Kant reasserts the prohibition against using persons merely as means at the end of this passage. A person must be punished only because he has done something to deserve it, not to promote some other end for society, no matter how admirable that end may be (such as deterring future crime). According to this view, if Sinestro were to be punished, it should be because he committed heinous crimes, not because it will make the universe a safer place to live—a desirable outcome, of course, but one that cannot justify the punishment itself while still treating Sinestro as a person with dignity.

Kant was not focused just on restricting punishment to the guilty, however. He also argued that criminals *must* be punished, out of respect for the criminals themselves. To respect a person's dignity is to treat him as responsible for his actions, including crimes with consequences involving punishment.

Perhaps Hegel made this point the best, writing that punishment is the criminal's "implicit will, an embodiment of his freedom, his right," as the predictable outcome of a voluntary action.[14] But as Kant wrote,

> No one suffers punishment because he has willed *it* but because he has willed a *punishable action*; for it is no punishment if what is done to someone is what he wills, and it is impossible to *will* to be punished.[15]

Likewise, contemporary philosopher Herbert Morris defends the idea that by voluntarily breaking a law, the criminal "has chosen to be punished," but prefers the language that the criminal "has brought the punishment upon himself" through his actions.[16] Hal says as much while discussing Sinestro's recent impending execution with Carol when he claims that Sinestro "dug his own grave a long time ago." And when he leaves Carol to visit Sinestro in his cell on Oa, he tells the villain, "You did this to yourself," to which Sinestro replies, "Yes. I did."[17]

Concern for justice in punishment explains the shock that Lanterns Guy Gardner and Kyle Rayner feel when they discover that the Alpha Lanterns (presumably internal affairs officers for the Corps) are summarily executing prisoners who escaped from their cells on Oa during the buildup to the Blackest Night. One Alpha Lantern explains that the new law allowing lethal force permits such executions, but Kyle responds that "the Corps has never sanctioned anything like this before," implying that the prisoners couldn't have known they would pay so high a price for escaping. As Kyle explains to one of the escaped prisoners who thanks him, "This isn't about saving your worthless lives—it's about preserving an ideal, damn it!"[18] One imagines that Kyle's concerns run deeper than due process, but due process does ensure that criminals receive the punishment they deserve as a matter of right—not as a matter of ad hoc punitive whim.

Wait—Maybe It's about the Rest of Us!

Other retributivists focus attention on victims and the community at large—not to consider their future well-being as deterrence theorists would, but rather to emphasize their need to express their condemnation and rage at the criminal for what he's done. The most famous exponent of this view, philosopher Joel Feinberg (1926–2004), wrote of the "expressive function of punishment" used to convey "attitudes of resentment and indignation, and judgments of disapproval and reprobation."[19] Feinberg used the expressive function to distinguish between punishments and mere "penalties," such as fines for parking violations that do not invoke the kind of societal outrage that crimes like murder do.

Feinberg draws our attention to the cathartic needs of the community. We see this kind of need on Sinestro's home world of Korugar after his recent execution was delayed. The citizens of Korugar City made their desires clear to Soranik Natu, the planet's current Green Lantern (and, unbeknownst to her at the time, Sinestro's daughter). The crowd chanted, "We've been cheated of Korugar's redemption!" and a woman shouted to Natu, "Sinestro's death was going to be a new dawn for Korugar, a chance to wipe away the sins of the past!"[20] Natu tries to calm them down, but her fellow Lantern Iolande explains the crowd's feelings to her: "I think the only way your planet will ever move forward is to have that bloodlust satiated. . . . Only Sinestro's death will free them."[21] Here, the concern of the Korugarians is less to express their outrage to Sinestro himself and more to show their neighboring planets—and themselves—that not all Korugarians are evil, that they don't identify with Sinestro, and that they can turn a new page in their history.[22]

Although the expressive theory of retributivist punishment pays attention to the often-neglected victims of crime, including those directly harmed and also the larger community, it violates the Kantian ideal of punishing the criminal for the sake of the criminal. Also, because of its emphasis on the emotions of victims and the community, the expressive theory naturally leads us to ask how these natural feelings of vengeance, anger, and hatred are related to retributivist punishment, in terms not only of society but also the individual.

All Together Now: "Justice!"

The distinction between vengeance and justice is a major theme in the *Justice League: Cry for Justice* miniseries, in which every participating hero says, at least once, "I want justice" for the death of a friend or a loved one. But is it truly justice they're after, or merely vengeance?

Contemporary philosophers Jeffrie Murphy and Jules Coleman describe "revenge or vindictiveness" as *personal* responses to perceived wrongs to oneself and motivated by a concern with one's own self-regard or self-respect," often pursued outside of the law, while retribution "grows out of respect for the law (not simply oneself)" and the belief that people who break laws should be punished within the law.[23] In one of their early team-ups, Green Lantern puts it well when he stops Green Arrow from killing a man who hit Black Canary with her own motorcycle and left her for dead: "You're neither judge . . . nor jury!"[24] But Hal seems to have changed his tune by the time he quits the Justice League, in frustration over the death of his friends, to lead a group of heroes in hunting down villains proactively.

Understood in this light, the heroes in *Cry for Justice* seem to want personal vengeance for their losses rather than impersonal justice, especially considering the extraordinary lengths they go to—including torture—to get it.[25] Things start to turn around midway through the series, when Starman stops Congo Bill from killing a couple of two-bit villains, saying "Vengeance isn't justice, Bill. Blood isn't justice!"[26] Later, after Animal Man accuses Bill of wanting to kill Prometheus (the villain behind the deaths of all the heroes' loved ones), Bill explains, "No, I've had a change of heart in that regard. When I say I want justice—I mean I want him *brought* to justice."[27] In the end, Prometheus rips an arm off Red Arrow (Roy Harper, Green Arrow's ward and original sidekick) and causes the destruction of Green Arrow's beloved Star City, during which Roy's daughter Lian is killed. Prometheus then forces the heroes who had captured him to set him free. Ollie then hunts him down and puts an arrow through his head, saying the single word "justice"—but it is clearly vengeance on which he acted.[28]

The issue of justice and vengeance also arose when Laira, a longtime Green Lantern and a fierce warrior, killed Amon Sur, a member of the Sinestro Corps (and the son of Hal Jordan's predecessor, Abin Sur). Sur had just slaughtered the family of Ke'haan, Laira's former partner and close friend (who had very recently been killed himself, during the Sinestro Corps War). Sur surrendered, but Laira cited the law allowing lethal force against Sinestro Corps members and executed him anyway, later screaming, "It was justice!"[29] At her trial on Oa for murder, Laira defended her actions, citing Sur's heinous murders and the fact that his ring was still a deadly weapon. But Boodikka, an Alpha Lantern, told her, "You lashed out with the anger that lurks in your heart," and a Guardian said, "You have misinterpreted the laws of Oa," implying that she acted outside the law.[30] Both of these accusations, of course, are indicative of vengeance, not justice—to which, incidentally, Boodikka tells Laira that she is "rededicated" since becoming an Alpha Lantern.[31]

Who Should Cry for Justice?

So while Hal told the Justice League, "I want justice," what he really wanted was vengeance—and he certainly wasn't alone in this, as we saw. But we must be careful not to lose sight of the justice inherent in retributivist punishment.[32] While pursuing personal vendettas based on revenge is not serving justice, exacting punishment on deserving wrongdoers is. Justice comes in many varieties—such as corrective justice, which deals with righting private harms, and distributive justice, which deals with the allocation of economic benefits and costs—but what they all have in common is a concern with fairness, equality, and desert. People should be treated as equals unless there is a morally relevant reason not to, and even then they should be treated the same as other people such a reason applies to. For instance, a murderer should not be treated like an innocent person—that would not be fair to either—but he should be treated the same as other murderers in similar circumstances, and only according to his desert. If a person feels that, in general, murderers deserve to die for their crimes, then that punishment constitutes justice in his or her eyes. But ultimately, the decision to punish wrongdoers should be left to representatives of the state, who are ideally more impartial with respect to the crimes at hand and therefore better suited to serve justice rather than vengeance.[33]

So let Hal and the rest of the heroes cry for justice if they want, as long as they remember what that really means, and who is ultimately responsible for it.

NOTES

1. *Final Crisis* #1 (July 2008).

2. *Final Crisis: Requiem* (September 2008). (Remember Ollie's words for later . . .)

3. Just to cite two recent and particularly brutal examples, the Rogues beat Bart Allen (the Flash at the time) to death in *Flash: The Fastest Man Alive* #13 (August 2007), and Deathstroke's new band of villains slaughtered Ryan Choi (Ray Palmer's successor as the Atom) in *Titans: Villains for Hire Special* (July 2010).

4. *Justice League: Cry for Justice* #1 (September 2009).

5. To be more precise, negative retributivists hold only that the innocent must never be punished, while positive retributivists add that the guilty must be punished. In this chapter, I'm discussing retributivism in its positive version, since this is the stricter (and more controversial) version.

6. For instance, the Green Lantern Skirl argued against killing Sinestro out of respect for life and the "larger plan" that created him. (Hal Jordan, too, was uncomfortable with putting Sinestro to death, but his concerns were unclear.)

7. G. W. F. Hegel, *The Philosophy of Right*, trans. T. M. Knox (Oxford, UK: Oxford University Press, 1821/1952), 69.

8. Immanuel Kant, *The Metaphysics of Morals*, translated by Mary Gregor (Cambridge, UK: Cambridge University Press, 1797/1996), 332. (All citations to Kant's work use the standard Academy pagination from his collected works, which appears in any reputable edition.)

9. *Green Lantern*, vol. 4, #37 (February 2009), reprinted in *Green Lantern: Rage of the Red Lanterns* (2009).

10. *Green Lantern*, vol. 3, #132 (January 2001), reprinted in *Green Lantern: New Journey, Old Path* (2001). The destruction of Xanshi happened in 1988's *Cosmic Odyssey* mini-series, and still haunts John to this day, as shown during the Blackest Night in *Green Lantern*, vol. 4, #49 (February 2010), reprinted in *Blackest Night: Green Lantern* (2010). However, John is no fan of the *lex talionis*: "Eye for eye, tooth for tooth. What does it get you? Bloody eyeball, broken tooth" (*Green Lantern*, vol. 3, #16, September 1991).

11. Immanuel Kant, *Grounding for the Metaphysics of Morals*, trans. J. W. Ellington (Indianapolis: Hackett Publishing Co., Inc., 1785/1993), 429.

12. For instance, see his very controversial 1799 essay, "On a Supposed Right to Lie because of Philanthropic Concerns," included in the edition of the *Grounding* cited above, in which he argues that you should not lie to a murderer who comes to your house to kill your friend who is hiding there.

13. Kant, *Metaphysics of Morals*, 331.

14. Hegel, *Philosophy of Right*, 70.

15. Kant, *Metaphysics of Morals*, 335.

16. Herbert Morris, "Persons and Punishment," reprinted in *On Guilt and Innocence* (Berkeley: University of California Press, 1976), 31–58, at 36.

17. *Final Crisis: Rage of the Red Lanterns* (December 2008), reprinted in *Green Lantern: Rage of the Red Lanterns*. This exchange has another layer, since Sinestro credits himself with forcing the Guardians to write a new law into the Book of Oa allowing lethal force to be used against Sinestro Corps members (and later, all enemies of the Corps), a law that is used to justify his execution.

18. *Green Lantern Corps*, vol. 2, #38 (September 2009), reprinted in *Green Lantern Corps: Emerald Eclipse* (2009).

19. Joel Feinberg, "The Expressive Function of Punishment," reprinted in *Doing and Deserving* (Princeton, NJ: Princeton University Press, 1970), 95–118, at 98.

20. *Green Lantern Corps*, vol. 2, #35 (June 2009), reprinted in *Green Lantern Corps: Emerald Eclipse*.

21. Ibid. In the same issue, Iolande also makes clear that one of the feelings that the Korugarian people need to express deals with the debt that must be paid: "They want Sinestro to pay—they need Sinestro to pay for his sins and theirs."

22. The case of Korugar also brings to mind the concept of *restorative justice*, which is focused more on the needs of victims and the community at large, and less on punishment as an end in itself.

23. Jeffrie G. Murphy and Jules L. Coleman, *Philosophy of Law: An Introduction to Jurisprudence*, rev. ed. (Boulder, CO: Westview Press, 1990), 120–121.

24. *Green Lantern*, vol. 2, #79 (September 1970), reprinted in *Green Lantern/Green Arrow Volume One* (2004).

25. See *Justice League: Cry for Justice* #3 and 4 (November and December 2009) for some very insightful debates between Green Lantern, Green Arrow, and the Atom regarding torture. (See also the chapter by Novy in this volume for Kyle Rayner's experiences with torture.)

26. *Justice League: Cry for Justice* #4 (December 2009).

27. *Justice League: Cry for Justice* #5 (January 2010), emphasis mine.

28. *Justice League: Cry for Justice* #7 (April 2010). (Compare this to his words to Hal over J'onn J'onzz's body, quoted at the beginning of this chapter.)

29. *Green Lantern*, vol. 4, #26 and 27 (February and March 2008), reprinted in *Green Lantern: Rage of the Red Lanterns*.

30. *Green Lantern*, vol. 4, #28 (April 2008), reprinted in *Green Lantern: Rage of the Red Lanterns*.

31. Ibid. In fact, in *Green Lantern*, vol. 4, #27, we see the Alpha Lanterns chosen with the words, "You have the ability to enforce justice." Furthermore, the "cosmic surgery" necessary to become an Alpha Lantern involves replacing the candidate's heart with a power battery, which represents the Guardians' wish to remove all emotion from the execution of justice.

32. And he seems to have forgotten telling Sinestro, who claimed to want justice, "Justice? You wanted vengeance. . . . I don't believe in vengeance" (*Green Lantern: Rebirth* #5, April 2005, reprinted in *Green Lantern: Rebirth*, 2005).

33. Hal Jordan did, of course, spend time as the host of the Spectre, God's spirit of vengeance, before his rebirth as Green Lantern. How does the Spectre's vengeance, which seemed horribly bloodthirsty at times, compare to justice? If God is impartial in His judgment, as we would like to imagine, they are one and the same, especially if God's law is considered to stand above man's law—but that didn't make it any less disturbing to Hal.

HATE CRIMES AS TERRORISM IN *BROTHER'S KEEPER*

Ron Novy

> Then I . . . then I kissed him . . . out on the street . . .
> I wasn't thinking. I just wanted to kiss my boyfriend.
> Somebody started whistling at us. . . . We heard
> them running up behind us. We ran.
>
> —David, Terry Berg's boyfriend[1]

Let's set the scene: Late last night, Terry Berg and his boyfriend David were chased by three men who had seen them walking arm-in-arm. There were catcalls and the noxious shouts of "Hey, faggots" as the three chased down the teenagers. David escaped the brutal assault; Terry didn't.

Terry Berg now lies in a coma. Holes have been drilled into his head to relieve the pressure on his brain; the skull fracture may cause him to lose his eye. His legs have been broken in multiple places, his left hand crushed. A lung has collapsed behind broken ribs. Terry is unable to breathe without a respirator; his prognosis is poor. Among family, friends, and loved ones sitting vigil at the hospital is Green Lantern—or rather, his alter ego Kyle Rayner, for whom Terry works as an intern at *Feast* magazine. New York's district attorney has announced that his office will pursue hate crime charges against Terry's attackers; President Lex Luthor—don't ask—has released a statement pledging that his administration will pursue "greater hate crime legislation at the federal level."[2]

So, what is it that justifies penalizing people more severely when their crime is motivated by hate? Fundamentally, hate crime is worse than its non-hate counterpart because the former brings about more harm than the latter. Terry is attacked *because* he is gay, which sends a ripple of fear and intimidation through the gay community. In this way, the attack on Terry is similar to terrorism, and the harsher penalties given for it reflect this recognition and express society's disgust with the act.

I Shouldn't Have Kissed Him

> The district attorney has also charged the three with
> a hate crime count stemming from allegations that
> assailants attacked Terry Berg because they believed
> him to be gay.
>
> —Reporter, Channel Nine[3]

Terry Berg now breathes through one tube and is fed through another, but the harm done to this individual gay man *because* he is gay reaches beyond him to harm all of those who identify (or are identified) as gay or lesbian. What constitutes a hate crime—sometimes called a "bias crime"—varies a bit from one jurisdiction to the next. The U.S. federal sentencing guidelines use the following definition:

> "Hate crime" means a crime in which the defendant intentionally selects a victim, or in the case of a property crime, the property that is the object of the crime, because of the actual or perceived race, color, religion, national origin, ethnicity, gender, disability, or sexual orientation of any person.[4]

For those convicted of a hate crime, these guidelines require "sentencing enhancement" (increased punishment) relative to those convicted of an otherwise similar act that lacks the bias motivation. So, if a pyromaniac were to burn down John Stewart's barn out of pathological desire to see things burn, she'd be charged with arson. But if the firebug instead torched the barn because Stewart is African American, her arson would be treated as a hate crime, so she would receive a harsher punishment.

Violence against a member of an oppressed group is not merely the victimization of the individual at whom the attack is directed; it is also a visceral reminder to all members of the group that "there but for the grace of God go I." In order to understand its severity, we must acknowledge the broader social context within which the violence against Terry took place.

Among the many functions of a good society is the promotion of justice among its citizens, a task usually understood as a matter of distribution (or redistribution) of resources, rights, opportunity, and so forth, in order to meet the basic needs of the citizens. As philosopher Iris Marion Young (1949–2006) pointed out, justice also requires that social conditions exist that enable "the development and exercise of individual capacities and collective communication and cooperation." This "enabling concept of justice" requires that the law must act as a guarantor that Terry, David, Kyle, and all other citizens are able "to develop and exercise their capacities and express their needs, thoughts, and feelings."[5] A large part of the oppression endured by citizens "based on what they look like, who they love, how they pray"[6] results from the lack of just such a guarantee.

In the case of gay-bashing, any and all gays and lesbians are potentially liable to come under such attack for no other reason than their group membership (or, more accurately, perceived membership in the group). After all, Terry and David were not selected by their attackers because they were Terry and David; rather, they were attacked because they were perceived to be members of a despised group. When the assailants shouted "Hey, faggots" and chased down their prey, it made no difference that it was Terry and David rather than Steve and Mike or Hannah and Mary. What mattered was that the victims were gay.

The knowledge that they and their partners must exist under this lurking threat each day severely limits the ability of gays and lesbians to participate fully in society and demands that they dedicate valuable time and energy to minimizing the likelihood of finding themselves on the receiving end of an assault. This is the hate crime's true terrorizing power: it "infects" other members of the victim's group such that in order to avoid negative attention, they police their otherwise unremarkable behavior—for example, by never walking hand-in-hand in the park. As David puts it, crying on Kyle's girlfriend Jade's shoulder in the waiting room, "If I hadn't been acting all queenie outside the club, those guys would never have known. I shouldn't have kissed him."[7]

Not only does the possibility of violence ripple through the lives of those who may become its victims, but its presence is understood by society as something to be expected, and so in a sense enables the perpetrators of hate crimes. Confusing their own bigotry for a feeling shared by all of the community, Terry's assailants would surely report that they act not only for themselves, but for society as a whole. As Young puts it,

> Often third parties find [incidents of gay-bashing] unsurprising because it happens frequently and lies as a

constant possibility. . . . It is a social given that everyone knows happens and will happen again. It is always on the horizon of social imagination, even for those who do not perpetrate it.[8]

For example, the detective who interviews Kyle minimizes—if not outright excuses—the assault as something the teens had brought upon themselves. First, he suggests that Terry and David may have been involved in a drug deal gone bad; he then tells Rayner that the police "have reports that these two left the club with those guys. A few said that they tried to pick them up; that the boys were hitting on those men." While Rayner is naturally outraged, asking, "What if they were?! Then it's okay to beat—to try to beat them to death?" the implication from the detective is clear: this is the sort of reaction to expect when someone violates social norms, acting "all queenie" in public.[9] In contrast to the detective, we can see clearly not only that Terry and David did nothing wrong but also that their victimization extends beyond them into the broader gay community. Thus increased penalties that attach to hate crimes are justified.

Hurt One of Us, Hurt All of Us

Incidents of gay-bashing carry a message to all gays and lesbians that they are hated and vulnerable. On the other hand, hate crime legislation expresses that despite the perpetrator's effort, society at large takes crimes against—and the citizenship of—gays and lesbians seriously. Hate crime legislation is thus justified by the *expressivist* theory of punishment, which the philosopher Joel Feinberg (1926–2004) explains in the following terms:

> Punishment is . . . [an] expression of attitudes of resentment and indignation, and of judgments of disapproval and reprobation, on the part of either the punishing

authority himself or of those "in whose name" the punishment is inflicted. Punishment, in short, has a *symbolic
significance*.[10]

Increased penalties for hate crimes may also be justified on
the grounds of the principle of utility, which tells us to act to
produce the greatest good for the greatest number. Utilitarians
typically think of the good in terms of happiness, and so
the principle of utility is often called the "greatest-happiness
principle." As the philosopher John Stuart Mill (1806–1873)
writes:

> Actions are right in proportion as they tend to promote
> happiness, wrong as they tend to produce the reverse
> of happiness. By happiness is intended pleasure, and
> the absence of pain; by unhappiness, pain, and the pri-
> vation of pleasure.[11]

Of course, crime in general disrupts society, but the com-
mission of a hate crime disrupts society in a more significant way. While hate crime reduces overall happiness just as
"regular" crime does, it also breeds a corrosive attitude among
people that prevents members of the direct victim's peer group
from living to their full capabilities. Simply put, all things being
equal, a crime motivated by hate is worse than one that is not
so motivated. Since there are more persons directly harmed
or threatened by a hate crime, more harm is caused and more
punishment is required in the interest of proportionality.

Further, this more severe penalty may also serve as both an
expression of social disgust and an instrument of moral education. Assuming Terry's attackers are found guilty of a hate
crime and are assigned the higher penalty, it is not because
the life and well-being of their victim is more valuable than
others', but rather because as bad as "normal" assault is, the
crime perpetrated against Terry was worse. Society benefits,
both from having these bad guys off the streets (as with a

"regular" crime), and also from the enhanced sentence, which demonstrates that such hateful actions will not be tolerated.

We can also justify enhanced punishment of hate crimes by comparing them to acts of terrorism, the purpose of which is to intimidate or create fear among a wide group of people. Like acts of terrorism, hate crimes not only harm the direct victim of the act, but also intend to intimidate some sector of the general population—the group to which the direct victim belongs. Terrorist actions are justly punished more severely than run-of-the-mill crime because of the wider yet more focused social harm they produce. Clearly, this reasoning should apply to hate crimes as well.

Extraordinary Crimes, Extraordinary Procedures

That was me breaking your wrist. Hurts, huh?

—Green Lantern[12]

At the core of *Brother's Keeper* is the story of seventeen-year-old Terry Berg being nearly killed in a gay-bashing frenzy and the effect this assault has upon his friend Kyle Rayner, aka Green Lantern. Soon after the attack, the police arrest Daniel Hirsh but have no leads as to where to find the other two assailants. Overhearing this, Rayner decides that he—that is, Green Lantern—will track them down. A short time later, he pays a late-night visit to Hirsh's cell on Rikers Island to convince him to give up his friends. What follows isn't pretty; suffice it to say that early the next morning, New York's finest find the two toughs in an alley slumped among the filth and their own blood.

If we see hate crimes as similar in effect to terrorism, *Brother's Keeper* raises one of the more challenging issues we face in our own post-9/11 world: Are there any limits to our legitimate behavior when it is aimed at preventing and responding to terrorist acts? That is, can extraordinary crimes justify the use of extraordinary procedures? While ostensibly a hero, Rayner does things to Hirsh that many would regard as less than heroic: he isolates him, suspends him upside-down, breaks his wrists, and threatens that he is "gonna have to get more creative" if Hirsh doesn't supply the information desired.[13] What follows is a more or less textbook justification for the benefits of the use of such "extraordinary procedures": the "prisoner" does have the information being sought, and he does give up the location of Terry's assailants. The pair is captured and all three are removed from society, unable to perform similar acts in the future.

Having successfully relied upon extrajudicial violence in Hirsh's interrogation, Green Lantern slips easily into that mode again. When he finds Hirsh's companions, Green Lantern provokes them into a fight—one that they have no possibility of winning, given that they are two frightened thugs with two-by-fours facing an enraged superhero wielding what may be the single most powerful weapon in the DC Universe. Rayner begins to grind them into hamburger with a vengeful green rage:

> Let me see some of that toughness! Some of that mus-cle it takes to beat a little boy to death!! I want to see it!! You gonna yell at me too?! Lemme hear it! Lemme hear what you said to Terry! "C'mon faggot!! You like this, you little queer!" . . . He's going to die because you're so screwed up and scared![14]

Green Lantern is on the verge of beating one to death, stop-ping only after the frightened, bloodied man begs for mercy.

Rayner is deeply shaken by his own brutality. His actions are strikingly similar to those of the men he is punishing: he has tortured a helpless prisoner and reigned blows down upon already defenseless opponents. Leaving Jade, David, and the rest at Terry's bedside, Rayner visits the watchtower of the Justice League of America to ask Flash to use the "cosmic treadmill" to undo the last twenty-four hours: to go back to a time before the assault on Terry. (Flash refuses, of course.) When confronted by Batman for his torture of Hirsh, Rayner reminds him that "You pull the same garbage a hundred times a day before the rest of us even eat breakfast." Batman replies, simply: "Maybe. But that is me, isn't it?"[15]

Rayner recognizes that his vicious actions do not fit with his sense of his own character. Even in pursuit of "good ends" such as the capture of Terry's attackers, there are moral limits to one's behavior, and failing to abide by these limits turns Rayner, as much as Hirsh, into a lesser person. In his reaction to the assault on Terry, Kyle sees a man he does not want to be. As he confesses to Jade,

> There is good in this world, but it doesn't measure up to the bad. In the hearts of humanity, there is anger, there is rape, there is brutality . . . there is hate. It took this happening to Terry to . . . to break me. I can't help these people now. I don't want to.[16]

In his good-bye note to fellow Green Lantern John Stewart, Rayner writes, "I haven't lost my faith in humanity, but I have lost my will to protect them. . . . Maybe it's shame. Maybe it's anger. . . . I hope I can find strength to return and be a guardian of our people."[17]

"This Isn't Just about Terry"

[No occurrence of a hate crime] is "isolated" in the United States. That is what makes the incidents so horrible, so scary. It is the knowledge that they are *not* the isolated [acts] of a dissident few that makes them so frightening.

—Charles Lawrence [18]

In the summer of 2002, this Green Lantern story line about Terry Berg, written by Judd Winick, drew the attention of an audience beyond the usual DC fandom.[19] Four years after the killings of Matthew Shepard and James Byrd, Terry Berg is the victim of a vicious and brutal hate crime. And less than a year after the terrorist attacks of 9/11 and the opening of the detention camp at Guantanamo Bay, Green Lantern recognizes that he has crossed a dangerous line by torturing one defenseless man and savagely beating others nearly to death. Due to its timeliness, the story was discussed in venues ranging from MSNBC's talk show *Donahue*[20] to the *London Times*[21] to the PBS newsmagazine *In the Life.*[22]

Yet the mere existence in the judicial system of the category "hate crime" has its detractors, most of whom are concerned either that it is a type of "thought crime"—punishing people for holding unpopular opinions—or that it implies that the well-being of some victims of crime is less important than that of others. But the category of hate crime doesn't have to be seen in those ways. Justice demands that we proportion punishment for a crime to the harm caused by that crime: lesser penalties for lesser infractions (a small fine for someone who jaywalks) and greater penalties for greater crimes (a long period of imprisonment for murderers). While any assault causes harm, that same assault committed for the purpose of instilling a broader sense of fear is deemed to cause greater harm than it would otherwise.

Like an act of terrorism, the hate crime gets its power— symbolic and otherwise—by reminding members of the victim's group that that membership is enough to bring violence upon them. In this way, the threat of violence coerces those individuals into certain behaviors. For instance, same-sex couples may take the attack on Terry and David as a warning against displaying affection in public or coming into that neighborhood or staying out after sundown. It is this broader effect, not the identity of the victim, that makes the hate crime worse than its counterpart and so deserving of additional punishment.

The existence of hate crime legislation expresses both our disdain for the act and our commitment to the idea that all citizens, including members of the gay community, have an opportunity to thrive. Or, as Flash reminds Green Lantern when he visits the JLA's watchtower:

> This isn't just about Terry. This about every teenager who is terrified of being different. Different because of race, because of appearance, because of who they love. This goes on every day, Kyle.[23]

Aristotle (384–322 BCE) tells us that a just society is one in which all members have it in their "power to act virtuously and live happily."[24] That some of us are not terrorized by others seems to be an obvious part of such a society. Hate crimes legislation is at least some small part of our own efforts to enable all citizens to fulfill their capabilities and so make society a little more just.[25]

NOTES

1. *Green Lantern*, vol. 3, #154 (November 2002); this issue and the following, #155 (December 2002), comprise the "Hate Crime" story line, the focus of this chapter, and have been reprinted in *Green Lantern: Brother's Keeper* (2003).

2. *Green Lantern*, vol. 3, #155.

3. Ibid.

4. The Violent Crime and Enforcement Act, H.R. 3355, §280003. When adopted in 1994, the list of recognized groups was less extensive and has since been expanded. On October 28, 2009, President Luthor's real-world counterpart Barack Obama signed the "Matthew Shepard and James Byrd, Jr. Hate Crime Prevention Act," which expanded hate crimes legislation to include gender, gender identity, and sexual orientation.

5. Iris Marion Young, *Justice and the Politics of Difference* (Princeton, NJ: Princeton University Press, 1990), 39, 40.

6. From President Barack Obama's proclamation at the signing of the "Matthew Shepard and James Byrd, Jr. Hate Crime Prevention Act," October 28, 2009.

7. *Green Lantern*, vol. 3, #154.

8. Young, *Justice and the Politics of Difference*, 62.

9. *Green Lantern*, vol. 3, #154.

10. Joel Feinberg, "The Expressivist Function of Punishment," in *Doing and Deserving* (Princeton, NJ: Princeton University Press, 1970), 98.

11. John Stuart Mill, *Utilitarianism* (Chicago: University of Chicago Press, 1864/1906), 9.

12. *Green Lantern*, vol. 3, #154.

13. Ibid. See also the miniseries *Justice League: Cry for Justice* (2009–2010), in which a group of heroes led by Hal Jordan (and including Green Arrow and the Atom) torture criminals to get information about their plans.

14. *Green Lantern*, vol. 3, #154.

15. *Green Lantern*, vol. 3, #155.

16. Ibid.

17. Ibid.

18. Charles R. Lawrence III, "If He Hollers Let Him Go: Regulating Racist Speech on Campus," in Mari J. Matsuda et al., *Words that Wound: Critical Race Theory, Assaultive Speech and the First Amendment* (Boulder, CO: Westview Press, 1993), 74.

19. Besides acclaimed runs on *Green Lantern* and *Batman*, Winick, a former *Real World* cast member, wrote *Pedro and Me*, a 2000 graphic novel about his friend, castmate, and AIDS educator Pedro Zamora.

20. With Phil Donahue, Winick appeared with the Family Research Council's Peter Sprigg to discuss the appropriateness of "gay story lines" in comic books (August 15, 2002).

21. David Thompson, "Men in Tights," *London Times*, August 23, 2002.

22. Initially aired spring 2003.

23. *Green Lantern*, vol. 3, #155.

24. Aristotle, *Politics*, translated by William Ellis, available at Project Gutenberg (http://www.gutenberg.org/etext/6762), Book VII, Chapter II (1324a 23–25).

25. Thanks to Dawn Jakubowski for our insightful discussions.

THE RING OF GYGES, THE RING OF THE GREEN LANTERN, AND THE TEMPTATION OF POWER

Adam Barkman

"Power tends to corrupt," wrote Lord Acton (1834–1902), "and absolute power corrupts absolutely." While many of us probably agree with the general sentiment of this saying, few of us who are comic book fans would go as far as Lord Acton does. The reason for this is that we have a slew of extremely powerful yet morally superior beings to prove our point—or do we?

Green Lanterns make particularly good case studies in this regard. Of all the DC Comics characters, the Green Lanterns show a whole spectrum of reactions to the temptation of power. Some appear unaffected by the siren call of power and use what they have been given with a reasonable degree of moral responsibility, while others—indeed, often the most experienced and celebrated of the Green Lanterns—have been corrupted by their desire for power, or even by their desires in general, which their power rings enable them to satisfy.

Indeed, it's no accident that one of the Guardians of the Universe says, "I was there billions of years ago when we first decreed that the ultimate cause of chaos was emotion."[1] With the belief that emotions and desires are the cause of disorder and lawlessness, the Guardians severed their own emotions and desires and formed the galactic police force known as the Green Lantern Corps, whose power rings are driven by willpower and rely on control over emotion and desire. So how can we make sense of this mess of desires, lack of desires, and the subsequent corruption or moral purity of those with or without desires? More to the point, what is the correct understanding of the desire for power?

"Now Suppose There Were Two Such Powerful Rings"

We could hardly ask for a more fitting guide to help us examine these questions than Plato (428–348 BCE) and his classic work, the *Republic*. In the second book of the *Republic* the character Glaucon argues that the only reason why people act morally is because they are afraid of the consequences of not doing so. To illustrate his point, Glaucon tells the story of the Ring of Gyges:

> An ancestor of Gyges of Lydia, a shepherd, was in the service of the Lydian ruler of the time, when a heavy rainstorm occurred . . . and a chasm appeared in the region where he was pasturing his flocks. He . . . went down into the chasm and saw there . . . a bronze horse, which was hollow and had windows set in it; he stooped and looked in through the windows and saw a corpse

inside. . . . The corpse was naked, but had a golden ring on one finger; he took the ring off the finger and left. Now, the shepherds used to meet once a month to keep the king informed about his flocks, and our protagonist came to the meeting wearing the ring. He was sitting down among the others, and happened to twist the ring's bezel . . . towards the inner part of his hand. When he did this, he became invisible to his neighbors, and to his astonishment they talked about him as if he'd left. While he was fiddling about with the ring again, he turned the bezel outwards and became visible. . . . As soon as he realized this, he arranged to be made one of the delegates to the king; once he was inside the palace, he seduced the king's wife and with her help assaulted and killed the king, and so took possession of the throne.[2]

After telling this tale, Glaucon declares, "Now suppose there were two such rings—one worn by our moral person, the other by the immoral person. There is no one, on this view, who has enough willpower to maintain his morality and find the strength of purpose to keep his hands off what doesn't belong to him."[3] In this respect at least, Lord Acton would agree with Glaucon.

Plato doesn't agree, however. He argues that power—even the power of magical green rings—will not corrupt the good man. The gist of Plato's argument is that injustice and immorality corrupt the soul, which has three parts—reason, spirit, and appetite. When those three parts are in proper balance a person acts morally and feels happy and at peace with himself. But when spirit or appetite (emotion or desire) override reason, a person acts immorally and is not at peace with himself. So the shepherd who uses the ring of Gyges to become king may have all the earthly goods he desires, but he will lack what is most important—the internal balance of his soul and its accompanying peace of mind. So, knowing that using power to indulge emotions and desires will bring unhappiness, the good person (and, thus, the good Green Lantern) will decline to abuse his power.

Who Guards the Guardians?

In *Tales of the Green Lantern Corps Annual* #3 (1987), we're presented with a pertinent question, "Who watches the Watchmen?," echoing the Roman satirist Juvenal's more ancient query, "Who guards the guardians?"[4] Plato's *Republic* divides the ideal society into three groups: the guardians (who are dominated by reason), the warriors (who are dominated by emotion), and the workers (who are dominated by desire). In Plato's *Republic*, the answer to Juvenal's question is simple: the guardians, being wiser and thus morally superior to everyone else, govern themselves in addition to governing everyone else. Nevertheless, Plato would be the first to admit that although the guardians, being wiser and morally superior to others, should rule, it doesn't follow that they're *morally perfect*. As limited beings, the guardians would still lack some knowledge and thus would be capable of making moral mistakes. Of course, it's important to keep in mind here that Plato had no clear conception of the will: he simply couldn't imagine a wise person, who knows that morality is essential to achieving true happiness, intentionally choosing to do evil, thus harming his own soul.

So how does this all apply to the Guardians of the Universe? Are they the universal equivalent of Plato's guardians? The answer appears to be yes for the following reasons. First, by virtue of their enormous longevity, the Guardians are among the wisest and most knowledgeable beings in the DC Universe. In one issue, a Guardian says, "My brothers and I have lived our lives by rational decision";[5] in another issue the Guardians are even referred to as "omniscient."[6]

Second, because of their great wisdom, the Guardians should be among the most moral beings in the universe; one piece of evidence supporting this is the fact that they have dedicated their lives to "promoting an orderly rational cosmos," largely by founding, and guiding, the Green Lantern Corps.[7]

Third, despite being among the wisest and most moral beings in the universe, the Guardians are still capable of moral mistakes. Nevertheless, because they are among the wisest and most moral, any mistakes they make should, at least according to Plato, be forgiven by less wise, less moral beings because we can assume that such beings would do an even worse job of ruling. For instance, the Guardians should be forgiven for neglecting their emotions (an error that, among other things, played a part in prompting Hal Jordan's killing spree after the destruction of Coast City[8]). They should also be forgiven for the massacres committed by their renegade androids, the Manhunters.[9] Of course, some Guardians are not wise or moral (Krona, anyone?), and some have mental illnesses that make them go mad, such as the Guardian Scar. Such Guardians should no longer be considered among the wisest beings in the universe, and so their moral mistakes should again not be tolerated.[10]

Consequently, Plato's explanation for the abuse of power—that power will only corrupt a person insofar as he is *ignorant* (wisdom teaching us to be moral)—goes a long way in explaining why the Guardians, among the wisest beings in the universe, do a lot of good for it and should be its rulers, even though, from time to time, they can make moral mistakes as well (though far less than the rest of us).

It follows, then, that if the Guardians are as Platonic as they, in fact, appear to be, we should expect that when they assembled the Green Lantern Corps, they only selected those whom they deemed, in their best but still imperfect judgment, to be wise and deeply moral beings, because the more moral a person is, the more likely he (or she, or it) will be able to control his desires and hence the Power Ring (a modern Ring of Gyges, to be sure). But is this what we see? Did the Guardians make wisdom and morality important traits in those they selected to be Green Lanterns?

"No Evil Shall Escape My Sight"

The most famous Green Lantern is Hal Jordan. Abin Sur, a dying Green Lantern who crash-landed on Earth, selected Jordan to be his replacement because Jordan possessed two qualities. First, he was honest, meaning that he was morally upright; second, he was fearless, which is to say that he wasn't afraid of evil or danger, and he had enough willpower to enforce his moral convictions.[11] Moreover, both of these qualities—commitment to morality and determination to uphold it—are evident in Jordan's famous Green Lantern oath:

> In brightest day, in blackest night,
> *No evil shall escape my sight*
> Let those who worship evil's might,
> Beware *my power* . . . Green Lantern's light!

Although wisdom isn't mentioned as a criterion for Jordan's selection, Plato believed that wisdom is implied in morality, for you can't act morally without wisdom. Hence, on this account, we could say that Jordan was chosen because he was wise, in addition to being moral and determined. His soul demonstrated a proper Platonic ordering, reason ruling the desires and indeed reason using the desires to enforce its moral dictates. Jordan, in other words, would have initially passed Plato's Ring of Gyges test.

Of course, this doesn't mean that Jordan, or any of the Green Lanterns selected for their moral uprightness, can't make moral mistakes: If extremely wise and moral beings like the Guardians can screw up, how can we expect mere mortals like Hal Jordan not to? Nevertheless, some might argue that the huge number of mistakes Jordan and other Lanterns made over the years is evidence that despite what Plato wrote, ignorance isn't enough to explain why creatures chosen for their wisdom and morality gave in to their desire for power and committed evil acts. Thus, the question is: Are there Green Lanterns who were chosen for their wisdom and morality but then gave in to their desire for power through something *other* than ignorance? In order to answer this question, let's look at the three worst cases in this regard: Yalan Gur, Sinestro, and Hal Jordan.

"You Have Never Understood Us"

Yalan Gur was an extremely powerful Green Lantern assigned by the Guardians to protect sector 2814 (Earth's sector). In the distant past, he was nearly killed by a yellow beast, since Green Lanterns' rings are traditionally powerless against the color yellow. The Guardians removed this weakness against yellow from Gur's ring and battery, thus granting him almost unlimited power.[12] Overwhelmed by this, Gur soon became a dictator, ruling his sector from his base in ancient China. However, seeing that Gur couldn't handle unlimited power, the Guardians added a new weakness to his Lantern: a weakness to wood. Consequently, Gur was defeated by angry Chinese peasants and their wooden weapons and, filled with "remorse . . . and guilt," he didn't bother to heal his own mortal wounds and so died, his life force being absorbed into his Lantern and merging with the mysterious Starheart, which later became the source of power to Alan Scott, the Golden Age Green Lantern.[13]

So what do we make of this story? Does it constitute a challenge to Plato's theory of desire and power? Probably not. Gur was almost certainly chosen by the Guardians, and so would have been chosen for his wisdom and morality. However, when Gur received new power, he was forced to deal with new possibilities that caused him to act wrongly insofar as he involved himself in local politics as a coercive force. Yet when Gur was shown the error of his ways, he became filled with remorse and guilt. Over the centuries, "the soul of Yalan Gur," we are told, "made peace with itself. It had repented. And so it gained control of its power."[14]

Although Yalan Gur was a hero-turned-villain-turned-hero, Sinestro, another extremely powerful former Green Lantern, is simply a hero-turned-villain (despite his temporary alliance with Hal Jordan during 2009–2010's *Blackest Night* event). Although the Guardians' initial "tests showed Sinestro to be a deserving one and absolutely without fear," they later admitted that they made a "mistake" insofar as they didn't scrutinize Sinestro's character as carefully as they should have. Sinestro, it turned out, didn't simply want the power ring to help the universe but also wanted to use it to set himself up as the dictator of his home planet, Korugar.[15] Thus, as one Guardian tells Sinestro point-blank, "You have never understood us,"[16] meaning that Sinestro *never* had the wisdom and morality that it takes to be a Green Lantern. Consequently, it's no surprise that he, like Gyges, was corrupted by "love of power."[17] And despite Sinestro's desire for power flowing from unwise, immoral intentions, his case poses even less of a challenge to Plato's theory of desire and power than Gur's.

"Understand, Hal's Not Evil . . ."

Hal Jordan was chosen by the Guardians for his wisdom, moral integrity, and willpower. In fact, he was the paradigm of what a Platonic Green Lantern looks like. Nevertheless, on at least two occasions, he made serious mistakes.

For instance, at one point he resigned from the Green Lantern Corps because he wanted to spend more time with the love of his life, Carol Ferris.[18] Although we romantic, emotional modern people might find this understandable, Plato would not, because according to him true happiness comes from being moral. Indeed, the only reason that Platonic guardians—and here we could substitute Green Lanterns—become guardians in the first place is because they realize that they have a moral duty to lead others. If they neglect this moral duty—say, for romantic entanglements or other temptations of a private life—they can't achieve true happiness. Thus, by valuing his personal life more than his moral duty as a Green Lantern, Jordan acted unwisely. Nevertheless, this error, brought on by ignorance of the proper value of things, was later rectified by Jordan when Earth was under attack. Understanding that the planet is more important than his personal life, Jordan saw that he "can't sit idly by" and watch it be destroyed, and so he asked for "a chance to do what is right."[19] The Guardians agreed to restore Jordan's power but, testing to see if he was truly wise and moral, required that he play second fiddle to Guy Gardner, one of his replacements. Jordan, realizing that doing what is right (following reason) is more important than his own pride (following desire), agreed.

Another time Jordan acted unwisely—to put it mildly—was after Mongul and the Cyborg Superman murdered the seven million inhabitants of Jordan's hometown, Coast City. Wandering through the crater that was once his hometown, Jordan dreamed about the "power to be God" so he could resurrect the city and its inhabitants.[20] Consequently, when the Guardians refused Jordan such power, he defied them and went on a mad rampage, even killing his close friend Kilowog, in order to acquire the energy of the Central Power Battery, which Jordan believed would give him the power to "set everything right."[21] Once again, Jordan acted out of ignorance of the proper value of things; as Alan Scott said of him later, "Understand, Hal's not evil. . . . He believes he's acting for the right reasons."[22] Indeed, some time later, Jordan—now known as Parallax—came to see that he "made mistakes . . . terrible mistakes,"[23] and so, in true Platonic fashion, sacrificed his own life to save Earth.[24]

Of course, some might still think that ignorance isn't enough to explain all the acts that Jordan committed as Parallax (in particular, the attempt at rebooting the universe in 1994's *Zero Hour*). Yet these people should keep in mind that it wasn't always Jordan doing these terrible things: it was revealed later that after absorbing the Central Power Battery, Jordan was possessed by the fear-entity named Parallax, who amplified Jordan's emotions—in particular, his fear—which in turn overruled the moral dictates of his reason. Thus, many of the evils Parallax brought about should be seen as ones committed by a mentally ill (and thus not necessarily evil) Jordan.[25] Consequently, the mistakes made by Jordan—like the mistakes committed by the Guardians, Yalan Gur, and Sinestro—do not pose a serious challenge to Plato's theory of desire and power.

"To End Evil"

Plato's theory of desire and power argues that because happiness comes from enjoying morality for its own sake, the person who understands this—the wise person—will thus be a moral person. Among other things, this means that he won't be corrupted by the desire for power, as Gyges the shepherd was. Even so, the moral person *will* desire power, but only insofar as he understands that it's his moral duty (and hence his happiness) to lead others by serving them.

A Green Lantern's ring is immensely powerful and brings with it its share of temptation, just like the Ring of Gyges. The universe is lucky that the Guardians and their chosen task force, the Green Lantern Corps, have mostly chosen to police the universe in order "to end evil," rather than pursuing power for its own sake. If Plato is right, their moral mistakes can be explained as the result of an acceptable level of ignorance. Let us hope—for the sake of the DC Universe and its readers—that they continue to strive for greater knowledge.

NOTES

1. *Green Lantern*, vol. 4, #43 (September 2009), reprinted in *Blackest Night: Green Lantern* (2010).

2. Plato, *Republic*, trans. Robin Waterfield (Oxford, UK: Oxford University Press, 1994), 359d–360b.

3. Ibid., 360b. (Most translators use "justice" instead of "morality" here, but we'll stick with "morality" for the sake of this chapter.)

4. Juvenal, *Satire*, 4.6.346–347.

5. *Green Lantern*, vol. 2, #200 (May 1986).

6. *Trinity* #1 (February 2008).

7. *Green Lantern*, vol. 3, #55 (August 1994), reprinted in *Green Lantern: Emerald Twilight/New Dawn* (2003).

8. *Green Lantern*, vol. 3, #49 (February 1994), reprinted in *Green Lantern: Emerald Twilight/New Dawn*. (See the chapter by Donovan and Richardson in this volume for more on the Guardians' rejection of emotion.)

9. *Green Lantern*, vol. 2, #141 (June 1981).

10. *Green Lantern*, vol. 4, #44 (September 2009), reprinted in *Blackest Night: Green Lantern*.

11. *Showcase* #22 (September/October 1959), reprinted in black and white in *Showcase Presents Green Lantern Volume One* (2005) and in color in *The Green Lantern Chronicles Volume One* (2009).

12. It is unclear (to say the least) how they were able to do this, as the yellow impurity was always explained as a structural necessity in the Central Power Battery on Oa (until it was later retconned to be the fear entity Parallax).

13. *Green Lantern*, vol. 3, #19 (December 1991). (See the chapter by Jones in this volume for more on Scott and the Starheart.)

14. Ibid.

15. *Green Lantern*, vol. 2, #7 (July/August 1961), reprinted in black and white in *Showcase Presents: Green Lantern Volume One* (2005) and in color in *The Green Lantern Chronicles Volume Two* (2009).

16. *Green Lantern*, vol. 2, #200.

17. *Green Lantern*, vol. 2, #7.

18. *Green Lantern*, vol. 2, #181 (October 1984).

19. *Green Lantern*, vol. 2, #197 (February 1986).

20. *Green Lantern*, vol. 3, #48 (January 1994), reprinted in *Green Lantern: Emerald Twilight/New Dawn*.

21. *Green Lantern*, vol. 3, #50 (March 1994), reprinted in *Green Lantern: Emerald Twilight/New Dawn*.

22. *Green Lantern*, vol. 3, #55.

23. *Green Lantern*, vol. 3, #0 (October 1994).

24. *Final Night* #4 (November 1996).

25. See the chapter by Michaud in this volume for more on Jordan's responsibility for the things he did as (or while possessed by) Parallax.

PART FIVE

DON'T TELL KRONA: METAPHYSICS, MIND, AND TIME

ALL FOR ONE AND ONE FOR ALL: MOGO, THE COLLECTIVE, AND BIOLOGICAL UNITY

Leonard Finkelman

Emerald rings cut through the void of space. Their task: to find intelligent beings worthy of wielding the greatest power in the universe! Their obstacle: the oldest riddles of existence itself!

These are the rings of the Green Lantern Corps, weapons of the universe's protectorate. Fueled by a user's willpower, the emerald rings must be wielded by rational beings. The will of a ringbearer must be focused and decisive. So the user must be a single individual; there can be no ring-wielding by committee. This is all straightforward, but life in this cosmos is diverse and often comes in scales beyond our reckoning. How can we recognize living individuals amidst this diversity? What are the boundaries between individuals, and how can we guard against false distinctions? For over two and a half millennia, these questions have plagued the greatest minds of sector 2814.

As they fly through the interstellar darkness, emerald rings find their answers to these questions in entities as diverse as organisms, genes, species, ideas, and planets. How have these pieces of jewelry unlocked the secrets of life's essence?

Carving Nature at Its Joints

The first time the bounty hunter Bolphunga the Unrelenting actually relented was upon the realization that the Green Lantern Mogo is a sentient planet.[1] Things might have gone differently if the philosopher Immanuel Kant's (1724–1804) famous saying that perceptions without concepts are blind had been more widely known outside of sector 2814.[2] What Kant meant is that one's conceptual framework—that is to say, one's *philosophy*—shapes perceptions taken in by the senses. Two people may *look* at the same object and yet *see* completely different things. Limited as he was by his concept of living things, Bolphunga looked at Mogo and saw an unconscious celestial body. The Guardians of the Universe, however, looked at the planet and saw an intelligent organism worthy of a power ring.

Looking through the Green Lantern Corps' Book of Worthy Names, we find listed those beings similarly recognized by the Guardians. In addition to Mogo we find Hal Jordan, a human of space sector 2814; Leezle Pon, a smallpox virus in sector 119; the Collective, a species of living puffballs from sector 1287; and Dkrtzy RRR, a mathematical equation first derived in sector 188.[3] Their exploits are the stuff of legend. How is it that these diverse entities each count as individuals?

Biology organizes living things into a hierarchical structure. Molecules are the building blocks of cells; cells aggregate to form tissues; tissues make organs; organs combine to form organisms; organisms group into species; species interact in ecosystems. But at which of these levels can a power ring find real living individuals? Ask this question about biology and you're engaged in the study of its *ontology*, the branch of philosophy that asks which things really exist, and how. The challenge before us, as Plato (428–348 BCE) first put it, is to divide reality "along its natural joints"—that is, where there are actual boundaries between things.[4] Since it must be used by an individual, a Green Lantern's emerald light illuminates these very joints, making plain which living things are real and how they are distinguished from others.

Although the power rings themselves seem to have it sorted out, the development of a biological ontology has become one of the central debates in the emerging field of *philosophy of biology*. The debate extends back to the beginnings of Western civilization and continues with the turn of this page. Reader, you have the will to overcome great confusion. Welcome to the Philosophy Corps.[5]

Tales of the Philosophy Corps

When confronted with profound questions, humans have tended to look up and beyond for answers. Why does the sun move across the sky? Perhaps it's pulled by some divine chariot. Why does it rain? Perhaps a goddess, when properly appeased, seeks to reward us with a bountiful harvest. Among the ancient Greeks, however, there came to prominence a group that looked down rather than up. They sought to resolve the riddles of existence with observations of nature, not speculation about what exists beyond nature.

Ontology proved a controversial subject for the Greeks, who realized that to succeed—to have reality submit before their understanding—would be to tame wild existence. Thales of Miletus (c. 624–546 BCE) made the first attempt. Realizing that ontology is ultimately a debate over counting—How many things are there?—he drew on the power of reason. The answer he derived: just one. Everything is made of *matter*, because matter is what we observe in nature.[6] This sort of ontology is called *monism*, and it became appealing to a number of Greeks in the century following Thales' death.

Let's count as a monist would. Mogo first appeared in *Green Lantern*, vol. 2, #188 (May 1985), an issue that also featured another human Green Lantern, John Stewart. In holding that issue, then, am I holding three things? No—the characters are *part of* the book and not separate from it. But if we are part of reality in the same way the characters are part of the book, then how many things are there in reality? One—*the* One! The universe is like a comic wherein each instant is a new panel. But should we see each panel as completely distinct from the next, in which case nothing ever lasts for any period of time? Or should we see the panels as bound together on the same page, in which case reality is like a printed volume, finished and unchanging? The philosophers Heraclitus (c. 535–475 BCE) and Parmenides (c. 520–450 BCE) pushed monism to these respective extremes.

Great confusion ensued. Maintain your will—help is on the way! To believe in a monist ontology is to reject individuality, casting reality as a single unjointed whole. Aristotle (384–322 BCE) thought it absurd to view things through this conceptual framework. We *do* recognize individuals; logically, there must be more to reality than matter alone. If Mogo can survive a collision with a meteor, as it does in *Green Lantern Corps*, vol. 2, #13 (August 2007), then changing matter must be unified by some other constant. Immaterial *form*, when united with matter, lays the foundation of individuality; Aristotle called this foundation *substance*.

Trying to lump all substances together, as the monists did, has severe limits. Consider that both Mogo and Hal avoid traveling to the planet Oa, home of the Guardians, whenever possible. Why? Aristotle's *pluralism* demands that we count substances separately because even the things they have in common are ultimately a result of things that make them different. Mogo avoids returning to Oa because Mogo's gravity would pose a danger to that planet. After all, Mogo is itself a planet. Hal avoids returning to Oa because Hal dislikes the Guardians. Hal, as we know, is prone to irrational sentiment because Hal is a human. Planets and humans may both exist, but each exists *in a different way*.[7]

Living substances in particular seem unique. Aristotle was impressed by the coordination of biology's hierarchy: the parts at lower levels work in the service of the higher levels. When Hal hunts an intergalactic criminal, every organ in his body—whether it's used for seeing, for talking, for grasping, or whatever—acts in harmony toward his goal. Aristotle therefore believed that an organism must be more than the sum of its parts or else its body would be a jumble of organs, each trying to do its own thing. Something in an organism's *form* unifies and coordinates its *material* parts. Aristotle called this something the *soul*.[8]

Aristotle enumerated his biological ontology. Count souls. Count organisms, "which we say are [unified] if anything is."[9] Do we count Mogo? Ecosystems are the parts of a planet, and organisms are parts of ecosystems; however, organisms have their own interests and don't always act in harmony with their host planets. The Resal species, for example, once settled into one of Mogo's ecosystems and ravaged the planet's resources.[10] Hey, Mogo needs those! This hardly seems like the unification of parts necessary to be counted as a biological individual. Put aside sentiment: we must admit that Mogo lacks a living soul. Mogo may *communicate* like a living thing; Mogo may *behave* like a living thing; but that doesn't mean that Mogo is *unified* in the same way as living things.[11]

Parts, wholes, and souls: this diverse reality challenges us with diverse objects of study. Mathematics! Physics! Astronomy!

Biology! Aristotle did his best to overcome great confusion in each of them; not for nothing did Dante (1265–1321) call him the "Master of those who know." For almost two thousand years, philosophers—especially those who studied biology—looked to Aristotle as the avatar of the Philosophy Corps. But the tales of the Corps were to be continued. . . .

"Soft"-Traveling Heroes

"No man escapes the Manhunters!" So goes the oath of the Manhunters, robotic predecessors of the Green Lantern Corps whose objective is to eliminate living substance from the universe. Their goals reflected those of their creators, the Guardians of the Universe, as if in a dark mirror: to bring order to a chaotic cosmos. The treacherous Guardian Scar described the Manhunters' logic: "The only way to eliminate chaos . . . is the annihilation of sentient life."[12]

The Philosophy Corps use the power of reason to bring the universe to similar order (in a somewhat less drastic way). Reason has discovered universal laws that govern the behavior of matter. Sir Isaac Newton (1643–1727), for example, read from the Book of Nature and found within it the Laws of Motion. $F = ma$: all matter—past, present, and future—exerts force equal to its mass multiplied by its acceleration. This codification of strict universal laws is sometimes called "hard science."[13] Like the Manhunters' mission, hard science comes at a cost. Where Aristotle once believed that different substances had different origins, reason found the origin of all things, from molecules to Manhunters to Mogo, in physics. The Master's pluralism has been *reduced*, once again, to a sort of monism: all matter is physical, and none of it is particularly unique. Only life resists this reduction.

Life is messy; life is *unpredictable*. Unpredictability is the impurity against which the power of reason falters. Biology stands against reduction because life gains new powers at each level of its hierarchy. We can view a robotic Manhunter as just a bunch of mechanical parts, but, as Aristotle pointed out, an organism can do things that a bunch of organs can't. What is the origin of biology's levels? What are their powers, and how did they come to be? Enter: Charles Darwin (1809–1882), biology's "greatest revolutionist!"

Sinestro, once the famed Green Lantern of sector 1417, fancied himself the Corps' own greatest revolutionist. After he was exiled by the Guardians, Sinestro antagonized his former comrades, killing many and forcing the rest to adopt new strategies for survival. When the prodigal Lantern was finally captured, Hal confronted him, and asked, "Why?" Sinestro answered simply: "Loyalty!" In forcing the Corps to adapt in the face of his threats, Sinestro had made them more fit to face upcoming challenges for which he saw the Corps as ill-equipped.[14]

Sinestro's machinations had so altered the Corps that some members, such as Honor Lanterns Guy Gardner and Kyle Rayner, barely recognized their changed organization. Through a process that we might call *artificial selection*, the Corps evolved because of Sinestro's selective rejection and preservation of preferred traits. Likewise, Darwin observed nature's diversity and wondered if some similar principle might be at work. The workings of nature might gradually change whole species of organisms. Darwin therefore called the process that causes evolution *natural selection*.

Sinestro's choices were motivated by foresight, but how can blind nature compare? All life faces a veritable rogues' gallery of challenges: Climate change! Food shortages! Predation! Competition for mates! Each of these elements selects in its own way, preserving advantaged organisms and eliminating those found wanting. If an organism succeeds in this struggle for existence because of some inborn trait, it might pass this advantage down to its offspring. Let time pass; preserve the useful traits and eliminate the harmful ones. Eventually, entire groups of organisms will be molded to fit their ecological roles. Sinestro had but a few years to prepare the Green Lanterns; nature, however blind, selects across the eons, and its works are all the grander for it.

In focusing reason through this argument, Darwin gained abilities beyond those of previous biologists. How do organs work in such well-organized unison? Why do organisms function so well in their ecosystems? What causes some species to resemble others? Evolution by means of natural selection answers all of these questions, and more, by suggesting that the struggles of organisms throughout history have created all of life's diversity. Darwin's true revolution was more ontological than biological.[15] Even in a world constructed of indistinguishable atoms, nature recognizes and selects organisms as individuals. According to Darwin, this must be biology's hierarchy: organisms, counted in different ways. Where the universal laws of hard science all but eliminate the concept, the "soft" science of biology preserves individuality by recognizing the uniqueness of organisms.

In concluding the argument that sparked his revolution, Darwin mused on the difference between the hard and soft sciences: "There is grandeur in this view of life . . . that, whilst this planet has gone cycling on according to the fixed law of gravity, from so simple a beginning endless forms most beautiful and most wonderful have been, and are being, evolved."[16] One reduces reality to atoms where the other has created a diversity of organisms. Let physics have its monotonous Manhunters; the organisms of the Green Lantern Corps have to get on with the business of living.

Hierarchy: Rebirth

Databank entry: sector 1287. Home to the Collective, a species of small puffballs that collectively absorbed the will, intelligence, and powers of the sector's previous Green Lantern, sector 1287 is among the safest in the universe. Its exemplary security can probably be attributed to the fact that the odds of running into the sector's resident Green Lantern is roughly one billion times higher than the odds in other sectors.[17]

Something is off here. A power ring must be wielded by an individual counted within the biological hierarchy, right? If organisms are the basis of that hierarchy, as Darwin insisted, then how can the entire Collective wield the emerald light? Summon your will to overcome great confusion, because we must understand how to count one billion as one.

Darwin counted organisms as individuals because, through selection, nature itself recognizes them as such. But biology is a soft science; it has no universal rules. What if there are organisms that don't behave like individuals? Worker termites, for example, are born sterile and sacrifice their lives in service to their reproducing queen. Nature should have selected against such behavior long ago, since these individuals can't pass their traits along to the next generation. Darwin's solution was to change scale. If we view the termite as an integral *part* of a larger colony that includes reproducing queens, then we can imagine the entirety functioning as a single organism would. Nature can then make its selections. Enter the *superorganism*: an individual formed from the concerted efforts of smaller organisms. Hence the Collective: one billion puffballs with one power ring between them.

The Philosophy Corps' Book of Worthy Names is voluminous; its entries often recall earlier pages. The superorganism had, in fact, made earlier appearances. Although Aristotle would have rejected the idea that planets have souls, the Master's followers explored the various analogies that hold between a healthy organism and a life-sustaining planet.[18] Mogo seeks equilibrium similar to that of a living body. When afflicted with disruptive pests—the Resal, for example, or a bombardment of corrosive meteorites—the planet takes measures to ensure that the "perfect symbiosis" of its parts is preserved.[19]

Thus it maintains a balance necessary to support life; without equilibrium, the planet becomes mere inanimate rock. Isn't this selection? Doesn't Nature recognize Mogo (or Earth, for that matter) as an individual?

There is a danger to counting puffballs and planets as we do people. We've added one Collective to one billion puffballs; one planetary superorganism to billions of less-super organisms. Each aggregation is essentially counted twice: once, as each of its parts, and again, as itself. An ontological explosion seems imminent. Perhaps we should replace puffballs in place of the Collective or count only the superorganism's parts. But why stop there? Look further down the hierarchy: Hal is made of organs, which are made of tissues, which are made of cells. The recipe for making a cell is encoded within an organism's genes. Nature preserves and eliminates organisms, but only because they exhibit particular *traits*, which are created by those genes. To avoid redundancy, we might think of genes as Darwin's true individuals; indeed, biologists George C. Williams (1926–2010) and Richard Dawkins (1941–) have suggested *gene reductionism* as a guide to biology's ontology.[20]

Aristotle counted only souls; Darwin counted only organisms. Each eliminated various levels from biology's hierarchy. Williams and Dawkins have gone further than that: their reductionism eliminates the full ontology of biology. The same genes in different bodies are like Manhunters: numerous, indistinguishable, and ultimately just a bunch of physical parts. When Hal, Mogo, and the Collective are all essentially the same sort of thing, life becomes physics. Soft science transforms into something harder.

"Not so fast!" comes the cry from another faction within the Philosophy Corps. Biology is not so easily overtaken. Among the laws written in the Book of Nature is that physical matter can be neither created nor destroyed. The transience of life cannot be denied; living things come to be and then perish. Without death, there can be no selection; without birth, no evolution. Darwin's individuals are historical figures: all life has a unique story to tell, and these unique stories define individuals. Thus the biologist Stephen Jay Gould (1941–2002) became the avatar of the new pluralism, arguing for the reality of different hierarchical levels in different contexts. Context makes the difference: it determines whether we count the puffballs *or* the Collective, avoiding the redundancy of counting the one billion *and* the one.

Shrouded in the mists of time though it may be, Mogo has an origin. According to the prophecy that spurred Sinestro to action, Mogo shall have an end. Such is the case with any Green Lantern: genes (Leezle Pon), organisms (Hal), species (the Collective), or even ideas (Dkrtzy RRR). Each can be selected, given the proper context. And why stop there? Perhaps a power ring may empower an entire space sector, or even a whole universe![21] So may biology's hierarchy be reborn, and with it the prospects of the Green Lantern Corps' full diversity.

Into the Wild Green Yonder

Troubled Green Lanterns are encouraged to make pilgrimage to Mogo. On the "planetform," Lanterns are given the opportunity to find perspective.[22] Philosophers may have their own Corps, but the pilgrimage may prove no less useful to them, because at this moment, a battle rages among them. Philosophers of biology are drawing on the power of reason to carve nature. The stakes run high: triumph of one faction over another will determine the fate of life as we know it—or, at least, life as we *see* it. Our pilgrimage to Mogo, now coming to an end, may shine an emerald light on the joints hidden within our own planetform.

NOTES

1. "Mogo Doesn't Socialize," in *Green Lantern*, vol. 2, #188 (May 1985), reprinted in *Tales of the Green Lantern Corps, Volume 2* (2010).

2. Immanuel Kant, *Critique of Pure Reason*, trans. Norman Kemp Smith (New York: Bedford/St. Martin's Press, 1787/1965), B75/A51. (This is the standard Academy pagination from his collected works, which appears in any reputable edition.)

3. *Green Lantern/Sinestro Corps Secret Files and Origins* #1 (February 2008).

4. Plato, *Phaedrus*, in John C. Cooper, ed., *The Complete Works of Plato*. translated by Alexander Nehamas and Paul Woodruff (Indianapolis: Hackett Publishing Company, 1997), 265e1–2.

5. Philosopher David Hume (1711–1776) noted that "reason is, and ought only to be the slave of the passions" (*A Treatise of Human Nature*, Oxford, UK: Clarendon Press, 1896, 415). For this reason, the Philosophy Corps—wielders of the power of reason— owe no allegiance to any particular color on the *emotional* spectrum; if you can't see a power ring on your finger, it's because the ring of the Philosophy Corps is completely transparent!

6. Thales took this matter to be water, and was famous for having claimed that "everything is water." Aristotle speculated that he might have believed this because all things that grow require moisture. See Aristotle, *Metaphysics*, in Jonathan Barnes, ed., *The Complete Works of Aristotle*, trans. W. D. Ross (Princeton, NJ: Princeton University Press, 1984), 983b20–27.

7. Ibid., 1003a33–34.

8. Ask a power ring to translate "soul" back to the original Greek, and that ring would give the answer "psyché." Regardless of the religious connotations we read into the term "soul," Aristotle defined "psyché" as "the definitive formula of a thing's essence" (*De Anima*, in *The Complete Works of Aristotle*, 412b12), meaning the organizing plan that makes a living thing what it is. For this reason, Nobel laureate for medicine Max Delbrück suggested (at least half-jokingly) that Aristotle should be posthumously awarded a Nobel for anticipating the discovery of DNA; see his "How Aristotle Discovered DNA," *AIP Conference Proceedings* 28 (1976): 123–130.

9. Aristotle, *Metaphysics*, 1032a20.

10. *Green Lantern*, vol. 3, #159 (April 2003), reprinted in *Green Lantern: Passing the Torch* (2004).

11. It is true that Aristotle believed that heavenly bodies have souls; however, it is important to understand that he meant "heavenly body" in a literal sense, meaning that he saw stars and planets as eternally unchanging divine entities. The word "planet," as it is currently used, denotes a purely physical entity, and so it's fair to say that we're talking about different things.

12. *Green Lantern*, vol. 4, #44 (September 2009), reprinted in *Blackest Night: Green Lantern* (2010). Paleontologist Peter Ward has recently suggested that this may be a scientific truth, and that all life is ultimately self-destructive, in his book *The Medea Hypothesis* (Princeton, NJ: Princeton University Press, 2009).

13. We mean "hard" in the sense of being rigid and inflexible; whether or not any such science is *difficult* is an entirely different question!

14. *Green Lantern*, vol. 4, #26 (February 2008), reprinted in *Green Lantern: Rage of the Red Lanterns* (2009).

15. Darwin was not the first to propose that evolution occurs, nor was he the first to give an explanation of how it happens. The ancient Greek philosopher Anaximander (c. 610–546 BCE) is the first member of the Philosophy Corps to be on record as believing that one species may give rise to another. More recently, Darwin's grandfather Erasmus Darwin (1731–1802) and Jean-Baptiste Lamarck (1744–1829) proposed that evolution is the result of organisms' self-improvement. Darwin's theory of natural selection is unique in that it is the only mechanism to have survived repeated testing. See Stephen Jay Gould's excellent *The Structure of Evolutionary Theory* (Cambridge, MA: Harvard University Press, 2002).

16. Charles Darwin, *On the Origin of Species by Means of Natural Selection, or the Preservation of Favoured Races in the Struggle for Life* (New York: Penguin Books, 1859/1985), 459–460.

17. *Green Lantern/Sinestro Corps Secret Files and Origins* #1.

18. The most recent proponent of the planetary superorganism idea is James Lovelock, a NASA physicist who proposed what has come to be known as the "Gaia hypothesis." However, Lovelock's claim that the Earth is nature's "largest organism" traces much further back into the Book of Worthy Names. Most prominently, Leonardo da Vinci (1452–1519) espoused similar ideas, having likely picked them up via the works of Jean Buridan (1300–1358). See James Lovelock, *Gaia: A New Look at Life on Earth* (New York: Oxford University Press, 2000); see also Stephen Jay Gould, "The Upwardly Mobile Fossils of Leonardo's Living Earth," in *Leonardo's Mountain of Clams and the Diet of Worms: Essays on Natural History* (New York: W.W. Norton & Company, 1988), 17–44.

19. *Mister Miracle*, vol. 2, #14 (April 1990).

20. Richard Dawkins, *The Selfish Gene* (New York: Oxford University Press, 1976).

21. Such an idea may not be so far-fetched—Sinestro enlisted the aid of a sentient space sector in *Green Lantern Corps Annual* #2 (1988).

22. *Green Lantern Corps*, vol. 2, #12–13 (July–August 2007), reprinted in *Green Lantern Corps: The Dark Side of Green* (2008).

GREEN MIND: THE BOOK OF OA, THE LANTERN CORPS, AND PEIRCE'S THEORY OF COMMUNAL MIND

Paul R. Jaissle

As any regular reader of the Green Lantern series knows, there is more than one Green Lantern. Although Hal Jordan is the main character of the comic, he is just one of the 7,200 members of the Green Lantern Corps. Indeed, he often reminds the reader: "My name is Hal Jordan. I am an officer in the Green Lantern Corps. Space sector 2814." What makes the Green Lantern Corps such an interesting concept is the seeming tension between the individual willpower that fuels the Corps members' rings and the collective nature of the Green Lantern Corps as a whole. The individual Green Lanterns rely on their rings for communications with one another and for access to the Book of Oa, the near-infinite database compiled and controlled by the Guardians of the Universe.

If the Corps is understood as a community, and the Book of Oa is understood as a sort of shared knowledge, then the relationship between the Corps members and the book illustrates the idea of communal mind found in the work of American philosopher Charles Sanders Peirce (1839–1914). (By the way, the last name is pronounced like "purse.") Peirce's theory of communal mind serves as a way of understanding how communities such as the Green Lantern Corps amass and share knowledge, as well as how such knowledge grows and changes over time, such as when the Guardians change what is written in the Book of Oa. This theory also explains how the individual members of the Corps stand in relation to the larger community, how the willpower that fuels the Green Lantern Corps differs from the emotions that drive the other Lantern Corps, and what makes them unique in relation to the other Lantern Corps.

Planets and Insects and Math—Oh My!

According to Peirce, "Thought is not necessarily connected with a brain. It appears in the works of bees, of crystals, and throughout the purely physical world,"[1] which means this notion of thought encompasses all that exists. Thus, Peirce's theory of mind explains how the ranks of the Green Lantern Corps are filled with such a wide variety of members, even those whom we would not usually think of as alive or sentient.

Because the rings bestowed upon the Green Lantern Corps require willpower to generate constructs, there are very few limits on who or what could possibly be a member of the Corps. As we know, here are many nonhumanoid creatures and beings among the Corps. A short list of such members would include Mogo, the sentient planet; Bzzd, a flylike insect from sector 2226; and even the android Stel of sector 3009. In Alan Moore's story "Mogo Doesn't Socialize," Green Lantern Tomar-Re actually mentions that the Corps ranks even include Leezle Pon, a "super intelligent smallpox virus," and Dkrtzy RRR, an "abstract mathematical progression."[2] While it may be difficult to understand how a mathematical progression could function as a Green Lantern, it does show that the properties of sentience and willpower are not exclusive to humans or even animals.

The Green Lantern Corps is so large and varied because the willpower and cognition that power the rings are common to all sentient beings. For example, there is a memorable moment in Geoff Johns's "Sinestro Corps War" in which Bzzd, while defending Mogo from attack, uses his ring to create a speeding locomotive—a literal train of thought—to run over members of the Sinestro Corps.[3] This scene demonstrates that even a tiny creature such as a fly is capable of sentient thought and can interpret the threat of an attack in order to will a defensive maneuver. While flies and insects as we know and experience them do not have Green Lantern rings, it would not be unreasonable to assume that these tiny creatures are able to interpret their experience, especially that of an imminent threat, and respond to their surroundings accordingly.

The ability to interpret a possible threat is important, since the main criterion for new members of the Corps is the ability to overcome great fear. Fear of violence or death is common to all living beings, as is the will to survive. Since this drive for survival is common to all sentient life, it would seem that any and all possible forms of life or sentience would be eligible for membership in the Corps. Despite the diversity within the Corps, the individual members are united by the fact they can overcome fear and use their individual willpower to bring justice and order to a violent and chaotic universe.

All for One . . .

Although Peirce believes that all thought takes place as part of the larger community of sentient beings, he recognizes individual consciousness. Thought itself is a semiotic chain of cognitions, and consciousness occurs when an individual knower comes to recognize his or her participation in this chain. By recognizing the chain of cognition, the individual realizes that the process has occurred and can actively will himself to focus on particular qualities of experience—such as the color green. The chain of cognition is happening constantly, but choosing to reflect on something in particular requires the willpower of an individual thinker.

The Green Lantern Corps, since they are associated with willpower, find strength in individual potential while at the same time working as a larger group. This can be contrasted with the other Lantern Corps that writer Geoff Johns has introduced into the Green Lantern mythos. Each Lantern Corps has a color and an emotion from which they draw their power, and each one has limits compared to the Green Lanterns. Members of the Sinestro Corps, associated with the color yellow and powered by fear, have abilities equal to Green Lanterns, but unquestioningly follow their totalitarian leader Sinestro. The members of the Sinestro Corps do not seem to have the individual willpower of the Green Lanterns, and as such are not as effective a group. The rage-powered Red Lanterns are limited in their power because in order to wield the red light, the Corps members must surrender themselves to rage, thereby relinquishing their own individual will. Fear and rage—which seem to rely on conflict rather than community—do not have the same potential as willpower, and as such, these Lantern Corps do not have the same power as the Green Lanterns. What makes the Green Lantern Corps so powerful is the balanced relationship between the willpower of each individual member and the shared experiences and knowledge of the larger community. The Book of Oa, as a collection of experiences that all Corps members share, suggests another element of Peirce's theory of mind: the importance of a community of thinkers.

. . . And One for All

Peirce perceives mind as a communal activity as well as a continuous one: "The very origin of the conception of reality shows that this conception essentially involves a COMMUNITY, without definite limits, and capable of an indefinite increase of knowledge."[4] In the largest sense, this community involves all creatures capable of thought, and it is the shared experiences of these thinkers that constitute the active, communal mind. Different beings will have different experiences, and the communal mind is the accumulation of these experiences rather than a force that controls or shapes individual thought. The Book of Oa serves as a database for all the experiences of Green Lantern Corps members past and present. The stories of each member are recorded in the book, and these experiences are accessible by each member through the Green Lantern ring. Thus, the book is a physical model of the sort of communal mind Peirce writes about. In short, knowledge is never held by an individual in Peirce's theory: all knowledge exists within a community.

In many ways, the Book of Oa may be more powerful and important than the ring each member wields. The Green Lantern ring offers its wearer enormous power: the ability to create physical manifestations, or "constructs," of whatever can be imagined. However, these rings depend on the willpower of the wearer in order to function; the ring itself would be useless without the guiding power of individual will. While the ring's main power, the creation of constructs, depends chiefly on the individual wearing the ring, many of its other functions, such as language translation, rely on connections to the Book of Oa and to the other members of the Corps. So the power of the ring also depends on the community of Green Lanterns, who are all connected to the Central Power Battery and the Book of Oa.

Although translation may not be the most glamorous ability of the Green Lantern ring, it may be one of the most useful, making communication with thousands of species and races of sentient beings from around the universe much easier. Translation also demonstrates how the ring and its wearer communicate with the Book of Oa. The ring may facilitate the translation, but it is only able to do so by accessing the database of previously known languages stored in the book. For example, in *Green Lantern: Rebirth* (2005), Kyle Rayner is unable to understand the sounds made by creatures he encounters in sector 3599. His ring then informs him that these sounds are a language, and it translates this language into English: "Language 1,456 of sector 3599. Translating to language 945,342 of sector 2814." The actual process of translation is not spelled out in the comic, of course, but the fact that both languages were cataloged in the Book of Oa suggests that prior experience with each language is necessary. Thus the ability of the ring to translate various languages is dependent upon the experiences of the Corps members. The ring, then, is limited in its ability not just by the willpower of the wearer, but by the shared experiences that constitute the Book.

The Green Lantern Corps resembles a community of thinkers whose shared experiences constitute the knowledge stored and shared by the database on Oa. The fact that each Corps member is involved in this large, communal mind is important because it is only in a community that knowledge and truth can be understood. Peirce does not mince words regarding the importance of a community when it comes to knowledge: "The individual man, since his separate existence is manifested only by ignorance and error, so far as he is anything apart from his fellows, and from what he and they are to be, is only a negation."[5] Truth, in this theory of mind, is only possible by means of shared experiences. Community, then, not only allows for a wide-reaching access to experiences and knowledge, but the community of thinkers also establishes which experiences and knowledge best resemble truth. However, establishing any sort of absolute truth is, in Peirce's model, incredibly difficult, even for such a vast, varied, and seemingly timeless community like the Green Lantern Corps and the Guardians of the Universe.

The Book of Oa: An Incomplete Truth

"Truth," in the communal model of mind, can only be recognized within the community. This community not only extends in a certain space, but also across time. "Absolute" truth would be the end result of an infinitely large community with an infinite amount of recourse to verify their findings over an infinite amount of time. Again, Peirce claims that whatever is understood as "real" is known as such only in a community "without definite limits, and capable of an indefinite increase of knowledge."[6] Not even the Guardians, an immortal race of beings who have existed for ten billion years, have achieved any sort of certainty in their vast knowledge. Despite their great resources and experiences, the Guardians simply do not "know it all," and they never will. Even the Book of Oa, filled with countless stories and experiences of all the various Green Lanterns over time, fails to be a catalog of absolute, immutable truth because the community that created and contributes to it is limited in number and has only existed for a finite time.

Unfortunately, an infinitely large and eternal communal knowledge is impossible. The notion of infinity here serves a limiting or ideal case: the infinite community defines what absolute truth would be, but is itself an impossibility. Despite being a powerful tool, the Green Lantern ring (along with the Book of Oa) would not be able to facilitate the translation of all conceivable languages because that would assume an absolute knowledge of all languages, which would require an infinitely large community over an infinitely long time. Even though the Green Lantern Corps has existed for millions of years and has had millions of members, there remain languages that have not been experienced, and that therefore remain untranslated. For example, in *Green Lantern: Secret Origin* (2008), neither Sinestro's ring nor the Guardians are able to translate Hal

Jordan's cursing, presumably because no other Lantern had heard those particular English words. But once those words had been experienced, there would be a record of them, and those words would be available to be translated into the various languages spoken on worlds throughout the universe.

The fact that English curse words would correspond to similar words in other languages is the sort of practical, dependable truth that can be established by a community of thinkers. Even though absolute truth is impossible to reach, the communal mind can establish facts that the members of the community of thinkers can agree upon. Things that are recognized as being practically true or real are those that the community of thinkers consistently recognize and agree upon. The consensus of what is true is not a formal agreement—there is not a vote that determines what should be considered true or false. As experiences are shared among thinkers, the consistent details and facts that bear out over time are those that are recognized as true. As ideas and experiences spread and influence one another over time, certain facts—such as "The color of the ring on Hal Jordan's finger is green"—become reinforced and can be considered reliable, true facts. If someone were to claim Hal's ring was not green, that statement would be suspect because it contradicts the established facts regarding the color green in general and Hal's ring specifically. Of course, someone could experience the color green differently from a larger community, and that experience would be part of the shared communal mind, but it would not have the consistency and duration over time that other facts would. In fact, these instances in which individual experience contradicts the communal cognitive stream are the very moments when individual consciousness can be recognized.

Room for Error?

Since truth is the result of a process of cognition, it is often the case that individual experiences turn out to be false. Since absolute truth requires infinite time and an infinite community, human knowledge is never fully complete. Thus there is always the possibility that humans can be wrong. As Peirce writes, "All human thought and opinion contains an arbitrary, accidental element, dependent on the limitations in circumstances, power, and bent of the individual; an element of error, in short."[7] That element of error is the reason Peirce suggests that mind is communal as opposed to individual: the consensus of the larger community of thinkers will always come closer to reality than any individual experience. But since the communal mind is the result of shared experience, there is still room for error in the larger sense of mind; it just has been greatly reduced from individual experience. Unless the community is infinitely large, there is no way to completely reduce the element of error present in knowledge.

Even the seemingly wise Guardians of the Universe are fallible in certain regards. In the "Sinestro Corps War" story line, the Guardians decided to remove the portion of the Book of Oa that foretold the War of Light and the Blackest Night, events that would lead to the destruction of the Green Lantern Corps and the universe as a whole.[8] These sections of the book were based on the Cosmic Revelations that were first revealed to Hal Jordan's predecessor, Abin Sur, by Qull of the Five Inversions, a prisoner held on the planet Ysmault in sector 666.[9] These predictions had been hidden from the Green Lantern Corps by the Guardians, but when aspects of these revelations began to occur and were experienced by members of the Corps, such as the existence of other Lantern Corps, the Guardians decided to remove the revelations from the Book rather than cause panic among the Corps.

Of course, the premonitions of the Blackest Night might have seemed suspect, but after the War of Light had begun and the Black Lanterns were summoned, it became clear that the Cosmic Revelations had had an element of truth. It was a small group of Guardians that had decided to remove those particular details from the communal database of the Book, but over time the larger community of Green Lanterns, as well as beings across the universe under siege from the Black Lanterns, began experiencing the details of the Revelations. The shared experiences of the larger community bore out the truth of the Cosmic Revelations despite the Guardians' belief that the Blackest Night was merely a superstitious myth. The "Blackest Night" story line serves as a powerful example of how arrogance and the fallibility of individual minds contrast with the shared experience of a larger community of thinkers.

The Spirit of the Corps

"My name is Hal Jordan. I am an officer in the Green Lantern Corps. Space sector 2814." Those words suggest that the power of the Green Lantern does not rest in the ring Hal wears on his finger, but in the larger group of Green Lanterns with whom he serves. The power of the Green Lantern ring depends on both the potential that comes with the power to will anything into being, and also on the knowledge and experiences of the other Corps members. As Peirce's notion of communal mind suggests, knowledge and truth come from individual experience and the active mind that is shared by all sentient life. Perhaps it is that balance of individuality and community that the Green Lanterns wield in order to bring order and peace to the universe. When each of the 7,200 Corps members takes the oath to defend the universe from "evil's might," they are part of a larger group that includes all life. And it is through this larger community that they must work together in order to make the universe a better, more knowledgeable place.

NOTES

1. Charles Sanders Peirce, "Prolegomena to an Apology for Pragmaticism," in *Peirce on Signs: Writings of Semiotic*, ed. James Hoopes (Chapel Hill, NC: University of North Carolina Press, 1991), 249–252, on 252.

2. *Green Lantern*, vol. 2, #188 (May 1985), reprinted in *Tales of the Green Lantern Corps, Volume 2* (2010).

3. *Green Lantern Corps*, vol. 2, #15 (October 2007), reprinted in *Green Lantern: The Sinestro Corps War Volume 1* (2008).

4. Charles Sanders Peirce, "Some Consequences of Four Incapacities," *Journal of Speculative Philosophy* 2 (1868): 140–157, available at http://www.peirce.org/writings/p27 .html.

5. Ibid.

6. Ibid.

7. Charles Sanders Peirce, "*Fraser's* The Works of George Berkeley," in *The Essential Peirce: Selected Philosophical Writings*, vol. 1, ed. Nathan Houser and Christian Kloesel (Bloomington, IN: Indiana University Press, 1992), 83–105, on 89.

8. *Green Lantern*, vol. 4, #23 (November, 2007), reprinted in *Green Lantern: The Sinestro Corps War Volume 1*.

9. "Tygers," in *Tales of the Green Lantern Corps Annual* #2 (1986), reprinted in *Green Lantern: In Brightest Day* (2008).

SHEDDING AN EMERALD
LIGHT ON DESTINY:
THE PROBLEMS WITH
TIME TRAVEL

Amy Kind

It's not easy being Green Lantern John Stewart, or "GL," as his Justice League friends in the DC Animated Universe affectionately call him. He finally gets together with the woman of his dreams—Shayera "Hawkgirl" Hol—only to discover that she's an advance scout sent by the Thanagarians as part of their plan to invade Earth. Though the Thanagarian invasion is ultimately thwarted, Hawkgirl resigns from the Justice League branded as a traitor, and the whole experience leaves GL with a broken heart. Some time passes, and after he develops a relationship with the superhero Vixen, he thinks he's finally moved on. But Hawkgirl's subsequent return to the Justice League fold makes him realize that his feelings for her are as strong as ever. Will the two star-crossed lovers ever be able to find happiness together?

Shortly after Hawkgirl's return, this question seems to be answered. In an effort to defeat the time-traveling Chronos, GL ends up more than a half-century into the future, where he meets his son, Rex Stewart, alias Warhawk. With wings like his, it's not at all difficult to guess who Warhawk's mother is.

Unfortunately, however, knowledge of his future doesn't make things any easier for GL. In fact, it seems to make things worse. The Green Lanterns have a legend that no one can see the beginning of time. As GL tells Batman, "It's a universal law."[1] But perhaps it should also be a universal law that no one can see the future—or at least that no one should be able to learn too much about his own future. As GL himself discovers, knowing too much about the future can make it awfully hard to live in the present. Once we know what the future holds in store for us, how can we still be the masters of our own destinies?

Hera, Give Me Strength

According to the philosophical position known as *fatalism*, each of us is powerless to do anything other than what we in fact do. For instance, fatalism would imply that when the executives at Cartoon Network ordered an additional thirteen episodes of *Justice League Unlimited* after the first two seasons aired, they couldn't have done anything else, and likewise when they cancelled the show in 2006. The network executives might have felt that they were making their own decision about the series' initial renewal and then eventual cancellation, and that those decisions could just as easily have gone the other way, but fatalists dismiss these feelings as mere illusions. Our sense that we can affect the future is allegedly just as illusory. What we will do in the future is no more up to us than what we do in the present.

We might be especially gripped by fatalist worries in light of the thesis of *causal determinism*, the claim that all physical events are causally determined by prior ones. Consider some physical event, like GL's arm movement when he reaches to remove Hawkgirl's mask as a prelude to their first kiss. According to causal determinism, this arm movement was causally determined by prior physical events, which were themselves determined by prior physical events, and so on. As the chain extends far enough into the past, we eventually get to some physical events that took place before GL was even born. But GL couldn't have any control over events that took place prior to his birth, so if his arm movement now is determined by those events, then it is hard to see how his arm movement could be free—and likewise for any other course of actions he might now pursue. In this way, causal determinism provides us with reasons to believe that our actions are not freely undertaken.

However, while these worries about causal determinism are clearly connected to worries about fatalism, discussion of them is usually treated under the heading of "the problem of free will" and segregated from the discussion of fatalism.[2] Rather than relying on deterministic considerations, fatalists typically motivate their view by an appeal to an omniscient and omnipotent God. As explained by philosopher Richard Taylor (1919–2003) in his discussion of fatalism, "If God is really all-knowing and all-powerful, then, one might suppose, perhaps he has already arranged for everything to happen just as it is going to happen, and there is nothing left for you and me to do about it."[3] In fact, the argument for fatalism can even be made by setting aside considerations of God's omnipotence and focusing solely on his omniscience. If God knows everything, then that really means *everything*—including the future.

Take the fact that my six-year-old son wore his Justice League T-shirt to school today—the shirt that, to his dismay, features Hal Jordan (or, as my son explains it, "some guy who was Green Lantern when my dad was a kid") instead of John Stewart. God's omniscience means that he has always known that my son would wear this Justice League shirt today—for instance, he knew it eighty years ago, long before my son was even born (long before I was even born!). And that means that this morning, when my son was getting dressed, it was not within his power to do anything else but put on this particular T-shirt; he couldn't have put on his *Clone Wars* T-shirt or his *Transformers* T-shirt instead. If he'd been able to do either of those things, then as philosopher Nelson Pike (1930–2010) has argued, he would have been "able to do something which would have brought it about that God held a false belief eighty years earlier."[4] But given our assumption of God's omniscience, God can't have made that mistake; it's not possible that some belief of his is false.

We know from Hawkgirl that the present-day Thanagarians refuse to bow down to any divine authority.[5] Faced with this argument for fatalism—with the idea that the existence of an omniscient God deprives us of the possibility of voluntary action—the Thanagarians' atheist perspective might well be tempting. After all, GL is not alone in his disgust at the thought of being destiny's puppet. Unfortunately, however, fatalism is not just a problem for people who believe in God. Even from a wholly secular perspective, the threat of fatalism remains—especially if we believe in time travel.[6]

The Savage Time

It takes GL a long time to get over Hawkgirl after the Thanagarian invasion of Earth. He mutters her name in his sleep. He even requests a transfer away from Earth in the hope that a tour of duty on Oa, the home world of the Guardians of the Universe, would help distract him from his troubles. But the Guardians are unsympathetic to his plight: "We will not alter our decisions, disrupt our plans, simply because of your personal problems. It's our business to know these things. You're going to have to work through it, John."[7]

He's only just begun to move on, dating Vixen, when Hawkgirl returns to the Justice League to help them battle the reanimated Solomon Grundy. And it's only a short time thereafter that he travels to the future and meets his son. But GL emphatically refuses to become a puppet of fate; like all of us, he wants to be the master of his own destiny. Thus, with the knowledge of the future weighing him down in the present, he keeps the revelation of their child a secret from Hawkgirl and stubbornly continues his relationship with Vixen—even when it becomes increasingly clear that Hawkgirl still has feelings for him, too.

It isn't easy, and he continually finds himself acting awkwardly around both Vixen and Hawkgirl. He keeps his distance from Hawkgirl, but he seems unwilling to fully commit to his relationship with Vixen. And though he wants to be free to make his own choices, he resents Hawkgirl's choice to enter into a relationship with the mysterious Carter Hall. As GL tells Batman, "This shouldn't be happening. When we traveled to the future, we met my son. Mine and Shayera's. We're supposed to be together. It's our destiny." Batman's response is typically pointed: "If you really believed that, why are you still with Vixen?"[8]

Almost an entire year in the present passes following his trip through time before GL finally tells Hawkgirl what he discovered:

> Green Lantern: I haven't figured out how to tell you this, or even if I should. When Batman and I went to the future we met a man named Warhawk. He's our son, yours and mine.
> Hawkgirl: Our son?
> Green Lantern: That's why I've been so awkward around you lately. I've been trying to figure out what to do with that knowledge, what it means for our future.
> Hawkgirl: Well, what else could it mean?[9]

What else could it mean, indeed? It doesn't really matter whether an all-knowing God sees the future if GL can see it himself. Time travel—even just the mere possibility of it— suggests that the future might already be written. So what role can we possibly play in the writing of it?

In Blackest Night

In trying to understand the connection between time travel and fatalism, it's helpful to think more about the nature of time; in particular, let's consider two opposing views about the existence of objects in time. The first view, *presentism*, claims that the only people and things that exist, the only ones that are real, are the people and things that exist *now*. At this moment in the twenty-first century, tigers still exist but dinosaurs don't. Likewise, the U.S. Treasury building exists but the Mars Treasury building doesn't. By requiring that people and objects be temporally present in order to be counted as real, the presentist claims that time functions in a very different way from space; after all, no one would claim that people and objects need to be *spatially* present to be real. When GL is on duty in the Watchtower, the lantern-shaped Power Battery that he left hidden in his apartment back on Earth does not become any less real for being *there* rather than *here*.

The second view about time, *eternalism*, claims that the presentist is mistaken in drawing a disanalogy between time and space. For the eternalist, temporally distant people and things have just as much claim to existence as spatially distant people and things; as the name of the view suggests, the eternalist claims that anything that exists enjoys its existence eternally. This means that even now dinosaurs are every bit as real as tigers, and the future Mars Treasury building is every bit as real as the present U.S. Treasury building. More generally, we can now say that future and past objects exist just as present objects do.

At first blush, presentism might seem to be obviously correct. To claim that a future object exists *now* almost seems to be a contradiction in terms, and one doesn't need to have a twelfth-level intellect like Brainiac 5 to laugh at the suggestion that everyday objects such as disposable cameras and diapers exist eternally. They may clutter up our landfills for a very long time, but a very long time is still a far cry from eternity.

Yet despite the fact that presentism seems to have common sense on its side, the view has trouble accounting for the fact that we can meaningfully talk about nonpresent objects. Even after his death in 2006, we can still talk about the great Martin Nodell, creator of Alan Scott, the original Green Lantern. But who are we talking about, if Nodell does not presently exist and thus (for the presentist) does not exist at all? It seems implausible that our talk about Nodell should be empty or meaningless, but the presentist has no way to explain what we're referring to. We can also meaningfully compare Nodell to other creative geniuses; for example, we might want to say that he made more creative use of ring imagery than the composer Richard Wagner. But how can the presentist account for our ability to make this comparison, given that neither Nodell nor Wagner exists now, nor did they ever exist at the same time?

Perhaps the presentist has the resources to solve these problems, but even so, a deeper problem remains: we have no way to make sense of the experiences of GL and his fellow members of the Justice League if presentism is true. The very phenomenon of time travel—the ability to travel *now* to times other than the present—seems to require that those times other than the present exist, and that they exist now (even though they're not "now"). Just as we can't take the Batmobile or the Javelin-7 to a nonexistent place, we can't take a time machine to a nonexistent time. If the past and future don't exist, if they're not real, then there would be no way to travel to them.

When the members of the League travel back to WWII France to undo the damage done by Vandal Savage, the people and things of that era are every bit as real as the people and things of their own era. There's no denying the reality of the Axis tanks bearing down on GL as he stands alone on the battlefield, his ring completely drained of power.[10] When GL, Supergirl, and Green Arrow are brought to the thirty-first century to help the Legion of Super Heroes battle the Fatal Five, the people and things of that era are also every bit as real as the people and events of their own era. There's no denying the reality of the Emerald Empress as she exercises her mind control over GL.[11] And when GL and Batman follow Chronos to the late twenty-first century, there's also no denying the reality of GL's son, Warhawk. He may not exist now, already, in the present. But he exists now, already, in the future.

Time travel itself is supposedly a dizzying experience. So, too, it turns out, is thinking about time travel. How could Warhawk already exist, given that he hasn't even yet been conceived? And more generally, how could it make sense to say that the future exists now? If the future already exists, then what distinguishes it from the present? It's no wonder that GL regards time travel with such disdain.

Back to the Future

To resolve the puzzles that time travel presents to us, proponents of eternalism suggest that we have to reconceptualize things—in particular, our notions of past, present, and future. Consider the argument of the contemporary philosopher (and eternalist) J. J. C. Smart: according to him, things seem puzzling only because we take the notions of past, present, and future to be objectively determined. The puzzle is solved if we realize that these notions really "have significance relative only to human thought and utterance and do not apply to the universe as such."[12] For Smart, temporal notions contain a hidden "anthropocentricity," which means that they characterize reality by way of an exclusively human perspective.

Consider the fact that GL's favorite movie is *Old Yeller* (something that earns him considerable ribbing from the women in his life). It would obviously be a mistake for him to take his subjective movie preferences to indicate anything about the objective superiority of the movie. But Smart thinks we are making a similar kind of mistake when we take claims about what's past and present as indicative of some kind of objective temporal order. Claims about the greatness of *Old Yeller* are relative to GL's personal taste in movies, and claims about some event being in the past are relative to our own personal position in time.

In Smart's view, ordinary people and things existing in the world should not be thought of as three-dimensional entities existing in space but rather as four-dimensional entities existing in space-time. Normally we think of people and things as completely and wholly present at any given time that they exist. Smart rejects this way of thinking. Just as people and things have spatial parts, they also have temporal parts. For example, just as the Watchtower is composed of the command center, the infirmary, the hangars, and so on, it is also composed of its *timeslices*: the-Watchtower-on-January-11, the Watchtower-on-February-16, the Watchtower-on-June-30, and so on. And just as GL is composed of his head, his shoulders, his legs, and so on, he is also composed of his timeslices: GL-on-January-11, GL-on-February-16, GL-on-June-30, and so on.

Some timeslices of GL have goatees; some don't. Some timeslices of GL have radiant green eyes; some don't. These claims are objective facts. But, according to the eternalist, it's not an objective fact that some timeslices of GL are *past* and some are *future*. This claim can be made only relative to a particular position in space-time.

Remember that the eternalist sees a close analogy between space and time. We already accept that spatial position is relative, that is, that objects have relative position in space without having any absolute position. The eternalist claims that just as no location in space can be objectively privileged as being *here*, no location in time can be objectively privileged as being *now*. Identifying something as being or occurring *now* has the same subjectivity as identifying something as being or occurring *here*.

When we classify an object as being here or there, we pick it out only relative to our own position in space-time. Likewise, when we classify an object as being now or then, we also pick it out only relative to our own position in space-time. I typed some sentences in this chapter before I typed this very sentence. That's all that it means to call some event "past." I will type some sentences in this chapter after I type this very sentence. That's all it means to call some event "future." Referring to some event as past just means that it is located in space-time prior to the typing of this sentence, and referring to some event as future just means that it is located in space-time subsequent to the typing of this sentence.

In Brightest Day

GL keeps his socks and underwear folded with military precision. He likes order. And these reflections about tense should help us to bring some order to our discussion, to unravel at least one of the puzzles that we described earlier. Eternalists would deny that their view commits us to saying that future beings like Warhawk somehow exist now. The past and the future do exist in space-time, as does the present, but for the eternalist it's misleading to take this to mean that the past, present, and future all exist *now* in space-time. When we make the claim that 2 + 2 equals 4, or that green is a color, or that Oa is a planet, we're making *tenseless* claims. We don't mean that 2 + 2 now equals 4, or that green is now a color, or that Oa is now a planet. There are no temporal aspects to these claims at all. The eternalist thinks that our existence claims are similarly tenseless and atemporal. To say that Warhawk exists is not to make a claim in the present tense; it is not to say that Warhawk exists now. Rather, it is to make a tenseless, atemporal claim.

None of this is likely to make GL a fan of time travel. But can it do anything to convince him that he's not a puppet of destiny after all? Smart, for one, thinks that it should. If we're going to banish tenses, says Smart, we must be serious about really banishing them: "Thus, when we say that future events exist we do *not* mean that they exist now (present tense)."[13] And this in turn might allow us to dismiss worries about fatalism:

> To say that the future is already laid up is to say that future events exist *now*, whereas when I say of future events that they *exist* (tenselessly) I am doing so simply because, in this case, they *will* exist. The tensed and tenseless locutions are like oil and water—they do not mix, and if you try to mix them you get into needless trouble.

According to Smart, once we embrace eternalism, we need to embrace it wholeheartedly. The only reason we still worry about fatalism is because we insist on tensed language, but that's just a sign of our misguided presentist thinking.

Even if we accept Smart's claim, that still doesn't tell us what to do with any knowledge of the future that we gain from time travel. But perhaps GL already has the answer. When he fights against the Jokerz side by side with his future son, our heroes seem outmatched, and the prospects for victory look grim. Warhawk turns to his father for guidance: "What are you supposed to do when you have the weight of the world on your shoulders?" GL's response? "Plant your feet."[14]

It's good advice, and advice that we might take to apply equally well in the face of worries about fatalism. Whatever knowledge we have, all we can do is to live our lives as best we can, and to make our choices as best we can so that even if we cannot escape our fate, at least we can take ownership of it.[15]

NOTES

1. Pursuing Chronos through the time vortex that he has opened, GL and Batman end up violating this universal law. It turns out that the beginning of time looks like a giant hand cradling the universe, as it does in the DC Universe of the comics (*Justice League Unlimited*, season 1, episode 13, "Once and Future Things, Part 2: Time, Warped").

2. For a useful introduction to the problem of free will, see Michael McKenna's entry on "Compatibilism" (especially section 1.5) in the *Stanford Encyclopedia of Philosophy*, available at http://plato.stanford.edu/entries/compatibilism/.

3. Richard Taylor, "Fatalism," *Philosophical Review* 71 (1962): 56–66, at 56.

4. Nelson Pike, "Divine Omniscience and Voluntary Action," *Philosophical Review* 74 (1965): 27–46, at 32. This argument for fatalism dates back at least to the sixth-century writings of the Christian theologian Boethius.

5. *Justice League*, season 2, episodes 41–42, "The Terror Beyond."

6. There is at least one other secular source of worry about fatalism, often referred to as the "logical argument for fatalism," which dates back to Aristotle. There is a helpful discussion of this argument, which is difficult to summarize briefly, in the entry on "Fatalism" by Hugh Rice in the *Stanford Encyclopedia of Philosophy*, available at http://plato.stanford.edu/entries/fatalism/.

7. *Justice League Unlimited*, season 1, episode 7, "The Return."

8. *Justice League Unlimited*, season 2, episode 28, "Shadow of the Hawk."

9. *Justice League Unlimited*, season 2, episode 37, "Ancient History."

10. *Justice League*, season 1, episodes 24–26, "The Savage Time."

11. *Justice League Unlimited*, season 2, episode 36, "Far from Home."

12. J. J. C. Smart, "The Space-Time World," in Michael Loux, ed., *Metaphysics: Contemporary Readings* (London: Routledge, 2001), 294–303, at 295. Ironically, his very way of putting the point also contains a hidden anthropocentricity. In speaking of "human thought," Smart presumably did not mean to make a distinction between humans and other sentient species such as Thanagarians, Kryptonians, Martians, and so on.

13. Smart, "Space-Time World," 302.

14. *Justice League Unlimited*, season 1, episode 12, "The Once and Future Thing, Part 1: Weird Western Tales."

15. This chapter is dedicated to my son Stephen, with whom I have spent countless hours watching *Justice League*.

PART SIX

CAN GREEN LANTERN MAKE A BOXING GLOVE HE CAN'T LIFT?: POWERS AND LIMITATIONS

ANOTHER BOXING GLOVE?: GREEN LANTERN AND THE LIMITS OF IMAGINATION

Daniel P. Malloy

Traditionally, there are two qualifications for joining the Green Lantern Corps: a candidate must be fearless and honest. Likewise, as Hal Jordan explains in 2001's *Willworld*, there are two capacities or "elements" one needs in order to use a power ring: willpower and imagination.[1] Willpower fuels the ring; imagination tells it what to do. But people often forget that a Green Lantern must be honest and imaginative.

There's a good reason we forget the importance of imagination to a Green Lantern. It's a longstanding complaint among comic book fans that members of the Corps tend to be unimaginative in their uses of their power rings. More often than not, Green Lanterns—particularly a certain Lantern of sector 2814 with the initials HJ—fall back on producing giant hands and boxing gloves with their rings in dire situations, rather than creating something new and innovative. Writer Ron Marz and penciller Darryl Banks even tried to address this fault in the aftermath of the much-maligned 1994 story line "Emerald Twilight." One of their ideas when creating the character of Kyle Rayner was that he would be a more inventive ringbearer, hence his profession as a graphic designer and artist. And for a while, the change paid off. Kyle was initially much more creative with his ring than Hal, Guy, or John had ever been. He started right away, redesigning the Green Lantern uniform. But as the years passed, Kyle grew a bit more staid until, inevitably, the giant hands reappeared.

We could find a number of reasons for a particular Green Lantern's lack of creativity: lazy or bored writers, a respect for tradition among the artists (regardless of how silly the tradition in question is), the need for the character to make snap decisions in life-or-death situations, characters who lack creativity, or maybe the number of adventures Green Lanterns have been through over the years (they're bound to repeat themselves sometime).

This chapter argues, however, that Green Lanterns fall back on hands and boxing gloves because of the inherent limits of the imagination itself, rather than a personal failing of theirs (or their writers). For the sake of convenience, I will focus on the most well-known Green Lantern, Hal Jordan.[2] The fact of the matter is that Green Lantern's ring, powerful as it is, is still incapable of creating anything that he can't imagine. And, contrary to widely held beliefs, the human imagination functions only within a set of strictly defined limits. A Green Lantern could no more exceed those limits than he could make a square circle.

Why Can't He Make a Square Circle?

To understand why Hal's imagination is limited, we have to understand what imagination is.[3] For convenience, let's define imagination as the mental faculty that enables us to create new images and ideas. Although imagination is most commonly associated with creative people like artists and inventors, all humans have imagination. We imagine when we dream, daydream, or fantasize. We imagine when we create something, be it a story or a picture or a house. We also imagine when we plan things—big things, like our futures, and small things, like what we'll wear tomorrow. Likewise, when we choose one action over another, say reading rather than watching TV, we do so because we have imagined the consequences of each action. Reading, we imagine, will provide more pleasure or good than watching TV, so we read.

By discussing all the ways in which we imagine each day, I seem to have made the case that the imagination is limitless. But that's not so. For the most part, our imaginations are limited to actions available to us—to what the philosopher William James (1842–1910) calls our "living options."[4] When I choose to read, for instance, I have to choose a place to read; I can read inside or outside. My imagination presents both options and allows me to weigh the pros and cons of each. It does not, however, present me with the option of hanging from the ceiling or floating in midair while I read. These are beyond my ability, and therefore are not living options. This is not to say that I can't imagine them, because I certainly can—I just don't (normally).

For me, reading on the ceiling or while floating in midair are physically impossible. So I don't imagine them with the same ease that I do having oatmeal for breakfast instead of cold cereal. However, they are living options for Green Lantern, who *could* read while floating in midair or hanging from the ceiling. There are, though, some things that are not living options for anyone, no matter how powerful he or she may be, because they are not logically possible. And I'm not referring to human limitations or the laws of physics, which don't seem to apply to Green Lantern. No, I'm referring to things that can't exist because they are impossible in and of themselves: things and actions, in other words, that are self-contradictory, or impossible by definition.

What does that mean? Imagine a circle. Now, make it the size of a football field. Easy enough. Now make it orange. Simple, right? Now make it square. Go on, try, I'll wait. Can't do it, can you? Don't feel bad—no one can. If it's square, then it's no longer a circle. A square circle can't exist, because the essence of a square contradicts the essence of a circle. No matter how much Green Lantern wants to, no matter how much willpower he directs toward it, he can never make his ring create a square circle, or a rectangle with three sides, or an octagon with ten sides. These things simply can't exist, so there's no way for Green Lantern to imagine them, much less command his ring to make them.

This really isn't much of a limitation, though. The fact that Green Lantern can't create a married bachelor or a clean-shaven bearded man—both standard examples in philosophy textbooks—doesn't explain his reliance on giant hands and boxing gloves. And, truthfully, it's difficult to imagine a situation where Green Lantern would be called on to produce self-contradictory things. A square circle might be interesting to see (if it were possible), but it would hardly do much good in a battle with Sinestro (other than confusing him momentarily).

So there is at least one set of limitations on the imagination imposed by the very nature of thought. We can imagine breaking the laws of physics—Green Lantern does it all the time—but not the basic laws of logic.

See No Evil, Make No Evil

Green Lantern's imagination is limited by logic; anything that contradicts itself can't be created by the ring. But that still leaves a seemingly endless variety of possibilities at his disposal. So why does he fall back on the same tired old weapons again and again? Instead of a hand to catch those falling civilians, how about some lobster claws, or flypaper, or fishhooks? Instead of aiming a giant boxing glove at the current evil menace, how about a flyswatter or a frying pan? Why not take a cue from classic cartoons and drop a giant anvil on him? Or better yet, show us something new—something fantastic, like no one's ever seen before. To understand why Green Lantern doesn't do this, we have to look a bit more closely at exactly *how* the imagination does what it does. In particular, we need to examine the materials that imagination draws upon.

Many novels, as well as many movies and television programs, include a disclaimer somewhere declaring that the characters and events depicted are fictional, and that any resemblance to any person, living or dead, is coincidental. This disclaimer serves to protect the producer from legal action, but it deceives its consumers. The fact of the matter is that every fictional person, from Hamlet to Hal Jordan, is based in some way or another on one or more real people. When artists are asked where they get their ideas from, they can be counted on to give a variety of answers. However, if you examine these answers closely, you quickly find that they come down to the same thing: experience. This is true of every artist, from the writer of the most prosaic short story to the most fantastical comic book illustrator. The same applies to Green Lantern; when creating a weapon to battle Sinestro or a contraption to detect invisible aliens, Green Lantern's options are limited by his experiences.

This limitation by experience means that our imaginations are closely linked to our memories. More specifically, our imaginations are subordinated to, and dependent on, our memories, meaning that our imaginations (and Green Lantern's) are much more limited than we may suspect. It also goes a long way toward explaining the giant hands and boxing gloves, because what we thought was our creative faculty is in fact a *reproductive* faculty. Rather than creating new things, our imaginations are limited to reproducing things we have already experienced. Hal has experienced his hands—he's got two, after all—and boxing gloves, so that's what he makes with his ring.[5] In our own cases, when we imagine the outcomes of possible actions, we're not creating new ideas—rather, we're remembering the outcomes of similar actions in the past. I choose not to place my hand in the fire, not because I create an image of flame, but because I remember being burned in the past.

This limitation isn't much of an excuse for Green Lantern, though, and it certainly doesn't explain the excessive reliance on hands and boxing gloves. Let's face it: compared to us power-ring-deprived individuals who have never flown around the universe or visited countless alien worlds, any Green Lantern—even G'nort—can draw on a far greater store of experiences as material for imagination.[6] They've all seen and done things that most of us can't even dream of. And a Green Lantern who's been at it as long as Hal must have plenty of otherworldly experiences at his disposal. But Hal is still limited by his experiences. He can't dream up something *completely* new to him; all he can do is reproduce what he's experienced before. And what he tends to reproduce are rather mundane items: hands, boxing gloves, eggbeaters, sponges, and so on. He could, in theory, reproduce more exotic things, but the imagination's connection to memory shows us why he doesn't: it's easier to remember things that we have been exposed to often and, hence, easier to imagine them. A hand is easy; a nuclear reactor is difficult. You can picture the inside of your own house much more easily than you can the White House (unless you're a member of the POTUS Corps, of course).

"Wait a minute, wait a minute!" I hear you saying, "Hal creates things that he hasn't experienced all the time!" And artists and novelists rarely re-create real people whole cloth—if they did, they'd be journalists or documentarians. Our imaginations are more than just sophisticated copying machines, exactly reproducing inputs. Even the hands and boxing gloves Green Lantern produces aren't exact copies. We've all seen hands, sure, but not many of us have seen hands big enough to topple buildings—at least, not without the help of mind-altering substances. And how many people have ever seen a clock melting, as in Salvador Dali's *Persistence of Time*, or a creature with the head and torso of a woman and the tail of a fish? To go even further, before they were invented, how many people had seen a clock? For that matter, if our imaginations are as limited as I've said, how did Gil Kane create Green Lantern's uniform? Had he met a member of the Corps previously? As cool as that would be, it seems doubtful. So how *did* these new creations come to be if imagination is limited to experience?

Seeing Giant Boxing Gloves

This problem can be broken down into two parts. First, we are confronted with the problem of how people create new ideas. Artists of every stripe do this all the time: painters create images no one has ever seen before, and novelists create characters no one has ever met, who go through experiences no one ever has. According to the theory of imagination as memory, this shouldn't be possible; let's call this the *problem of artistic creation*. Second, there are people who figure out how to do things no one else has. Thomas Edison figured out how to record sound and create light from electricity. Alexander Graham Bell discovered how to send and receive sounds via wires. The Wright brothers learned to fly. None of these discoveries should have been possible if our theory is correct; let's call this the *problem of invention*.

Each of these problems points to a different aspect of imagination. Take artistic creation: however vast our experiences are, not many of us have seen a giant boxing glove or a plug for an erupting volcano. If our imaginations are dependent on our memories, then Hal shouldn't be able to create these things.

The problem is that so far we've been operating with a rather dull sense of the term "experience." When imagination reproduces an experience, it is not confined to reproducing a single experience. Also, each of our single experiences has multiple aspects, so the creative aspect of imagination comes in when we combine and recombine different aspects of our experiences. For instance, in reading this book, one aspect of your experience is visual: you see the words on the page. Another aspect is tactile: you feel the texture of the paper. The distinct texture of the cover provides another aspect. Each of these aspects is what philosopher David Hume (1711–1776) called an *impression*.[7] Each and every experience we have is made up of a variety of impressions: some are external, like our senses, and some are internal, like our feelings.

Each of these distinct impressions, according to Hume, is copied into our memories, thereby becoming an idea. When we imagine something new, like Hal's giant boxing glove or the series of pipes and clamps he uses to hold the Earth's tectonic plates in place (as in 1999's *JLA: Year One*), what we are doing is putting together some of these ideas, these copies of our impressions, in a new way. Furthermore, there is a logic to this process. According to Hume, our imaginations have a set of *rules of association* that determine how different ideas are put together. He claims that there are three such rules: contiguity, resemblance, and cause and effect. When you imagine something, say a bowling ball, your mind is likely to be led to something you often find in close proximity to a bowling ball, like pins, an alley, or bowling shoes; or to something that resembles a bowling ball, like a melon; or to an effect that the ball often creates, like knocking down pins or breaking toes.

So the way any artist (or Green Lantern) creates is by combining various ideas, drawn from experience, in a new way. This is what I meant when I referred to the legal disclaimers of fictional works as deceptive. When a novelist creates a new character, he or she is drawing on experiences with people to make that character. It's a bit like mixing paints—you add a bit of yellow and a bit of blue and you get something that's neither yellow nor blue, but green. In Green Lantern's case, he takes the idea of a boxing glove and adds the idea of largeness. He could create a wide variety of other things: elephant trunks, charging rhinos, or parades of leprechauns riding on poodle-back. No matter how creative a particular GL like Kyle Rayner is, he is still limited by his experiences—what's new is how he pulls from this or that experience and adds it to this or that other experience.

So it seems that we've answered the problem of artistic creation. We now know how Green Lantern can alter the ideas he gets from experience: just add another idea or two. Have to clean up a spill? Make a sponge. Big spill? Giant-size sponge—no sweat. Fighting a giant monster? Giant fists—easy. This sort of situation covers the majority of Green Lantern's uses of his power ring that don't simply consist of flight, energy blasts, or force fields. But occasionally even a Green Lantern encounters something completely new—or, more accurately, a problem that is not a giant-size analogy for an everyday Earth problem, and therefore can't be solved by creating a giant-size version of a common Earth object. Occasionally, Green Lantern is called on to do something he's never done before—indeed, something no one's ever done before. At times like these, he has to invent something, which is the second part of our problem.

When Boxing Gloves Won't Do

Before proceeding, let's note that invention works in two stages—what we might call the *idea* stage and the *execution* stage. In the idea stage, the inventor decides what needs to be done or created; in the execution stage, he or she works out how to do it. For example, we all know that Henry Ford invented the assembly line. In the idea stage, he knew what he wanted: a more efficient way to manufacture cars. The execution stage brought us the "how" of the assembly line. In a certain sense, it is this latter part of the process that separates inventors from dreamers and artists. Lots of people dreamed of flight before the Wright brothers, but Wilbur and Orville figured out how.

As brilliant as they may be, inventors are still limited to their experiences when trying to create something new, and this limitation applies to both sides of the invention process. In the idea stage, inventors must be inspired by an experience of some unfulfilled want or need. Thomas Edison, in inventing the light bulb, was inspired by the lack of reliable light. Candles and gas lamps of various kinds provided wavering and undependable light—fine for staring at your boss at Ferris Aircraft across a dinner table, not so good for reading or working. His previous experiences with electricity led him to consider it as a possible reliable source of light. And now we move to the execution stage. Edison's problem was simple: he needed to find a material with two properties. It had to glow when exposed to a sufficient electrical current, and it had to be sturdy enough to withstand a sustained electrical current over a relatively long period of time. He found it, after many trials. The thing was, he could only discover it through experience— by conducting experiments.

In Green Lantern's case, his inventions take less work— which is good, since he's usually creating them on the fly in some life-or-death situation in which there's no time to experiment. Fortunately, Green Lantern doesn't really need to do the experimentation part of the invention, since he's essentially left out of the loop in the execution stage. That stage is left largely to the ring itself. Green Lantern is the idea man; all he needs to do is recognize a need and imagine what a tool that would fill that need might look like. For instance, in *JLA* #40 (April 2000), the Flash asks Kyle Rayner to make a machine that will translate speed into sound. The need is identified by the Flash, and Kyle knows basically that the machine needs two parts—something to take in the input, and something to produce output. So he imagines a machine that looks like a treadmill with a tuning fork stuck on top, and the ring creates it. Input: speed. Output: sound. The idea is there, still restricted by experience.

If you were to ask Kyle how this miraculous machine worked, he'd be clueless. He's the idea guy—he's not worried about execution. But if that's the case, it would seem that he should be able to create a machine that only *looked* like it could turn speed into sound—the same as any of us might, if asked to draw such a thing. He shouldn't be able to create a machine that could actually do it without knowing how the machine would work. It would be like going to a comic book artist for medical advice. He or she knows how the human body looks, not how it works. But this is where we have to bear in mind the nature of the power ring. Aside from being the most powerful weapon in the universe, a Green Lantern's power ring is also a semisentient computer. It knows things that the ringbearer doesn't. So it's possible that when Green Lantern wishes for something like this speed-to-sound machine, all he has to supply is the idea and the willpower. The execution is all in the ring.[8]

The fact that Hal Jordan can rely on his ring to provide some input seems to make his reliance on simple, pedestrian objects all the more puzzling. He has on his finger a weapon with almost limitless power *and* at least some knowledge and expertise beyond human experience.[9] And yet, when it's time to knock out a bad guy, out comes the boxing glove again. The ring, despite its capabilities, has its limits. The ring can help him create something he has already imagined, but it can't help him imagine it. That is, the ring can provide a kind of technical support to help the bearer realize what he or she imagines, but it can't provide him or her with new impressions to draw upon when imagining new constructs.

Making Impressions Stick

Knowing how the imagination works doesn't seem to have gotten us any closer to figuring out Green Lantern's obsession with hands and boxing gloves. But let's think a little more about it. Hume actually showed us the way by referring to the components of experience as "impressions." Imagine that you have a piece of clay that you wish to impress with a print of your hand. You're going to have to press hard, or repeatedly, to get the impression to stick. The same is true of memory and, hence, imagination. We remember things (like people's names) better after many experiences with them. The more reliably we remember a thing, the more apt we are to call it to mind when we're imagining something. For instance, imagine a dog. If there's a dog you've been particularly fond of, when you imagine a dog it probably looks like that dog. For instance, whenever I imagine a dog, it starts out looking like Cha-Cha, a dog I grew up with (I didn't name her).[10]

If this is true for us, then it should hold equally for Green Lantern. Yes, he's had a much wider range of experiences than we have. But his most common experiences, and therefore the ones that have made the deepest impressions, are more or less like ours. Though he's responsible for all of sector 2814, Green Lantern spends most of his time on Earth, doing "Earth-y" things with "Earth-y" people. It's no wonder that when he is called on to use his immense powers, he most often uses them to create rather mundane "Earth-y" things. If you wanted to knock out a giant monster, a giant boxing glove or fist would probably be the first thing to pop into your mind as well.

What can we take from this? If you wish to be a creative person, go out and experience new things—as many as possible, as often as possible. And to ensure that all your new experiences don't go to waste, make sure that they form lasting impressions. Then, later, when you try to create something, whether it's a plan for the future or a new dinner recipe, you'll have that store of impressions to draw upon. So after you've finished reading this book, go out and do something new. Who knows—maybe you'll get lucky and stumble upon the crashed ship of an alien member of an intergalactic peacekeeping force, and he'll make you his successor and bequeath an incredibly powerful piece of alien jewelry to you, and you'll . . . well, you'll never know unless you get out there! Good luck!

NOTES

1. *Green Lantern: Willworld* (2001), 84.

2. Editors' note: Surely you mean G'nort?

3. There are a variety of philosophical discussions of the imagination. In this chapter, I draw primarily on the work of David Hume; see, for instance, his *A Treatise of Human Nature* (1739), Book I, Part I. Other useful and interesting discussions of the imagination may be found in Immanuel Kant's *Critique of Pure Reason* (1781/1787) and Jean-Paul Sartre's two books on the subject, *The Imagination: A Psychological Critique* (1936) and *The Imaginary: A Phenomenological Psychology of Imagination* (1940).

4. This term is used throughout William James's *The Will to Believe, and Other Essays in Popular Philosophy* (Cambridge, MA: Harvard University Press, 1979).

5. In fact, when Kyle Rayner asks Hal's best friend, Oliver Queen (Green Arrow), "What was the thing with the boxing gloves?", Ollie answers, "The fights. We loved the fights" (*Green Arrow*, vol. 3, #19, January 2003, reprinted in *Green Arrow: The Archer's Quest*, 2003).

6. Editors: That's better—represent.

7. Hume, *A Treatise of Human Nature*.

8. There seem to be variations on how the ring works on this score. In some stories, the ringbearer has to fully understand what he or she is creating. In others, like the one under discussion here, the Lantern only needs a general idea. (See the chapter by Jaissle in this volume on the ability of the Green Lantern rings to tap into the communal knowledge of the Guardians of the Universe and the Book of Oa.)

9. To see what "almost limitless power" might mean, see the chapter by Nielsen in this volume.

10. My editors, apparently, would think of G'nort. (Sad.)

"BEWARE MY POWER": LEIBNIZ AND GREEN LANTERN ON GOD, OMNIPOTENCE, AND EVIL

Carsten Fogh Nielsen

The reason Hal Jordan is often considered the greatest Green Lantern ever is quite simply that Hal Jordan was the most determined, strongest-minded person to ever wear a power ring. It just makes sense. The Green Lantern power ring is limited only by the willpower of the bearer. So the stronger the will of the person wielding the ring, the more powerful the ring will be.

Since the willpower of the wearer is the only limitation on the Green Lantern power ring, does that mean a Green Lantern could be omnipotent, all-powerful? Would an omnipotent Green Lantern be a god? One of the all-time superheroes of philosophy, Gottfried Leibniz (1646–1716), will help us to answer these questions.

Absolute Perfection

According to Leibniz, the concept of God refers to the most perfect being imaginable, a being that possesses all conceivable perfections to the highest degree. Leibniz also notes, however, that this definition doesn't really help us unless we also have some notion of what "perfection" means. The claim that Hal Jordan is fearless would have no meaning for us if we did not already have some understanding of what it means to be fearless. Likewise, to say that God is an absolutely perfect being tells us very little about God, for, as Leibniz writes, "We must also know what perfection is."[1]

Perfection, as Leibniz goes on to explain, is a concept that is not applicable within every domain. To take one of Leibniz's own examples, there can be no such thing as "a perfect number." Why? Because the most obvious and plausible way of understanding this term, namely as "the greatest of all numbers," is a nonsensical, self-contradictory idea. After all, the greatest of all numbers would be a *number*, which means you can always add 1 to it and get an even greater number. The very notion of a perfect number, understood as the greatest of all numbers, involves a contradiction and therefore makes no sense.[2]

From this, Leibniz concludes that perfection implies non-contradiction. For something to be capable of perfection, it must be possible to think of it "to the highest degree" without involving ourselves in self-contradictory statements. Numbers are not capable of perfection because we cannot think of "the greatest of all numbers" without contradiction. Knowledge and power, on the other hand, involve no such impossibility—or so Leibniz claims: "The greatest knowledge, however, and omnipotence contain no impossibility. Consequently knowledge and power do admit of perfection."[3] We can think of knowledge

and power "to the highest degree" without any apparent con-
tradictions, which means that knowledge and power *do* admit
of perfection. And since God is an absolutely perfect being
who possesses all possible perfections to the highest degree,
it follows that God must be both *omniscient* (all-knowing)
and *omnipotent* (all-powerful). And though Leibniz does not
specifically mention it at this point in his work, it is safe to
assume that he also holds God to be *omnibenevolent* (all-good
or all-loving), since goodness appears to be an obvious example
of perfection, and the idea of a highest degree of goodness does
not imply a contradiction.

Perfection in Action

So God is an absolutely perfect being, one that possesses all
perfections (all inherently noncontradictory capacities, powers,
and attributes) to the highest degree. Since he is an absolutely
perfect being, God (quite obviously) acts absolutely perfectly.
However, as with Leibniz's preliminary definition of God, this
turns out to be one of those statements that make sense only if
we have a more detailed understanding of what it means to act
absolutely perfectly.

Unfortunately, Leibniz thinks that finite minds like ours
are not well-suited for understanding divine providence or for
understanding how and why God acts the way he does. As he
puts it, "To know in particular, however, the reasons which
have moved him to choose this order of the universe, to permit
sin, to dispense his salutary grace in a certain manner,—this
passes the capacity of a finite mind."[4] According to Leibniz,
however, this does not mean that we can't know anything
about God's reasons for acting the way he does. God may
move in mysterious ways, and human beings might very well
be incapable of understanding the specifics, the exact hows and
whys, of God's actions, but the general principles according
to which he acts *are* discernible by human intellects. We can

come to (partly) understand the perfection inherent in God's actions by looking at people whose actions to some degree approach this perfection: ordinary human beings who are very good at their jobs.

Take Hal Jordan. Hal tests airplanes for Ferris Aircraft with great efficiency, skill, and competence, solving whatever problems pop up through creative use of the available resources. But Hal is only human, which means that he is both finite and fallible. His actions are therefore never completely flawless. Still, by looking at the near perfection of Hal's actions, we can get some inkling of the perfect nature of God's actions, because God's actions must exhibit all possible perfections to the highest degree. This implies that God's actions must exhibit the very same virtues—such as simplicity, efficiency, and creativity—as Hal's do, but even more so, because God is an absolutely perfect being. Just like others who are really, really good at what they are doing, God achieves what he sets out to do in the most efficient way possible, using the available resources in the best possible manner.

Creating a World from Scratch—a User's Guide

Despite the similarities between the actions of God and the actions of extraordinary human beings like Hal Jordan, there are also a number of profound and important differences. One of these is the scale on which they operate. God, as opposed to a Green Lantern, does not simply create particular objects or use his powers to make people fly. After all, God's primary act—or at least the one for which he is most widely known—is nothing less than the creation of the entire world! The question is whether we can say anything about how he went about doing this. More precisely, can we say anything about how an absolutely perfect being would go about creating a world and what such a world would look like?

Consider another Green Lantern example. Whenever a Green Lantern creates an object, he (or she, or it) wants this object to be as good—we might say, as close to perfect—as possible. If he produces a jackhammer to clear away an obstruction put in place by a criminal, then he wants the jackhammer to work efficiently, get the job done as quickly as possible, and not break down halfway through the task at hand. The Green Lantern thus strives to create a tool that is as physically perfect as possible given the circumstances, the time at hand, and the resources available to him—which, in the case of Green Lantern, primarily means his willpower.

A Green Lantern is not interested only in the physical perfection of objects. He also intends his creation to improve the state of the world. After all, the primary reason that the Guardians of the Universe created the Green Lantern Corps was to combat evil and chaos and create a better, more orderly universe. Green Lanterns are supposed to act as a force for good: to apprehend criminals, stop natural disasters and catastrophes, help the weak and the innocent, and prevent unnecessary suffering.

Leibniz claims that God's actions are structured by the same basic concerns as those of a Green Lantern: they are aimed at establishing the highest possible degree of both physical and moral perfection. *Metaphysics* is the philosophical discipline concerned with the ultimate nature of reality, so metaphysical perfection is perfection in relation to the ultimate structure of reality. *Morality* (or *ethics*) is the branch of philosophy concerned with the virtues and vices of rational beings and with the rightness and wrongness of their actions. Moral perfection thus has to do with perfection concerning the character and actions of rational beings. From these considerations, it thus follows that God and Green Lantern alike both want their actions to exhibit metaphysical *and* moral perfection to the highest possible degree. As Leibniz explains, "God who possesses supreme and infinite wisdom acts in the most perfect manner not only metaphysically but also from the moral standpoint."[5]

If this is true of all of God's actions, then it must also be true of the act through which God creates the world. This act must, therefore, at one and the same time be seen as establishing the perfection of the ultimate structure of reality and the perfection of human character and human action. Put in slightly different terms, when God creates the world, he creates the best of all possible worlds in both metaphysical and moral terms.

Hey, Wait a Minute—Did You Say "the Best of All Possible Worlds"?

At this point, an objection naturally presents itself: If the world that God has created actually is the best possible world, which exhibits the highest possible degree of metaphysical and moral perfection, then why does it appear to contain so much suffering and evil? When we look around us, what do we see? Not a world in which goodness reigns supreme and every human being is an exemplar of moral perfection. No, what we see are natural disasters killing thousands of people around the globe, people inflicting all kinds of suffering upon one another, and tyrants oppressing their populations. Of course, the world also contains quite a few real-world versions of Hal Jordan, John Stewart, and Kyle Rayner, people who are willing to dedicate their life to the fight against evil and injustice. But such self-sacrificing behavior is only necessary because evil exists—because the world is not made up entirely of good people, but also contains creatures like Sinestro, Parallax, and Black Hand, whose sole purpose seems to be to pervert and destroy all that is good.

So if God really is an absolutely perfect being, one who possesses all possible perfections, including omniscience, omnipotence, and omnibenevolence, then how do we explain evil? As the Scottish philosopher David Hume (1711–1776) succinctly put the problem: "Is he [God] willing to prevent evil, but not able? then is he impotent. Is he able, but not willing? then is he malevolent. Is he both able and willing? whence then is evil?"[6]

Among philosophers and theologians, the question of why evil exists in a world supposedly created by an all-powerful and all-good God is known as *the problem of evil*. Leibniz explicitly acknowledged the existence of this problem, and in fact invented a new philosophical term specifically to describe the project of explaining and justifying God's goodness in the face of the existence of evil. By combining two Greek concepts—*theós*, which means "god," and *díke*, which means "justice"—Leibniz created a new term, *theodicy*, which literally means "the justice of God," and used this term as the title of one of his books.[7] The term caught on, and ever since Leibniz published his book in 1710, responses to the problem of evil have usually been known as *theodicies*.

How does Leibniz respond to this problem? How does he go about justifying God's goodness despite the fact that evil so often seems to prevail in the world around us? One obvious response would be to deny that God is omnipotent. If God were not omnipotent, then the existence of evil could be explained as a result of limitations in God's power. After all, at any given moment, the actions of human beings are constrained by the limited resources available to them. This is true not only for ordinary human beings but also for Green Lanterns in possession of a power ring. Green Lanterns are constrained by the time available to them for deciding what they should do, and they are further constrained by the amount of willpower they are capable of mustering. Although a Green Lantern is incredibly powerful, he or she is not in fact truly omnipotent. Perhaps the same is true of God? Perhaps he is also not fully omnipotent, but only nearly so?

Leibniz flatly denies this. Limitations that constrain the actions of finite creatures like humans do not apply to God:

"Nothing costs God anything, just as there is no cost for a philosopher who makes hypotheses in constructing his imaginary world, because God has only to make decrees in order that a real world come into being."[8] God, Leibniz maintains, *is* omnipotent. Whatever God wills to be comes into existence simply because he wills it. God is thus not bothered by the petty considerations that constrain the actions of finite creatures, whether they are ordinary human beings, aliens, or Green Lanterns with power rings.

Crisis on Infinite Possible Earths

All of this brings us back to the question of how Leibniz explains the existence of evil in a world created by an all-powerful and all-loving God. Well, let's take a step backward and consider God at the moment of creation. Since God is omniscient, he has direct and immediate knowledge of all the possible worlds that he might create. Since he is omnipotent, he can create any one of these worlds by simply willing it into existence. And since he is omnibenevolent, the world he actually chooses to bring into existence must, by definition, be the best of all of these possible worlds: "His goodness prompted him *antecedently* to create and to produce all possible good; but that his wisdom made the choice and caused him to select the best *consequently*; and finally that his power gave him the means to carry out *actually* the great design which he had formed."[9] This seems to follow from the very conception of God as an absolutely perfect being.

So far, so good. Human beings, however, are *not* omniscient, which means that we do not possess the necessary knowledge to evaluate and judge God's decisions. Just as the members of the Green Lantern Corps are occasionally dumbfounded by the purpose of the decisions made by the Guardians of the Universe, so human beings can be dumbfounded by the purpose of God's actions. In both cases this inability stems from lack of knowledge, which in both cases leads people to criticize and sometimes rebel against the decisions made by their superiors. However, if the Green Lanterns were in full possession of the relevant facts, then they would (at least in most cases) come to see the wisdom of the Guardians' decisions. Likewise, if human beings were in possession of full knowledge about everything, then we would comprehend the wisdom and inherent goodness of God's actions.

These considerations provide Leibniz with a possible response—a theodicy—to the problem of evil. If it is generally true that we do not and cannot fully comprehend the specific details of God's actions, then this is most certainly also true of God's most fundamental action: the creation of the world. We do not have direct and immediate knowledge of all the possible worlds that God considered at the moment of creation. In particular, we know nothing about the precise nature of those worlds God discarded in favor of this one. We only know the world he actually created, namely *this* world.

We have no way of comprehending the actual magnitude of the evils and suffering of this world, since we have no other world to compare it to. For all we know, every other possible world, the worlds God *could* have created but chose not to, are far worse than ours. Imagine that all of these possible worlds are something like Qward in the antimatter universe, where evil rules supreme and everything good is considered bad. If this were the case, then God *did* in fact create the best of all possible worlds when he created the world in which we actually live, since this world, though it contains pain, suffering, and evil, is in fact much better than any of the other possible worlds (each of which is as bad as Qward).

And, in fact, this is precisely what Leibniz argues. His response to the problem of evil is to claim that however bad the evils we see around us seem to be, they are in fact necessary features of the best of all possible worlds. "God, having chosen the most perfect of all possible worlds, had been prompted by his wisdom to permit the evil which was bound up with it, but which still did not prevent this world from being, all things considered, the best that could be chosen."[10] God permits the existence of the particular evils of our world because they are a necessary part of the structure of the best of all possible worlds. If God had changed any aspect of the world, if he had removed even the slightest instance of evil, then this world would no longer be *our* world, but another world, and hence not the best of all possible worlds.

Omnipotence, Schmomnipotence

A Green Lantern whose willpower was unlimited would be omnipotent, but would such a Green Lantern be a god? Leibniz would answer this question with a resounding *no!* Leibniz would deny that a finite creature, however powerful, could ever be truly omnipotent. No matter how much power a particular Green Lantern possesses, no matter the strength of will he or she exhibits, there will always be limitations on how this power can actually be employed. Lack of time and insufficient knowledge are just two examples of the kinds of limitations that finite creatures have to deal with, preventing such creatures from employing their powers as easily and efficiently as a truly omnipotent being. Even Kyle Rayner, during his periods as the godlike Ion, faced these kinds of limitation.[11]

Leibniz would also object to the idea that omnipotence is possible without possession of every other possible perfection. How, he might ask, can you be omnipotent if you are not omniscient? If there are things you do not know, then obviously there are things you cannot do. Omnipotence thus seems to require absolute knowledge of absolutely everything that is, or omniscience. Furthermore (as Stan Lee once famously pointed out), with great power comes great responsibility, and responsibility is fundamentally a moral notion. You cannot be a responsible human being without having some pretty reliable understanding of what morality dictates. This must also be true of an omniscient and omnipotent being. Such a being would always know precisely what morality demands and would be under even greater obligation than the rest of us to do what morality prescribes.

According to Leibniz, no creature should be called omnipotent unless it is also omniscient, omnibenevolent, and in full possession of every other possible perfection. For this reason Leibniz would deny that extremely powerful creatures such as Parallax and the Anti-Monitor should ever be called omnipotent. When Parallax possessed Hal Jordan, he (or perhaps it) was extremely powerful, but he was definitely not benevolent. And the Anti-Monitor might very well (in the *Crisis on Infinite Earths* miniseries) have had the power to destroy entire universes, but he was immoral—certainly not omnibenevolent. So if omnipotence implies omniscience, and if omniscience implies knowledge of (and willingness to follow) the basic demands of morality, then neither Parallax nor the Anti-Monitor deserves to be called omnipotent.

For Leibniz the term "God" is not simply a shorthand way of referring to very powerful beings. Rather, it is a term reserved for the most perfect being imaginable, a being that embodies all possible types of perfection to the highest degree. As we have seen, no finite creature, no matter how strong-willed and powerful, can ever possibly rise to that level. Hal Jordan, Kyle Rayner, Kilowog, and the other members of the Green Lantern Corps are all good-hearted and powerful creatures, but they are clearly not omniscient, nor are they perfectly and absolutely good. They use their considerable powers to make the universe a better place, but they are not always sure what the right thing to do is, and they occasionally fail to live up to their own moral ideals. They are admirable and worthy of praise, but they are not gods.[12]

NOTES

1. Gottfried Leibniz, *Discourse on Metaphysics*, trans. George Montgomery (LaSalle, IL: Open Court, 1973), § 1.

2. Ibid.

3. Ibid.

4. Ibid., § 5.

5. Ibid., § 1.

6. David Hume, *Dialogues Concerning Natural Religion*, ed. Martin Bell (London: Penguin Classics, 1990), part 10. In formulating his version of the problem of evil, Hume is paraphrasing the ancient Greek philosopher Epicurus (341–270 BCE), who was the first to explicitly state the problem.

7. See Leibniz's *Theodicy—Essays on the Goodness of God, the Freedom of Man and the Origin of Evil*. I quote from the English translation by E. M. Huggard, edited by Austin Farrer (London: Routledge & Kegan Paul Ltd., 1952).

8. Ibid., § 5.

9. *Theodicy*, Part Two, § 116.

10. Ibid., Preface, 67.

11. See especially *Green Lantern: The Power of Ion* (2003), collecting *Green Lantern*, vol. 3, #142–150 (2001–2002), in which Kyle first became Ion and had to deal with issues of godlike power.

12. Of course, Hal Jordan did spend several years (in real-world time) as the human host for the Spectre, God's agent of vengeance, and therefore shared in godlike power for that time. But as detailed most clearly in *Green Lantern: Rebirth* (2005), Hal struggled against the Spectre, uncomfortable with the latter's wrath, and the Spectre similarly resisted when Hal wanted to use their incredible power for positive good (rather than retribution). (See the chapter by Darowski in this volume for more on Hal's motivations during that period, and the chapter in this volume by White titled "Crying for Justice" on retributive punishment.)

MAGIC AND SCIENCE IN THE GREEN LANTERN MYTHOS: CLARKE'S LAW, THE STARHEART, AND EMOTIONAL ENERGY

Andrew Zimmerman Jones

Science fiction author and futurist Arthur C. Clarke famously claimed that "any sufficiently advanced technology is indistinguishable from magic."[1] This principle is at the core of most great science fiction, including most superhero comic books, which often make at least a nod toward a scientific basis for magic. Perhaps no other comic book has taken the concept of "advanced technology" as far as *Green Lantern*. The power rings of the Green Lantern Corps utilize technology that is limited mainly by the bearer's willpower, and the Guardians of the Universe resolutely insist that the power of the rings is based in science.

Fortunately, the Green Lantern mythos also provides us with a counterpoint for the comparison in Clarke's proposal: Alan Scott, the Golden Age Green Lantern, whose power is not derived from the Guardians' Central Power Battery, but instead from raw mystical energy called the Starheart, magic that the Guardians isolated and expelled to preserve the pure scientific basis of their green energy.[2] Yet, in many ways, Scott's power manifests itself in the same way as a modern Green Lantern power ring does. These two power sources, the Central Power Battery and the Starheart, provide a convenient basis for comparison between science and magic.

Do You Believe in Magic?

What do we mean by magic? Is a sunset magical, for example? Is an illusionist practicing magic when he pulls a rabbit out of a hat? The answer in both cases is no. So what, then, is magic?

One frequently cited element of magic is that there are set rules for performing it.[3] If someone meets the conditions for a spell, including elements such as visualization, concentration, intensity, energy, time, knowledge, courage, silence, and, of course, willpower, the spell's effect transpires. Notably, many of these traits are of paramount importance to Green Lanterns as well, especially willpower. Whatever other emotion is part of the magic, it must be supported by willpower; the magic user must intend a certain result, and though physical effort is not often necessary, mental effort often is. (Note the beads of sweat often shown on a mystical hero's brow while weaving a spell!)

The same rules also place restrictions on what magic can do. For example, Jakeem Thunder of the Justice Society of America, master of the mystical genie Thunderbolt, is unable to wish his predecessor Johnny Thunder back to life because it is against the rules governing the wishes that Thunderbolt is allowed to grant.[4] And while Green Lantern Kyle Rayner is able to "wish" his mother back to life with the near-godlike powers of the Starheart-enhanced Ion willpower entity, she recognizes that it's only an illusion and forces him to release her: "This isn't me, Kyle. It's just a shell you brought back."[5]

In our own world, the simple empirical observation that magic doesn't work is enough for those who embrace science and reason to oppose magic as superstitious nonsense. The DC Universe, however, is far more complicated. After all, the Guardians of the Universe, often portrayed as exemplars of wisdom, were well aware that magic *does* work, yet they sought to replace it with the structured logic of scientific rationality by collecting the magical power together to create the Starheart and expelling it from their home world of Oa.

The Social Side of Spellcasting

Since in the real world there are no magical effects to study, many scholars have instead opted to study the social relationships between three types of quests for knowledge: magic, science, and religion.[6] Sociologist Marcel Mauss (1872–1950) saw magic as a social phenomenon similar to but distinct from science and religion in many ways. According to Mauss, magic and religion bear strong resemblances to each other, mainly because of the importance of belief and ritual in both. The distinction between them is mostly social: magic, he claims, is a fundamentally private matter, whereas religion is usually communal. In fact, according to his ultimate definition, "a magical rite is any rite which does not play a part in organized cults—it is private, secret, mysterious and approaches the limit of a prohibited rite."[7]

Obviously, this doesn't mean that religion can't be practiced in private, but the point is that if a religious experience is held purely in private, then it never becomes part of the (organized) religion. Such an unshared experience would instead be a personal mystical experience, which straddles the line of magic and religion in some way. On the other hand, magical experiences can be communal, but the magic user rarely shares his experiences in detail with the world at large, or even with the other magic users hanging out at the Oblivion bar. The magical experience is fundamentally solitary, in contrast to the religious experience, the point of which is often precisely that it should be shared with others.

The private nature of magic provides a barrier between magic and science, as well. Though some early scientific work, such as attempts at alchemy or even Thomas Edison's famous experiments leading to the lightbulb, has been performed in secret, modern science is characterized by the open and collaborative nature of the inquiry.[8] Publication of results, peer review, scientific conferences, and replication of experiments are hallmarks of the scientist's work. The distinction between magic and science is mostly based on this difference in methodology; as Mauss points out, "We can only concede that if its formulas were simplified, it would be impossible not to consider magic as a scientific discipline, a primitive science."[9]

Trying to Rule the Unruly

It gets more complicated when we consider other aspects of magic, religion, and science, such as the role of rules, goals, and the will in each. One characteristic that magic and science have in common is their reliance on rules. Religion has rules, too, of course, but they have a fundamentally different purpose, because religion is not seen as means to an end. Even if you do everything "right" in a religious ritual (such as prayer rites), there's no guarantee a miracle will occur. Further, religious miracles are the work of divine will, while magical rites are based on mortal will. In contrast, the will of the scientist is not necessary to the actual scientific process itself (other than actively conducting experiments). In science, the behaviors of natural processes are separate from our opinions about them, as opposed to magic, where the beliefs of the magic user are of vital importance.

One way that these three classes of inquiry could be broken down is as follows:

- **Religion:** public, divine, focus on moral laws, powered by belief and emotion
- **Magic:** private, rule-based, focus on tangible results, powered by belief and emotion
- **Science:** public, rule-based, focus on tangible results, belief and emotion are irrelevant

In the DC Universe, the Guardians—not being divine beings (except possibly in their own minds)—are not interested in forming a religion, so that's off the table. They are then left with the options of creating a system built around either science or magic, and clearly they were so afraid of magic that they quarantined and shunned it.

While I'm very reluctant to question the wisdom of the original Blue Man Group, what were they so worried about? Perhaps they feared loss of control. Science, in which results are determined by initial conditions and firm laws, is far easier to control than "wild" magic, which often takes on a mind of its own, as the Starheart did. This is the most likely reason why the Guardians would focus on the creation of a scientific system in which the chaotic, emotional elements of reality can be controlled. As a Guardian explained to Hal Jordan and Oliver Queen (Green Arrow), "Being charged with the task of creating order . . . we gathered together the mystic force loose in the starways . . . for we had decided that science should prevail."[10] This need to cleanse the reality of chaotic elements—such as emotion—is shown throughout the history of the Guardians to be one of their strongest motivating factors.[11]

Vessel of Chaos: The Starheart

But in attempting to cleanse the universe of this chaotic emotional magic, they first had to gather and contain it. As the recipient of the resulting "green flame," Alan Scott and his power have undergone many transformations (and revisions) over the years. But it began in *All-American Comics* #16 (July 1940), in which he discovered a mysterious green lantern after a train crash. The lantern provided him with the power to manifest his will, and he eventually forged a ring from the metal of the lantern, taking the name Green Lantern. Unbeknownst to Alan at the time, the lantern was actually a fragment of the Starheart, "all the wild magic collected and contained by the Guardians of the Universe."[12]

But if magical power is fundamentally tied to willpower, then it shouldn't surprise us that the wild mystical energy gathered by the Guardians eventually gained sentience. The Starheart is therefore not only a power source, but also a living being of pure mystical energy. Consider the Starheart's explanation of why the Guardians had issues with its existence:

Do you want to know what true power is? Possibility. The absolute absence of structure and reason and limit. Everything the order imposed by the Guardians wasn't. That's what I am. I am chaos! I'm the stuff of creation. Before the Guardians, before anything, there was chaos![13]

This may seem confusing: we have already established that magic users need to obey certain rules in order to get the results they want, and yet the Starheart is wild, chaotic, and seemingly unbound by rules. Perhaps one of the ways in which magic differs from science is that the objects of scientific work are bound by the rules of natural causality, whereas the objects of magical work are themselves chaotic. While the sources of magical power are chaotic, their wielders must follow rules if they hope to get anything done, or else results might spiral out of control.

Over the years of wielding the Starheart's power, Alan Scott absorbed a significant portion of the Starheart's essence. This is one reason why, despite his age, he has a young, vibrant body.

And his children, Obsidian and Jade, bear powers based on their heritage not from Alan Scott himself, but from the Starheart. In fact, Alan Scott's body is now made of the Starheart energy (although he prefers to call it the "green flame" these days after it lost its sentience in a battle with Jade). He continues to wear the ring merely for symbolic purposes.[14]

Alan Scott has stepped away from the traditional Green Lantern powers. Instead of just wielding a piece of technology that allows his will to become manifest, he has actually become a repository for the energy itself. As Mr. Terrific puts it to Alan, "Essentially, your body, your being, is composed entirely of green flame. You bleed because you think you should. Your age, your appearance—everything, it's all based on your willpower."[15] We should note, however, that although the Starheart is a mystical force, Alan Scott is not a magic user or a sorcerer of any kind. He does not have the skills needed to manipulate mystical energies in more traditional ways. He has not been trained to cast spells, though he has intuitively wielded mystical energy for over half a century.

The Starheart, as a mystical power source, provides Scott with some advantages that the Green Lantern rings don't. He can duplicate certain powers, such as Jay Garrick's speed, and can manipulate mystical energy to alter spells. Recently, he has also gained the power to see ghosts and other mystical energy, thanks to Jade's ghost imbuing him with a portion of her Starheart power.[16] So while in large part the green flame replicates the abilities of the power rings that modern Green Lanterns wield thanks to science, these additional capabilities serve to emphasize that Alan's power comes from a different source altogether, magic.

The Color of Willpower

The Guardians sought to eliminate the wild chaos of magic from the universe by capturing it in the Starheart. Likewise, they sought to harness the greatest power that their science could muster for their order-keeping Green Lantern Corps: the willpower of sentient life throughout the universe. As explained by the Green Lantern Kyle Rayner (whose ring is obviously powerless against sentence fragments):

> The power that flows through our rings—it's not just light . . . The Central Battery the Guardians made. It collects willpower from every living being in the universe. Raw emotional willpower converted into energy. Amplified by our own a million times over. There's an emotional electromagnetic spectrum out there that can be harnessed and used. Green willpower is the most pure.[17]

This is the closest we have ever come to a scientific explanation for the Green Lantern Central Power Battery. In the words of the Guardian Sayd (shortly before being banished from Oa), "The greatest powers in the universe are manifested from emotion."[18]

In fact, the "emotional electromagnetic spectrum" and the various Lantern Corps associated with it, has become the defining theme within recent *Green Lantern* titles, culminating in the *Blackest Night* event in which Nekron and the Black Lanterns threaten life throughout the universe, and the *Brightest Day*, in which the effects of the former event and the arrival of the White Lantern is felt. The Guardians had foreknowledge of "the blackest night" in the form of an almost religious prophecy,[19] which most choose to ignore, except the Guardians Ganthet and Sayd (and Scar, who serves as a herald of the Black Lanterns).

In the familiar "Roy G. Biv" electromagnetic spectrum (red, orange, yellow, green, blue, indigo, violet), willpower (green) is the center. The "negative" emotions of hate (red), avarice (orange), and fear (yellow) are on one side, while the "positive" emotions of hope (blue), compassion (indigo), and love (violet) are on the other. Hate and love, being furthest from the center, are the most powerful emotions, and therefore the ones that willpower must work hardest to control. Consider this description in the villain Black Hand's journal, *The Book of the Black*:

> When the first living creature gained sentience and voluntarily moved, willpower was born. It is the most basic element of sentient existence, often obscured by the complexity of life. The Guardians knew this as they knew the secret of life.[20]

Indeed, this is why the Guardians chose willpower as a power source for their keepers of order—it can keep all of the emotions in check. Willpower helps focus the emotions, as tangibly demonstrated by the fact that it is the green light of willpower, together with at least one other color/emotion, that is able to destroy the reanimated corpse of a Black Lantern.[21]

Guardians: Scientists or Sorcerers?

We come now full circle, back to the original statement by Arthur C. Clarke: "Any sufficiently advanced technology is indistinguishable from magic." The Green Lantern power rings are sufficiently advanced to be (mostly) indistinguishable from magic. In a world where magic and science coexist, it seems like when you go too far in one direction, you might just come around the other side.

There is, however, something that distinguishes the Green Lanterns from the other Corps and also from the Starheart, but that is not accounted for in Clarke's law. And this also cuts to the heart of why the Guardians chose science as their modus operandi in imposing order on the universe. Magical power has an inherent will of its own, as evidenced by the Starheart's fall toward evil.[22] It is the power of chaos and is therefore opposed to order. Similarly, the other emotions—the positive ones as well as the negative ones—are out of balance. Both the Sinestro (Yellow Lantern) Corps, based on fear, and Blue

Lantern Corps, based on hope, are compatible with order, and in fact they seek to maintain it. The further out you go on the spectrum, the less clear it is how order could be maintained by, say, everyone giving in to hate, avarice, love, or even compassion. This is why, of all of the Corps, only the Green Lantern Corps is governed on the basis of order above all.

Despite Clarke's axiom, the Guardians are wise enough to know that there is a fundamental difference between science and magic. Magic in their universe is always tainted by some aspect of the emotional energy spectrum other than pure willpower, whereas willpower in its rawest form does not appear to have this random emotional corruption. Had they formed a Corps utilizing mystical energy rather than the Green Lantern power rings, their power would have been clouded by the chaotic emotions that are linked to mystical energy. They would be facing the Blackest Night with a Corps that is out of balance.

But while the Guardians forged a weapon in the form of technology, the way in which they operate is far closer to sorcery. They are secretive about their goals and knowledge, reminiscent of how Mauss defined magic.[23] Their methodology is not the one of open inquiry that defines the human sciences, and they lack one key trait that drives human scientists: curiosity. Unlike the scientists who have achieved greatness in our world, the Guardians are unwilling to explore boundaries of knowledge and risk making mistakes (especially after Krona brings evil to the world while trying to witness the creation of the universe).[24]

The rule that "any sufficiently advanced technology is indistinguishable from magic" is actually the third of Clarke's three laws. The second says, "The only way of discovering the limits of the possible is to venture a little way past them into the impossible." The Guardians (as a rule) fail to follow this second law. Finally, in considering the pronouncements of the Guardians, we should also keep in mind Clarke's first law: "When a distinguished but elderly scientist states that something is possible, he is almost certainly right. When he states that something is impossible, he is probably wrong."[25]

NOTES

1. Arthur C. Clarke, *Profiles of the Future: An Inquiry into the Limits of the Possible* (London: Phoenix/Orion Publishing Group, 2000). (The claim originally appeared in the 1973 edition.)

2. The concept of the Starheart served to reconcile Alan Scott's origin with the modern Green Lantern mythos, and was first introduced in *Green Lantern*, vol. 2, #111–112 (December 1978–January 1979). However, in *Green Lantern*, vol. 3, #19 (December 1991), Scott's ring and lantern are tied to an ancient renegade Green Lantern of section 2814 named Yalan Gur, with no mention of the Starheart. (This tale did explain the weakness of Scott's ring to wood rather than to the color yellow.) Some versions of Scott's origins involve the Starheart merging with Gur's essence (such as *Green Lantern Corps Quarterly* #7, Winter 1993), while most leave Gur out of the picture entirely; for the sake of this essay, I'll ignore Gur. (See the chapter by Barkman in this volume for more on Gur himself.)

3. In fact, one goal of the "revision" of the status of magic in the DCU following the *Infinite Crisis* event (2005–2006) was to restore regularity and order to it by reinstating the power of rules. (Not much has been seen from this initiative, however.)

4. *JSA* #37 (August 2002), reprinted in *JSA: Stealing Thunder* (2003).

5. *Ion* #12 (May 2007), reprinted in *Ion, Guardian of the Universe: The Dying Flame* (2007). (This was paralleled later by the reanimation of the dead as Black Lanterns during the Blackest Night.)

6. As well as the work by Marcel Mauss referenced in note 7, interested readers may also wish to investigate the writings of S. J. Tambiah, Bronislaw Malinowski, Robin Horton, Sir James Frazer, and Edward Burnett Tylor.

7. Marcel Mauss, *A General Theory of Magic*, trans. Robert Brain (London: Routledge and Kegan Paul, 1902/1972), 30.

8. An obvious exception to this is corporate research, which is often kept relatively private. Even in these cases, they build upon the public results of other researchers, so the scientific enterprise remains collaborative, even if the private researchers don't reciprocate their information.

9. Mauss, *General Theory of Magic*, 79.

10. *Green Lantern*, vol. 2, #111 (December 1978).

11. See the chapter by Donovan and Richardson in this volume for more on this point.

12. *Green Lantern/Sentinel: Heart of Darkness* #1 (March 1998).

13. *Green Lantern/Sentinel: Heart of Darkness* #3 (May 1998).

14. Ibid.

15. *JSA* #27 (October 2001), reprinted in *JSA: Fair Play* (2003).

16. *JSA* #85–86 (July–August 2006). At the time of this writing, the Starheart has just returned to Earth with the reborn Jade in the *Brightest Day* story line, and its final effects on her, her brother Obsidian, and Alan Scott have yet to be seen.

17. *Green Lantern: Rebirth* #3 (February 2005), reprinted in *Green Lantern: Rebirth* (2005). For more on the relationship between willpower and emotion, see the chapter by White in this volume titled "Flexing the Mental Muscle."

18. *Green Lantern: Sinestro Corps Special* (August 2007), reprinted in *Green Lantern: The Sinestro Corps War Volume 1* (2008).

19. Originally presented in Alan Moore's story "Tygers" in *Tales of the Green Lantern Corps Annual #2* (1986), and reprinted in *DC Universe: The Stories of Alan Moore* (2006).

20. *Blackest Night* #4 (December 2009). The journal entries are in the back material after the comic book proper.

21. *Blackest Night* #3 (November 2009).

22. *Green Lantern/Sentinel: Heart of Darkness* #3 (May 1998).

23. See, for instance, the revelation of *Green Lantern: Ganthet's Tale* (1992) and its effect on Hal Jordan's faith in the Guardians.

24. This was first shown in *Green Lantern*, vol. 2, #40 (October 1965; reprinted in *Showcase Presents Green Lantern Volume Three*, 2008), and has since become a central part of the mythology of the DC Universe. It's important to note that it's unclear whether the Guardians would qualify as scientists by many of the definitions of science that we use today. It's hard to picture them proposing hypotheses, conducting experiments, and putting up with peer review, for example. They use and rely on science, but they don't practice science as scientists do.

25. These first two laws were proposed in the original 1962 edition of Arthur C. Clarke's "Hazards of Prophecy: The Failure of Imagination" essay in *Profiles of the Future*. The third, and most famous, law was added in the 1973 edition.

CONTRIBUTORS

Tales of the Philosophy Corps

Adam Barkman is assistant professor of philosophy at Redeemer University College in Ontario, Canada. He is the author of *C. S. Lewis and Philosophy as a Way of Life* and *Through Common Things*, and is the coeditor of *Manga and Philosophy*. Ever since his dad bought him his first superhero action figure—of the Emerald Crusader, of course—Adam has wanted to be a hero, and hopefully he will be one someday.

Joseph J. Darowski is a Ph.D. candidate in the American Studies program at Michigan State University and is an editorial assistant for *The Journal of Popular Culture*. He has an M.A. and B.A. in English from Brigham Young University. His research interests include popular culture, comic books, American literature, and Latino/a culture and theory. He has coedited *The Entertainment Society* and *Movies, Music, and More: Advancing Popular Culture in the Writing Classroom* and is one of the event organizers of the annual Michigan State University Comics Forum. He is fairly certain that wearing a gaudy green ring would quickly tip his family and friends off to his secret identity if he were ever enlisted into the Green Lantern Corps.

Sarah K. Donovan is associate professor in the Department of Philosophy and Religious Studies at Wagner College in New York City. Her teaching and research interests include feminist, social, moral, and continental philosophy. Donovan suggested some ideas to DC Comics for new, cool power rings like the "logic ring" and the "reading ring," but they never seem to understand her vision.

Jane Dryden is assistant professor of philosophy at Mount Allison University in New Brunswick, on the east coast of Canada (which seems to have been spared by all the DC cross-over events—perhaps it would be a good place for rookie GLs to train?). Her research is focused on German idealism and feminist philosophy, and her teaching extends to aesthetics and biomedical ethics. She thinks Kyle Rayner is sweet, but she has a good sense of self-preservation and will leave him to Soranik Natu.

Leonard Finkelman is a graduate student in philosophy at the City University of New York Graduate Center. In his secret identity, he is hard at work on a dissertation in philosophy of biology; since he takes metaphysical issue with the idea of multiple identities, that endeavor takes up most of his time. He was first drawn to Green Lantern comics back when Kyle Rayner wore the original "crab mask." Now Leonard enjoys reading about the evolutionary history of arthropods. Correlation or causation? You decide!

Paul R. Jaissle is currently adjunct professor of philosophy at Grand Valley State University in Michigan. His research is primarily focused on continental philosophy, phenomenology, and the pragmatic philosophy of James, Peirce, and Dewey. Specifically, he is interested in how the work of these philosophers can inform our experiences of art. He has presented papers on phenomenological approaches to reading comic books as well as his own work in collage art. Paul can personally identify with many members of the Green Lantern Corps: he has the reckless attitude of Hal Jordan, the creativity of Kyle Rayner, and the social skills of Mogo.

Andrew Zimmerman Jones is the physics guide at About .com and author of *String Theory For Dummies*. He always appreciates hearing from readers at azjauthor@gmail.com or through his Web site at www.azjones.info/. He is an Eagle Scout, a Freemason, and a member of the National Association of Science Writers and Toastmasters International. But his application to join the Green Lantern Corps is still pending.

Amy Kind is associate professor of philosophy at Claremont McKenna College in California, where she teaches classes in philosophy of mind, metaphysics, and logic. Her research has been published in journals such as *Philosophy and Phenomenological Research*, *Philosophical Studies*, and the *Philosophical Quarterly*. She has also written frequently on philosophy and popular culture, and her articles have appeared in *The Ultimate Harry Potter and Philosophy*, *Battlestar Galactica and Philosophy*, and *Star Trek and Philosophy*. She probably shouldn't be trusted with a power ring, as she'd undoubtedly forget to recharge it.

Daniel P. Malloy is adjunct assistant professor of philosophy at Appalachian State University in Boone, NC. His research is focused on political and continental philosophy. He has published on the intersection of popular culture and philosophy, particularly dealing with ethical issues, as well as on Leibniz, Spinoza, Foucault, Hegel, Horkheimer, and Adorno. Daniel has based his approach to teaching on Kilowog's, which is appropriate, since all his students are poozers.

Nicolas Michaud teaches philosophy at the University of North Florida and at the Art Institute of Jacksonville. He is under the impression that he would make an awesome Green Lantern, but his friends know better. How do they know that he would never make it in the Corps? It is the fact he lacks the sufficient will to walk past a plate of cookies without eating all of them or a pan of brownies without stuffing his face and greedily licking the pan. He has even been known to steal candy bars from small children. Perhaps if there were a cookie-charged ring . . . then he would be an unstoppable chocolate powered villain!

During the day **Carsten Fogh Nielsen** pretends to be a post-doc at the Center for Subjectivity Research at the University of Copenhagen, hard at work at unraveling the mysteries of the human mind, moral psychology, and moral philosophy. At night, however, when nobody is watching, he transforms into a superhero fanboy and contributes chapters to books such as *Batman and Philosophy* and *Iron Man and Philosophy*. Though he is well aware that Mogo doesn't socialize, he still thinks it would be wicked cool to meet him and discuss the morality of sentient planets.

Ron Novy is lecturer in philosophy and the humanities in the University College at the University of Central Arkansas. He has recently taught courses in metaphysics, moral problems, Marx, and mind. Ron has written chapters for *Batman and Philosophy*, *Supervillains and Philosophy*, *Iron Man and Philosophy*, and the forthcoming volumes *Spider-Man and Philosophy* and *Dr. Seuss and Philosophy*. Alan Scott remains his favorite Green Lantern because . . . um, he wears a cape. Did he mention it's purple? Classy.

Brett Chandler Patterson studied literature, theology, and philosophy at Furman University, Duke University, and the University of Virginia. He has taught ethics at Meredith College and Anderson University, including an honors course in character ethics and comic books. He is currently serving as a pastor and freelance writer. Brett rediscovered comic books in graduate school to escape all those books without pictures.

He still thinks that a Lantern ring would be helpful whenever he helps his children clean up their toys.

Nicholas P. Richardson is associate professor in the Department of Physical Sciences at Wagner College in New York City, where he teaches general, advanced inorganic, and medicinal chemistry. He is still waiting to receive a green power ring, but would consider a yellow one in the meantime.

Jason Southworth is a graduate student at the University of Oklahoma, Norman, OK, and adjunct instructor of philosophy at Barry University, Miami Shores, FL. He has written chapters for other philosophy and pop culture volumes, including *Batman and Philosophy*, *X-Men and Philosophy*, and *Stephen Colbert and Philosophy*. He is g'not crazy about writing cute tags for the ends of his bios.

Ruth Tallman is an assistant professor of philosophy at Barry University, Miami Shores, FL. She has written chapters for several pop culture volumes, including *Heroes and Philosophy* and *Christmas—Philosophy for Everyone*. She prefers her Guy Gardner with a little more Bwa-Ha-Ha than does your typical Green Lantern fan.

Andrew Terjesen is currently a visiting assistant professor of philosophy at Rhodes College in Memphis, TN. He had previously taught at Washington and Lee University, Austin College, and Duke University. Andrew has combined his long-standing passion for comic book superheroes with his interest in ethics, especially moral psychology, in contributions to *X-Men and Philosophy*, *Watchmen and Philosophy*, and *Iron Man and Philosophy*, as well as the forthcoming *Spider-Man and Philosophy*. Andrew has aspirations of patrolling sector 2814 (or anything in the low 2800s) himself someday, but that is unlikely until the Guardians lower the requirement to a being without fear of clowns. Until then, he'll have to settle for the Darkstars' stingy benefits plan.

Mark D. White is a professor in the Department of Political Science, Economics, and Philosophy at the College of Staten Island/City University of New York, where he teaches courses combining economics, philosophy, and law. He is the author of *Kantian Ethics and Economics: Autonomy, Dignity, and Character* and editor of a number of books, including *Iron Man and Philosophy*, *Watchmen and Philosophy*, and *Batman and Philosophy* (with Robert Arp), all from Wiley. He takes great comfort in knowing that after people read this book, they will understand why he yells "Will! Fear! Rage!" at traffic lights.

INDEX